The Developmental Scientist's Compan

Written by one of developmental science's ~~~~~~~~~~~~~~~~~~~~~~~~~~
Developmental Scientist's Companion provi~~~~ ~~~~~~gaging and accessible
guide to the scientific techniques that have been devised to investigate human
development. Adopting an original approach to what can be a dry yet essential
topic, Reznick enlivens his coverage of key issues in developmental methodology – measuring psychological phenomena, assessing reliability and validity,
experimental design, interviews and surveys, data collection and analysis, and
interpreting research results – with discussion of his own experiences of those
various techniques, gained over a substantial research career. The Companion
concludes with practical tips for improving the field and navigating a path
to professional success. Reznick's "behind-the-scenes" view of empirical
research and career progression, told with wit, wisdom, and insight, is essential
reading for students, young researchers, and other academics launching their
careers in developmental science.

J. Steven Reznick was Professor Emeritus in the Department of Psychology
and Neuroscience, University of North Carolina at Chapel Hill. Dr Reznick
published numerous books, articles, and chapters on a wide array of topics
in developmental psychology; his research is most notable for the measurement tools he developed, including the MacArthur-Bates Communicative
Development Inventory, which remains the most widely used child language
assessment tool in the world, and the First Year Inventory (developed with colleagues at UNC), used by researchers worldwide to identify infants at risk
for autism spectrum disorder. He also founded the Cognitive Development
Society, served on the editorial boards of many scientific journals, and held
several administrative roles for the Society for Research in Child Development.
Dr. Reznick completed this book during the final year of his life while living
courageously with amyotrophic lateral sclerosis.

The Developmental Scientist's Companion

Improving Research Methodology and Achieving Professional Success

J. STEVEN REZNICK

University of North Carolina, Chapel Hill

CAMBRIDGE
UNIVERSITY PRESS

CAMBRIDGE
UNIVERSITY PRESS

University Printing House, Cambridge CB2 8BS, United Kingdom

One Liberty Plaza, 20th Floor, New York, NY 10006, USA

477 Williamstown Road, Port Melbourne, VIC 3207, Australia

4843/24, 2nd Floor, Ansari Road, Daryaganj, Delhi – 110002, India

79 Anson Road, #06-04/06, Singapore 079906

Cambridge University Press is part of the University of Cambridge.

It furthers the University's mission by disseminating knowledge in the pursuit of education, learning, and research at the highest international levels of excellence.

www.cambridge.org
Information on this title: www.cambridge.org/9781107194281
DOI: 10.1017/9781108155359

© J. Steven Reznick 2017

First published 2017

Printed in the United States of America by Sheridan Books, Inc.

A catalogue record for this publication is available from the British Library.

ISBN 978-1-107-19428-1 Hardback
ISBN 978-1-316-64560-4 Paperback

To my dear friend and colleague, David S. Moore,
who took up the baton to ensure that this book got published
when I could no longer lift that baton myself.

Contents

Preface

Developmental science is generally defined as the study of cognitive, social, and other behavioral processes that emerge and change in human beings from conception through death. Thus, the relevant phenomena within developmental science begin with the post-conception emergence of the nervous system, the sensory systems that provide the nervous system with information, the muscle systems that allow the nervous system to produce behavior, and the mechanisms whereby early experience shapes the developing brain and is stored as representations and changes in how information is processed. Developmental scientists categorize the emergence and change of these components into separate domains such as cognitive development, language development, emotional development, social development, developmental disorders, etc. Theoretical approaches to developmental science often identify a progression of age-related or ability-related stages within each of these areas, and focus on typical development with some acknowledgment of individual differences, particularly at extremes labeled "atypical development" or "developmental psychopathology." Other prominent issues within developmental science include innate versus acquired knowledge, environmental influences, social influences (e.g., parenting, peer relations), nutrition, the effect of formal education, epigenetics, etc.

A general characterization of developmental science can be used to identify many of the challenges that developmental scientists face, but contrasting the phenomena addressed by developmental science with the phenomena addressed by physical science also helps us see the challenges. A useful first step toward identifying these challenges is to cite Paul Meehl, a psychologist who is well known for persistently and persuasively addressing problematic aspects of research methodology. In a lecture that he delivered at a meeting of the American Psychological Association over three decades ago (Meehl, 1978), which I believe should be required reading for all developmental scientists, Meehl described 20 reasons why psychology is a difficult topic and all of these difficulties are relevant for developmental science. Unfortunately, researchers who are interested in developmental science still face these issues, and many of us are disappointed in our lack of progress in solving them. Other prominent critics have also articulated challenges. I will not reiterate all of these challenges here, but my goal in this book is to address our challenges and to help us navigate toward solving them.

It has been difficult to find an appropriate title for this book. The primary topic of the book is research methodology in developmental science, but I have not written it as an introductory textbook that teaches students the basic skills needed to conduct developmental science research. I describe many essential skills such as measuring psychological phenomena, assessing reliability and validity, designing experiments, recruiting participants, conducting data analysis, drawing conclusions, etc. However, my goal in this book is to provide a broader perspective that offers my fellow developmental scientists some interesting, important, and innovative ideas to ponder as they plan, conduct, analyze, and interpret their research. I am attempting to speak to a broad audience. The young extreme of the audience includes students who are advanced undergraduate psychology majors and assistants in research laboratories and who hope to conduct independent research someday. The old extreme of the audience includes ready-to-retire developmental scientists (like me) who have played the research game so long that they feel empowered, if not obliged, to point out research methodology mistakes that could be corrected. The salient center of the audience contains graduate students and young professionals who are launching their research-oriented careers in developmental science. My decades of dialog with this group have set the tone of voice that I will use in this book.

Although my suggestions obviously make me sound like an opinionated curmudgeon at times, I prefer to see myself as more of a pluralistic meliorist, as defined by my role model William James. I am confident that we can improve our world if we work toward its betterment and that we have an obligation to do so. My goal is to express my suggestions in a way that will contribute to our ongoing dialog about how research in developmental science can be improved, and I am trying to do so with a perspective that includes my crazy/creative insights and also my openness toward learning from my own mistakes and adjusting my own strategies when I can improve them.

My view of research methods is strongly affected (and probably biased) by my own research interests and experience. My primary research interest has been infant cognitive development and how cognitive abilities change over the first years of life. Within the broad palette of infant cognitive abilities, I have been particularly interested in the typical and atypical development of memory, attention, language, categorization, perception, etc. and how these phenomena are influenced by experience and various aspects of the environment. I have also been involved in several collaborations regarding parent perception of infant intentionality and how this aspect of parenting behavior can be related to child maltreatment and abuse. Finally, I have collaborated in many research projects on autism spectrum disorder (ASD) including the development of the First Years Inventory (FYI), which is a parent-report instrument designed to identify infants who might eventually receive a diagnosis of ASD.

I have played various roles in the research world that have provided me with the wide perspective that I will present in this book. My interest in psychology dates from my years as an undergraduate psychology major at UNC-Chapel Hill, working with Dr. V. M. LoLordo on studies of operant behavior in pigeons. I received an M.A. in General Psychology at Wake Forest University in 1975 studying adult cognition with Dr. Charles Richman. I then entered the Ph.D. program in Psychology at the University of Colorado at Boulder with a primary interest in cognitive topics, initially working with Dr. Lyle Bourne, Jr. Under the influence of my advisor and dear friend Dr. Elizabeth Bates, I became interested in understanding the cognitive development of infants. In 1978, I moved to Harvard University to conduct my dissertation on infant categorization and language with Dr. Jerome Kagan, and I remained at Harvard as Director of the Harvard Infant Study, collaborating with Kagan and other colleagues on studies of behavioral inhibition. I joined the faculty at Yale University in 1987, and renewed my focus on infant cognitive development. Most of my research at Yale was conducted in collaboration with colleagues in the MacArthur Network on Developmental Transitions and with graduate students. I returned to UNC-Chapel Hill Psychology Department in 1998, and I am delighted to have returned to my "home sweet home" with its great cuisine, climate, and culture. My local affiliations include the Center for Developmental Science (CDS), the Frank Porter Graham Child Development Institute (FPG), the Carolina Institute for Developmental Disabilities (CIDD), and the Program for Early Autism Research, Leadership & Service (PEARLS).

I have served in many administrative positions directly relevant to research methodology, and I have also done extensive teaching on this topic. My first course on this topic was an undergraduate course at Yale. The 10 renditions of my graduate course on this topic at UNC-Chapel Hill have evolved into this book. One of the main seeds for the book was my chapter "Research design and methods: Toward a cumulative developmental science" in *The Oxford Handbook of Developmental Psychology* (2013), edited by my first Ph.D. student, Philip D. Zelazo. One additional perspective on research methodology has emerged through my editorial work including leading the development of the Society for Research in Child Development's (SRCD) recent journal,

Child Development Perspectives; serving on the editorial boards of *General Psychology Review*, *Developmental Science*, *Infancy*, etc.; and actively listening to talks in a wide array of contexts.

I could add an entire chapter describing and praising the people who have assisted me in various ways and my authorship of this book. Particularly salient at the present moment, I thank the following students for helping me form this important synthesis by reading my chapters and editing them: Rebecca Stephens, Dana Pettygrove, Priscilla San Souci, Kelly Sheppard, Heidi Vuletich, Dana Wood, Erika J. Bagley, Nicholas Wagner, Maura Sabatos-DeVito, and Jen Gibson. Recent editors of the book include Grace Baranek, Barbara Goldman, Phil Zelazo, and Jed Elison.

The course that I taught on this topic (Psychology 216 then 762) definitely evolved, and in its final rendition was described as addressing a broad array of perspectives on research on human development with the goal of facilitating the pursuit of an optimal cumulative developmental science. Our weekly discussions were based on specific readings and any other articles that students discovered and read if they wanted additional perspectives on the topic for that week. Students were asked to email me a one-page ~400-word reaction paper (not a summary paper) prior to class each week. The goal of the reaction paper was to encourage students to read the relevant material, ponder the topic, and to formulate questions and observations that would fuel our discussions. Grades in this class were based on reaction papers, class participation, and a take-home final exam. The primary criteria for success in each aspect of this course were active and appropriate participation, conceptual depth, and creative synthesis.

The final exam evolved and eventually became my effort to motivate my students to review the topics that we covered and to consolidate a set of ideas that students would find useful during their career. Here is the specific assignment:

We have addressed a broad array of perspectives on research on human development with the goal of facilitating the pursuit of an optimal cumulative developmental science. I hope that our discussions have helped you develop many ideas that will help you with your subsequent research and with your evaluation of research conducted by others. For the final exam, please review the articles that you have read for this course, your reaction papers, your notes, and your brain, and use this information to formulate a document that describes the top 10 insights/guidelines/commandments that will improve your developmental science research methodology and/or that will improve the quality of research in developmental science more broadly and that you will use when you are engaged in activities like reviewing articles or grants, or handing out tenure, awards or other evaluations. The balance between items that are relevant for your research versus items that are more generally relevant will probably depend upon how far you have advanced in your own research, so either type of item is fine.

To facilitate the document's gradability for me and long-term functionality for you, please state each idea in specific headings numbered 1–10 and then use approximately 1 page (using the ~400-word per page format you used in your reaction papers) to articulate the idea, how you expect to use it (with specific examples if possible), and why the idea is important to you as an individual scientist and/or as a member of the larger research community. You can mention the idea's history or the articles that support it, but I am much more interested in your description of how you expect to use the idea and why you see it as important. Some of your items might be quite narrow and specific, and others might be broad. Some ideas might be direct quotes from articles and that's fine, but I will be even more impressed if you include some original ideas that you have synthesized across sources and/or the broader expanse of topics we have covered (or that we should have covered).

Please view this document as a resource to help you remember some strategies for pursuing an optimal cumulative developmental science. I'll save it and if I hear that you have won an Early Career Award or that you have been elected president of SRCD, APA, or another professional organization, I will send you a copy and ask you if it helped.

To facilitate student participation in class, I began each class by asking students to answer an interesting question that would help us learn more about our fellow participants. Here is the most recent list of questions that I used:

1. What magazines do you read on a regular basis?
2. Best concert you ever attended?
3. Where would you shop for 2 hours?
4. Favorite local restaurant?
5. Where did you grow up and who were your siblings?
6. Best vacation site and most amazing natural wonder?
7. In the world you grew up in, what were your religion, SES, and region?
8. What instrument do you play or would you like to play?
9. Your background in statistics?
10. What sports are you good at and/or enjoy playing?
11. Most useful website you found recently?
12. Thanksgiving plans?

Class begins now:

1   The Broad Goals of Science

My goal in this book is to describe, evaluate, and lay the groundwork for improving the empirical research techniques that developmental scientists use for accruing knowledge. This goal could seem relatively isolated without some initial focus on the historical and contemporary contexts of knowledge accrual, and on the criteria used to amass knowledge and evaluate its strength. Understanding the term "knowledge" is an activity pursued by many philosophers, historians, and other scholars who could be described as epistemologists (i.e., individuals who explore the definition, source, and relevance of knowledge). Writing a book on the epistemology of human development would certainly have been a viable and productive project. However, lacking that tool, I have crafted a broad skim of the history of how humans accumulate knowledge with the goal of providing a context to help us understand the challenges and opportunities posed in developmental science.

1.1   Historical Roots of Knowledge Accrual

We can easily assume that most of our human ancestors lived in circumstances in which survival was the primary motivation. The range of viable activities that human beings participated in was constrained by fundamental needs such as food, shelter, health, successful reproduction, and protection from predators. As civilization has evolved, society has become increasingly able to delegate survival needs to a subset of humans who specialize in areas such as farming, cooking, carpentry, law enforcement, and health care. This delegation has allowed many of us to engage in an array of peripheral activities that are not directly linked to survival (e.g., professional sports, art, music, etc.). One salient domain of peripheral activities indirectly linked to survival is the accrual and articulation of knowledge via science. Our long history of epistemogenic activity (i.e., creating knowledge) is directly tied to human progress via the creation of modern civilizations and improved quality of life. A large proportion of contemporary human beings actively support scientific pursuits because most of us realize that epistemogenic accomplishments have enhanced our ongoing evolution beyond mere survival.

We can only guess about the early history of knowledge accrual. However, commonalities across cultures suggest that as human language, intelligence, and social communities evolved, knowledge began emerging when individuals began pondering and asking peers questions regarding the physical environment (e.g., the rising and setting of the sun, the progression of seasons, astronomical events) and health (e.g., birth, disease, phases of human development), and broader questions like the origin of life, the implications of death, and the relevance of social justice. The initial answers to these questions were probably articulated as stories, and it seems reasonable to assume that the popularity and longevity of individual stories reflected the degree to which the story met criteria of being interesting, memorable, consistent with obvious phenomena, and broadly acceptable. Further articulation of knowledge occurred in the narrative format (e.g., while humans were sitting around the fire, huddling in the cave, foraging for low-hanging fruit, etc.), and in the graphic format (e.g., when humans created rudimentary carvings, paintings, pottery, or sculptures). It is likely that some humans were born with notable story-telling or graphic skills, and others enhanced their skills through their ongoing activities. These skills can be viewed as peripheral daily activities with limited longevity. However, these effective communicators eventually became the professional knowledge accrual experts who were called shamans, artists, prophets, judges, astrologers, priests, rabbis, etc. The initial effectiveness of these individuals was affected by their ability to convince others via brute force, leadership, or clever instantiation. These initial criteria were enhanced eventually by subjecting new knowledge to possible refutation because of incorrect logic, unpopularity, or the lack of empirical support.

Preserved texts and traditions suggest that there has been continuity in some articulated knowledge for millennia, which is impressive given the changes during those years in language, culture, and technology. For example, contemporary explanations of creation, life, and death, and contemporary behavioral constructs like friendship, loyalty, and greed, were described in various religious texts, the archives of cultures in a wide array of countries and across many millennia. A more specific example, Euhemerism, which is the tendency to interpret myths as reflections of historical events and to interpret mythical characters as real people, is attributed to Euhemerus, a writer in Sicily in the 4th century B.C., and this idea remains present today. We also see frequent manifestations of many persistent folk insights. For example, when I sneeze, I will probably hear someone say "bless you," which historians suggest is built upon the assumption that my soul has made a temporary exit from my body. When we await news regarding an impending decision, we sometimes cross our fingers, which historians interpret as a strategy for evoking the power of the Christian cross. Some people would claim that having 13 guests at dinner or spilling salt predict bad outcomes, and historians link these theories to details in Leonardo da Vinci's painting titled "The Last Supper."

1.2 Science as a Source of Knowledge

The roots of science as a source of accrued knowledge began with observations that were more or less structured or specialized, and the systematic formulation, preservation, and communication of discoveries based on these observations. Science evolved further by developing increasingly sophisticated methods for conducting observations, often including the contextual manipulations that we label as experiments in the specialized environments that we label as laboratories using refined observational mechanisms like microscopes, telescopes, or MRIs. The amalgamation of scientific observations into an expanding body of knowledge has gone beyond description and simplistic explanations of causality and has attained additional utility through applications such as prediction, control, and the formulation of complex and powerful theories and models.

For several centuries, science rested comfortably in two different nests, which Francis Bacon labeled as lucriferous and luciferous in the 1600s. Lucriferous, from the Latin lucrum (gain), refers to science being useful (e.g., being profitable and providing material gain). Luciferous, from the Latin lucifer (light), refers to science providing insight and enlightenment. Profitable usefulness is a practical target, but it became clear that usefulness was unlikely to be achieved without a general understanding of the relevant phenomena. Alchemy was an early scientific activity with an obvious lucriferous goal, and despite alchemy's failure to find a technique for creating gold, the scientific techniques that emerged in alchemy supported the luciferous progress of chemistry and physics.

The transition to contemporary science emerged in the context of Logical Positivism, which refers to the innovative perspective on science that began in the late 1920s among a group of philosophers, physicists, and mathematicians from Austria, Germany, and Poland. Many members of the so-called Vienna Circle migrated to the United States to escape the rise of Nazism, and their Logical Positivism continued to dominate the philosophy of science for decades. Many books have been written on this topic, and Bechtel (1988) provides a notably readable description.

A literal definition could define Logical Positivism as referring to science conducted by people who think logically and have positive attitudes. However, that is not how the Vienna Circle used this phrase. They referred to logical in the sense of using symbolic logic for formal expression of scientific theory, and they referred to positivism as knowledge that is based on experience. Thus, the Logical Positivists attempted to promote greater clarity in scientific discourse by proposing normative standards that could serve as criteria for good science. They were motivated by the beliefs that 1) science needs constructs that have clearly articulated definitions, 2) accrued knowledge should be expressed and manipulated within a system of logic, and 3) contributions to knowledge should be based on empirical experience rather than conjecture.

Logical Positivism stipulates that science must be built upon constructs that have an operational definition that establishes a specific technique that can be used to define, identify, and measure the construct. Constructs are then combined in protocol sentences or observation sentences that clearly specify relationships among the constructs. This leads to the Logical Positivist verifiability theory of meaning, which defines the meaning of these protocol or observation sentences based on the set of conditions that would demonstrate that they are true. For example, to verify the sentence, "If atmospheric pressure is low, it will rain," a Logical Positivist would require us to measure the atmospheric pressure using an operational definition, determine whether or not the atmospheric pressure is low, measure whether or not it is raining using an operational definition, and evaluate whether or not the observed combinations of atmospheric pressure and rain are consistent with the outcome entailed by the logical definition of "if-then."

An obvious implicit step in articulating cumulative knowledge based on this form of science is creating an epistemic vocabulary that can be used to represent the results that are discovered and the interpretations and generalizations that are proposed. This epistemic vocabulary should also facilitate the integration of new knowledge within the body of existing knowledge. This topic will receive extensive attention in subsequent chapters in which I describe how we define constructs and variables, but the history of Logical Positivism provides an opportunity to introduce this issue. At one extreme within the range of possible vocabularies, scientists could establish a set of ad hoc terms based on operational definitions of specific phenomena, and then represent the accrued knowledge about these phenomena as a set of statements that explicitly describe the logical relations among the phenomena. For example, we could first express operational definitions for the terms blafuka, smagali, reflugel, and a polygoy of repugna. We then conduct research and make the discovery that when 2 units of blafuka are combined with 7 units of smagali and the mixture is reflugeled, the result will be a polygoy of repugna. Depending upon the operational definitions of the terms, this discovery could be more or less interesting and important. At the opposite extreme of possible vocabularies, scientists could incorporate traditional terms based on historic folk knowledge. For example, we could formulate operational definitions of the terms happy and healthy, and then conduct research that leads to the discovery that happiness makes us healthy. From a Logical Positivist perspective, abstract terms like happiness and healthy would probably be considered too vague to support scientific discourse, and the implications of the claim that happiness makes us healthy would thus be too vague to allow the statement's confirmation or disconfirmation.

Logical Positivism was an important step in the evolution of science because it reflects a significant departure from the traditional strategy, particularly for behavioral science, which was mired in anecdotal observation (e.g., Darwin's diary), vague definitions of constructs and theory (e.g., Freud's differentiation among id, ego, and superego and descriptions of processes like the pleasure principle), and the use of questionable paradigms for conducting empirical research (e.g., Wundt and Titchener's use of introspection). The Logical Positivist operational definition perspective was appealing to many behavioral scientists. Abandoning the questionable validity of introspection and case study observation, these behavioral scientists thrived by linking constructs like learning to easily observed behaviors in rodents like button presses, and linking constructs like motivation to easily manipulated environmental factors like limiting access to food. Moreover, behavioral scientists found that these constructs could be combined in a structured network of specific laws and then incorporated into a hypothetico-deductive model reflecting the cumulative knowledge. For example, Clark Hull (1943) crafted axioms based on assumptions and postulates about behavior, and combined these axioms into a complex description of learning with specific tests of model-based predictions and extensive discussion about seemingly important questions like whether motivation and drive are additive or multiplicative, or whether reinforcement is more effective when massed or distributed. Despite the eventual demise of Logical Positivism, this approach to behavioral science led to a legacy of precisely defined behavioral constructs, well-designed and creative experiments conducted in controlled contexts, data derived from meticulous recordings of objective observations, and definitive conclusions based on results from statistical analysis of data used to evaluate specific hypotheses.

My description of this phase in the history of behavioral science is based on my own personal experience. When I was an undergraduate at UNC-Chapel

Hill in the early 1970s, I had the wonderful experience of working in the laboratory of Dr. Vincent LoLordo in the Psychology Department, maintaining pigeons at 80% of their free-feeding weight so that they would all have equivalent hunger/motivation, testing them in a "Skinner box" in which their pecks led to reinforcement administered in various contingencies (e.g., LoLordo, 1971), and then counting the number of pigeon key pecks recorded on a strip chart. When I pursued a M.A. degree in Psychology at Wake Forest University, Dr. Robert Dufort had us read a photocopied version of Clark Hull's *Principles of behavior* (Hull, 1943), which was already out of print, and memorize the details of Hull's mathematico-deductive theory of learning with constructs like sHr (habit strength), D (drive), and K (motivation). Ah – the good old days of relatively straightforward behavioral science! Psychologists were definitely proud of our strategy for accruing knowledge: I have a clear mental image of a display apparatus in the lobby of Davie Hall (the location of the Psychology Department at UNC-Chapel Hill) that contained a pigeon in a Skinner box pecking a key to open a feeder. As students walked by, they could see that science was marching forward based on the ongoing research we were conducting!

1.3 What Is Explanation?

If a clearly articulated hypothesis regarding the logical relations among operationally defined constructs has been tested, have we ipso facto attained the goal of our science? The Logical Positivists might say yes, but contemporary philosophers of science would be less enthusiastic due to concern that Logical Positivism endorses a relatively weak definition of explanation. Specifically, Logical Positivism defines explanation as a description of an event based on 1) operational definitions and 2) the logical rule that links statements of initial conditions with outcomes, which is more or less the same as the formal articulation of a prediction. To expand a previously stated example, we could live in a world in which low atmospheric pressure is associated with higher likelihood of rain, whereas high atmospheric pressure is associated with lower likelihood of rain. This prediction is impressive and practical, but from the perspective of accrued knowledge, the conditional relation between atmospheric pressure and rain does not explain the mechanism that causes this phenomenon. And, as explanation emerges, collateral issues can emerge (e.g., is the relation limited to rain or does it include snow? Is the effect the same at all altitudes? Will the effect be altered by global warming?). Although explanation is enhanced by finding the cause of an outcome, explanation should also include positioning the phenomenon within a broader context of related laws and the categorization of the conditions and the outcomes. As pointed out by Salmon (2003), explanation is an answer to a "why" question and not simply the description of the relations among a subset of laws and events. Science can sometimes predict without explaining or it can induce specific alterations, but attainment of broader epistemic goals requires including an explanation of how we can make the prediction or cause the alteration.

Within the world of explanation, it is also important to recognize that explanation can have different definitions. The phrase "ultimate explanation" can be used to define why a behavior exists, and the phrase "proximate explanation" is more concerned with the mechanism whereby that behavior works. Scott-Phillips, Dickins, and West (2011) explore this distinction using the example of an infant's crying. When a human infant cries, the ultimate explanation would address the probability that crying evokes care from someone and thus promotes the infant's survival. In contrast, the proximate explanation of crying would refer to the specific context that makes the infant cry and also to the internal mechanisms that underlie the physical state that we label "crying." These two zones of explanation can be completely separate, but as pointed out by Scott-Phillips et al., a comprehensive explanation of behavior should include both perspectives.

Applying the definition of explanation to a topic that is currently very salient for me, it would be very interesting if we could attain a broad understanding of amyotrophic lateral sclerosis (ALS). There are presently some molecular explanations that focus on aspects of epigenetics, but other explanations will need to explain why ALS is more likely in certain geographical areas or in individuals who have had certain life experiences. Researchers who explore the proximate explanations of ALS try to explain the underlying neuromuscular phenomena that lead to the wide array of symptoms encountered by people with this diagnosis. And, proximate explanations of ALS would also address the challenges faced by human beings who encounter this problem and the decisions that they face as the disease progresses. Finally, and to be optimistic, a thorough ultimate and proximate understanding of ALS could also lead to the development of interventions that delay the progressive neuromuscular deterioration or reverse it. I hope that scientists will conduct the wide array of research that we need to develop this broad view!

1.4 Is Scientific Knowledge Truth?

As described above, Logical Positivists can use operationally defined constructs to make scientific progress by accruing observations designed to explore the truth of statements such as "If atmospheric pressure is low, it will rain." However, we quickly encounter another logistical and logical problem: How many observations of the same phenomenon would we need in order to prove that a statement describing the phenomenon is true? As David Hume noted in the 1700s (Hume, 2003), inductive inferences (i.e., broad generalizations based on descriptions of evidence) can suggest truth, but they cannot be verified directly. Even if every low-pressure moment we have observed thus far has been associated with rain, observations of these occurrences do not prove that the same phenomenon will occur forever (which is a particularly salient example for scientists who have noticed that our climate is probably changing!). The Logical Positivists initially took comfort in their assumption that confirmatory evidence provides confidence in a theory's truth, but their friend Karl Popper (Popper, 1934) noticed a flaw in this inductive logic. From a broader perspective, the world of rigorous research can not only never prove that a current phenomenon will be true in the future, but also almost always has too few tests to provide strong confidence that a hypothesis is completely true now.

Popper offered a radical remedy to this problem, and his proposed remedy has had a dramatic effect on science. Given that we cannot confirm a theory because there is always the possibility that counter-evidence will emerge eventually, a more effective strategy is to replace confirmation with the opposite approach: Rather than trying to prove that a theory is true, we should diligently attempt to acquire evidence that proves that a theory is false. A theory that has been subjected to a strong challenge (i.e., what Popper labeled a "grave risk of refutation") and survives this challenge has thus been corroborated and is a stronger candidate for being true. From this perspective, instead of focusing on verification, science should be oriented toward identifying theories that are incorrect, and the potential falsification of incorrect theories becomes a major component of scientific progress. For example, Einstein's theory of relatively became increasingly testable as physics progressed, and it has continued to survive grave risk of refutation and is currently accepted as a virtual fact. In contrast, the psychoanalytic theories proposed by Freud, Jung, Adler, and others were not amenable to translation into definitive and testable hypotheses. Evidence exists that could be considered consistent with these theories, but their lack of grave risk of refutation has undermined the status of these theories as accrued knowledge, their scientific credibility has abated, and from some perspectives they are viewed as poetry rather than science. The scientific focus on grave risk of refutation as a path toward truth has continued to grow and has affected how scientists design experiments, conduct statistical analyses, and draw inferences from their research findings. Each of these topics will be explored in subsequent chapters.

Returning to the broad approach to knowledge accrual that I described at the beginning of this chapter, scientific methodology has continued to evolve, which could support an increasingly strong case for credibility in knowledge accrual. However, consensus among scientists regarding the optimal approach to knowledge accrual can encounter additional challenges when knowledge accumulation is viewed from a social/political perspective. For example, Frank Sulloway (1997) used historical data from scientific rebellions to demonstrate the birth order effect known as deidentification, in which later-born scientists were more likely to reject normal science in contrast to first-born scientists, who were more likely to accept contemporary perspectives. Historian Thomas Kuhn (1962/1970) explored the history of various scientific theories and discovered that prominent scientific perspectives often go through distinct stages: They begin as immature science and eventually become widely known and accepted in the context that Kuhn labeled normal science. As scientists continue to gather knowledge, alternative theories and methods often emerge, which can lead to a crisis for the reigning perspective, a revolution, and eventually a resolution in which the new perspective replaces the previous perspective and becomes normal science as long as it can withstand subsequent challenges. Kuhn thus suggests that accrued knowledge is not necessarily truth: it emerges via a process by which a particular perspective is designated as normal science based on somewhat arbitrary political and sociological factors, as well as on issues of taste or persuasion.

The accrual of knowledge is thus not simply adding facts to an ever-increasing library. As noted by Popper, removing facts that have relatively low probabilistic support could be considered a more efficient and authoritative process than simply adding new potential facts. And, from the Kuhnian perspective, whole shelves in the library may get abandoned on the basis of revolutionary disciplinary changes. The somewhat arbitrary nature of this knowledge development process could undermine respect for the efficacy and validity of science, but looking at the science-based technological advances that have occurred in recent centuries (e.g., longer life span, cures for many diseases, indoor plumbing, television, computers, etc.), science is not easily dismissed.

I see no value in getting enmeshed here in an argument about absolute truth that would eventually tap into fundamental personal questions such as our spirituality and our conjecture about the future. Instead, I take comfort in embracing Donald Campbell's description of a process that he labeled "evolutionary epistemology." I had the good fortune of working with Donald Campbell during his semester as a visiting faculty member at Harvard University, which culminated in his William James lecture in 1977. I audited the course on evolutionary epistemology that Donald taught during his semester at Harvard. I also escorted him to several of the talks that he presented that semester in the Boston area, mostly in philosophy departments.

Evolutionary epistemology provides an interesting perspective on how science leads to the accrual of knowledge. Borrowing from biological descriptions of evolution, the general idea is that although the prominence, credibility, and survival of knowledge is affected by various influences, a piece of knowledge that is an accurate reflection of the world will have more long-term utility than a piece of knowledge that is incorrect. Thus the more accurate piece of knowledge will have a better chance of survival in comparison with knowledge that perseveres because we have not established an improved methodology that would refute it or found different knowledge that would be more functional, or because the knowledge has become broadly accepted in our culture. From this perspective, Popper's suggestion that hypotheses be subjected to grave risk of refutation could be seen as a selective elimination process designed to promote an evolutionary "survival of the fittest" among hypotheses. The longevity of accrued knowledge provides increasing confidence that the knowledge is correct, particularly when the knowledge has been subjected to grave risk of refutation. A particular piece of knowledge might rise or fall as a function of the contemporary view of normal science, but from an evolutionary perspective, knowledge that has long-standing consistent credibility could claim higher probability of being true than knowledge that emerged recently or was discredited long ago and has not re-emerged. Slow fluctuations in reigning worldviews, such as the millennia of belief that the sun orbits the earth, the centuries of belief in Newtonian mechanics, or the decades of belief that "refrigerator mothers" and infant immunizations cause autism spectrum disorder can add to our concern that knowledge that is being published and is popular is not necessarily true. In contrast, the re-emergence or consistent longevity of knowledge despite the vagaries of the knowledge acquisition process and the presence of ongoing challenges gives us confidence that selective retention can be viewed as epistemogenic evolutionary progress: Truths will flourish in the world of science and allow us to move forward with our collection of accrued knowledge.

A more contemporary perspective on the truth of knowledge is the distinction between realism and instrumentalism. Scientific realism is the idea that all of the constructs that we are talking about as scientists actually exist in some sense and that our scientific endeavor is thus an attempt to explore and describe entities that actually exist. In contrast, instrumentalism sees scientific discoveries as convenient representations that have usefulness for predicting what will happen or explaining why something happens, but these discoveries do not have any claim regarding what actually exists. Philosophers and researchers could engage in battles in which particular constructs are judged as more or less realistic and more or less instrumental, but I see little to be gained in that debate. Indeed, I agree with Cacioppo, Semin, and Berntson (2004) in their suggestion that our most critical goal as scientists is to form a synthesis of realism and instrumentalism. That is, scientists should adopt both approaches in an integrated way to guide their theory and research. Scientists who lean toward instrumentalism are less likely to believe in the existence of underlying constructs, but they take comfort in the fact that some research leads to models or explanations that become increasingly effective at predicting outcomes or dictating interventions that alter the apparent course of ongoing development. These scientists are not concerned with truth per se: Their explicit goal is to posit structures that describe, predict, and explain particular phenomena. Realists and instrumentalists can easily and effectively share the goal of helping science become increasingly accurate in its description, prediction, and explanation of relevant phenomena.

2 Developmental Science in Context

Each developmental scientist could offer a unique definition of developmental science, and here is my extremely broad rendition: Developmental science is the systematic exploration of human behavior and mental processing and how these attributes emerge, change, and dissipate from conception until death. Our exploration of developmental science generally seeks description, prediction, explanation, and/or modification of relevant phenomena. The primary academic perspectives of most developmental scientists are developmental psychology, clinical psychology, developmental neuroscience, or education. Additional topics that are relevant for this exploration include philosophy of mind, sociology, economics, religion, neurology, genetics and epigenetics, psychiatry, pediatrics, muscles and bones, nutrition and gut brain, animal models, statistical analysis and mathematical modeling, environmental pollutants, physical and mental health and illness, and other domains that can be added to this list now or that will be added based on the evolution of technology.

I sometimes use the metaphor of seeing developmental science as a valley between the mountain of philosophy of science and the mountain of biology. We need to appreciate and understand our connection to each mountain, but climbing them is a very rigorous activity. When I began reading about philosophy of science (and particularly philosophy of mind), the references I encountered were usually citations of books rather than articles. I pursued this at one point in my career, and I currently have many shelves of books on this topic. Reading them was virtually impossible because each book was built on other books and it takes a long time to read a book. So, I recommend picking up an awareness of what we learn from that mountain, but if you are tempted to climb it, I also recommend finding a feasible strategy for exploring it (e.g., find an undergraduate or graduate course and audit it). Various philosophical topics (e.g., Logical Positivism) will be mentioned in many chapters, and this will not be an amply articulated theme. My exploration of the mountain of biology began with learning the terms used to describe various parts of the brain, the structure of cells within the nervous system, and the general architecture of the connection between the brain and sensory organs or muscles. More rigorous training occurred when I used my flexible schedule during a semester of research leave to audit a course in the Yale medical school on neurology. I attended lectures and read materials, but I quickly realized that my performance on exams would be embarrassing. Courses and collaborations will introduce this topic, and hands-on experience gathering and analyzing biological data will provide the most relevant perspective. I will mention various biological topics, and this too will not be an amply articulated theme.

My goal in this chapter is to review the challenges that developmental science faces in comparison to the challenges associated with various other sciences. And, I will address the importance of linking developmental science to other relevant sciences, particularly neuroscience, and handling appropriately the potential problems that these linkages can evoke.

2.1 Exploring an Open System

Many of the challenges in developmental science emerge due to the fact that we are exploring an open system. The term "closed system" is used to describe phenomena that are isolated from the broader environment and thus can have a relatively deterministic predictability. In contrast, the term "open system" often describes phenomena that have an interactive relationship with a broader environment, thus accommodating a wide array of influences and a relatively non-deterministic predictability. For example, imagine a research study that is investigating how individuals are affected by the ambient temperature they are experiencing. A closed system experiment could include a group of rodents with similar genetic configurations whose activity level is being measured while they are experiencing a range of ambient temperatures. In contrast, an open system experiment could include a group of people who are experiencing a particular temperature depending upon their access to, and choice among, alternative locations. Ambient temperature in the closed system could predict internal change in the metabolism rate in the rodent. Ambient temperature in the open system would be experienced differently by individual people and thus would be less predictive of internal change. Extending this to the world of developmental science, the people in the open system might also be affected by their previous experiences with ambient temperature, skills at coping with ambient temperature, access to resources that provide protection from ambient temperature, or political beliefs about climate change.

Another example of a research project in a relatively closed system could include a group of young adults who have agreed to participate in a research project in which they will be "on vacation" for several days during which they will be housed in a laboratory, receive meals with specific types of food, engage in specific activities, be allowed to sleep at a specific time, and have their weight monitored on a predetermined schedule with multiple measurements. A relatively open system could include a comparable group of young adults whose participation includes describing the foods that they are eating, the activities that they engage in, their amount of sleep, and their weight. Metabolic processing in both systems could be explored using models that link caloric intake with various metrics of activity and sleep. However, parameters in the open system will include each participant's personal food, activity, sleep choices, accuracy in reporting, pre-established expectations, etc. The variables that influence behavior in an open system not only exist at different levels but also can play very different roles. For example, some relevant variables remain relatively constant, some can be manipulated within the context of an experimental setting, and some change randomly. Within any open system, some variables will be identified as nuisance variables in the sense that they have strong, possibly systematic influence, and scientists can neither control nor measure them. For example, consider the challenges facing a developmental scientist who is attempting to measure the efficacy of an intervention that is designed to improve reading skills in children who live in a poor environment. Variables such as the parents' attitudes, the child's motivation, the interventionist's relationship with the child, the child's interest in the reading materials, the child's level of nutrition and sleep, etc. are all influential and difficult to control or measure. Even if all variables in an open system are accessible, the number of variables that could be relevant for describing a person's experience or ongoing behavior in an open system is virtually infinite and could include variables that have influenced a person's representation of the world, altered a person's appearance, or induced epigenetic changes that might not be manifest until evoked by some external influence on that person or on that person's progeny. The obvious implication here is that it is extremely difficult to measure the constructs and variables that are relevant for developmental science.

2.2 Meeting Translational Goals

The previous chapter offered the broad perspective that science is a contemporary mechanism that is used to accrue knowledge that is not necessarily focused on immediate survival per se, but long-term survival and quality of life. Looking now at the research choices that scientists make, we can see that some scientists are fascinated by questions in domains that are primarily theoretically relevant (e.g., cosmology, particle physics, quantum states). And, some scientists investigate phenomena that move practical knowledge forward but are not necessarily or obviously related to anything that would improve the quality of human life (e.g., aspects of animal behavior, linguistics). Within the various domains of developmental science, I have seen an evolution in the past four decades from an approach to research that was once referred to as applied research to what is now labeled as translational research. Looking at this from a personal perspective, I would describe this as a shift from what was sometimes described as relatively mundane applied science to what is now becoming an increasingly important target for successful developmental science.

The solution to human problems does not always emerge directly from a focus on a specific problem: some solutions emerge from a broader understanding of how humans function. For example, for many decades researchers focused directly on applying specific therapeutic interventions to remove cancerous cells. However, from a broader contemporary perspective, our more innovative and effective cancer treatments seem to be emerging from research on fundamental cellular process, epigenetics, nanotechnology, and other basic phenomena that can lead to effective translational treatments for cancer. Thus, we should support science on theoretically interesting and important questions and not limit ourselves to research that is explicitly translatable. However, I do recommend that we keep "translation" in mind in all research that we conduct, and that we make strong efforts to use collaborations as an opportunity for translating our research into its practical implications. For example, we could use our knowledge regarding infant development to diagnose infants who are at-risk for eventual health issues and then create possible therapeutic interventions for infants who are developing atypically. Moreover, our translational opportunities for making optimal use of developmental science also include political opportunities such as helping practitioners in our judicial system make wise decisions regarding parental problems, helping clinicians remediate parents who are having problems, and helping legislators become able to make wise decisions regarding funding and implementation of public education in North Carolina and other states. Developmental science is a discipline that has extremely broad and deep relevance for human life, and we should attempt to make optimal use of this opportunity.

2.3 Social Science versus Physical Science

Empirical research evokes unique challenges in both social science (e.g., psychology, sociology, etc.) and physical science (e.g., physics, chemistry, etc.), and both are important because they contribute to the accrued knowledge that supports our contemporary civilization. Both domains of science have made progress, and both are bordered by a vast zone of mystery that reflects all that we do not know about ourselves and our world. Given this lack of knowledge, it is impossible to predict the exact value that any new discovery could have that might allow us to predict or control threats like oil wells leaking in the Gulf of Mexico, suicide bombers, ALS, cancer, or attention deficit/hyperactivity disorder (ADHD). And, given that talented, highly motivated scientists have spent centuries exploring the frontiers of ignorance in both domains, it is likely that the easy answers have already been harvested, and advancement in either domain will entail addressing increasingly difficult questions.

As described in the previous chapter, Logical Positivism confers credibility on empirical science and is an obvious model for research on the phenomena studied in physics, chemistry, biology, and related fields. However, the guidelines suggested by Logical Positivism become problematic when we address the increasingly complex phenomena that constitute the social sciences. Physical scientists encounter problems when their research leads to phenomena that are at the extremes of size (e.g., galactic astronomy, sub-atomic particles), time (e.g., cosmology, evanescent new elements), or complexity (e.g., epigenetics). Social scientists encounter problems when there is more than one way to measure a particular construct, and when influences cannot be observed, phenomena are dispositional or probabilistic, or causal paths are complex and co-directional. Unfortunately, developmental scientists are social scientists who encounter these problems constantly.

The difficulty of social science calls to mind the linguistic convention of labeling the physical sciences as "hard" in comparison to nonphysical sciences that are labeled "soft" in the sense of ambiguous, inexact, or not rigorous. This distinction has relevance, but as applied to the physical sciences versus social sciences, it is important to note that the distinction emerges as a description of the science's target phenomena rather than the science itself. Social phenomena are almost always characterized as being underlying abstract constructs that are measured via more or less indirect behavioral manifestations. And, the complexity of causal relations in open systems preclude the exactitude that sometimes can be manifest in physical phenomena in closed systems. Finally, rigor as applied to a synthetic, inorganic phenomenon in an experimenter-controlled environment is very different than the rigor that can be applied in research with fellow human beings who have consented to participate in research that adheres to ethical and legal constraints.

Most people tend to underestimate the difficulties faced by peers and overestimate their own personal challenges. I acknowledge that my limited view of the physical sciences might blind me to the inherent problems in that world as compared to the exploration of social sciences, but I do see measurement in the physical sciences as relatively simple and easy in comparison to measurement in social sciences, and particularly in developmental science, which is notably complex and difficult. Any direct comparison of the problems encountered when exploring physical sciences versus social sciences will be inherently limited because so many different phenomena and methods are used within each type of science, and many phenomena are targets of interest in both domains. I will offer a compromise: let's adopt a vocabulary that reflects the fact that all sciences are hard (i.e., difficult) by definition, and that some are most focused on physical phenomena while others are more focused on social phenomena. Social science would be the most obvious domain referred to as hard science, but to reduce competition and animosity, this ambiguous term should be replaced with the more accurate terms physical science and social science, with neither tagged as a hard or soft science.

2.4 Going Beyond Research on Human Behavior

My definition of developmental science refers to the exploration of human behavior and mental processing, but this exploration can be advanced via exploration of the broad array of animals who behave and have mental processes, the underlying biologic infrastructural levels in human and nonhuman animal bodies such as muscles, bones, nerves, hormones, genes, etc. and how this array of participants and their underlying infrastructure can enhance our understanding of behavior and mental processing. For example, what are the advantages and disadvantages of using nonhuman animals to investigate behavioral constructs like learning, mothering, aggressiveness, autism spectrum disorder, etc.? And, what is the relevance of the underlying infrastructure for describing, predicting, controlling, and understanding behaviors and mental processes like memory, emotion regulation, self-concept, attachment, etc.?

From one perspective, recognizing the relevance of a wide array of animals and their underlying biological infrastructure is yet another reminder that behavioral development is an extremely complex open system. Many scientists tend to focus on human behavior and conduct research with human participants, but related behavior and mental processes emerge in many ways in various animals, with the habitat, lifestyle, and research contexts differing across all species. In addition to our focus on behavior, we also measure many obvious observable structural differences in human beings like height and weight, locomotion and fine-motor skills, visual acuity and aural sensitivity, etc. and we can see that these biological parameters obviously affect behavior and mental processing in relatively straightforward ways. Advances in biological measurement have opened an additional perspective, which is less obvious, but even more exemplary of a complex open system: Behavior and mental processing are also affected by underlying differences in genes, hormones, brain structure, nutrition, environmental toxins, neurotransmitters, muscle fibers, cardiac responsiveness, etc. These underlying parameters can be measured in various ways, almost all of which are cumbersome and intrusive, and thus difficult to align with a specific behavior at that behavior's time of occurrence. For example, contemporary techniques for assessing the brain involve constraints like wearing a head net filled with electrodes and/or lying without moving in a large, loud apparatus. Human and nonhuman participants in most research that taps underlying biological variables are thus in an atypical context that obviously affects their behavior in both obvious and subtle ways.

We have realized for centuries that the brain is relevant for understanding behavior and mental processing. The phrenological examination of the human skull was a popular and inefficient step in the correct direction. Researchers have recorded electrical activity in individual neurons using the insertion of electrodes for almost one century. This technique has advanced our understanding of underlying neural mechanisms and functions, but with obvious, strong limitations such as focusing on one cell and ignoring billions of others, only using animal models, and causing pain and damage through the data-gathering process. Recent advances in technology have boosted brain-measurement progress by creating an extensive array of sophisticated measurement techniques that give us access to many aspects of the brain's functionality.

Electroencephalography (EEG) measures voltage on the head to monitor the brain's broad array of electrical activity. The metaphor I use to describe EEG is standing outside of a baseball stadium and monitoring the noise produced by the audience in the stadium to differentiate a hit from an out, or the home team at-bat versus the visiting team at-bat. EEG is relatively primitive in comparison to contemporary neuroimaging, but has various advantages such as being very accurate as an index of the time course of neural processing, much less expensive, easily implemented and conducted, no background noise, and virtually no risk. Neuroimaging is the use of various technologies to monitor the structure and function of the nervous system, and thus provides a much more detailed spatial, but not necessarily temporal, description.

Neuroimaging has evolved dramatically in recent decades to include various techniques such as magnetic resonance imaging (MRI) that uses magnetic fields and radio waves to produce images of brain structures; functional magnetic resonance imaging (fMRI) that monitors blood flow that is correlated with neural activity; magnetoencephalography (MEG) that measures the magnetic fields produced by neural electrical activity; and positron emission tomography (PET) that measures emissions from radioactive chemicals that are absorbed during brain activity.

EEG and neuroimaging have become increasingly prominent in developmental science research. However, as we navigate toward a cumulative developmental science, it is important to avoid the siren's song of measurement techniques that have the imprimatur of science simply because they provide the straightforward quantification that is associated with measurement of closed-system physical and mechanical phenomena. Our critical and difficult challenge is to examine the role that these variables can play in our measurement techniques in order to use them to our best advantage and to also remain aware of the obvious complications that must influence our interpretation of brain data. The following paragraphs describe several examples of potential problems associated with neuroimaging.

One obvious problem with neuroimaging is that it is complex and expensive, and thus must be conducted by professionals in a relatively sophisticated laboratory. This inherently imposes constraints on the population of researchers who have access to neuroimaging and how many participants can be enrolled in research projects. As noted by Cacioppo, Berntson, and Decety (2012), relatively small neuroimaging studies do not provide a sufficient basis for broad generalizations, thus evoking the need for meta-analytic methods to create definitive analyses of neuroimaging data. Another obvious problem is that the neuroimaging assessment is never natural and always includes levels of potential discomfort and distraction associated with wearing equipment, maintaining stillness, ignoring extremely loud noises, and being in an extremely unusual context. Almost all participants in neuroimaging will experience some level of uncertainty and stress.

Another problematic aspect of neuroimaging is the tendency to assert that participants are manifesting a specific mental state that is being indexed. At a behavioral level, a participant might be engaged in a task that is challenging working memory, might be processing a visual image that is being presented, or might be pondering a question that has been asked. Any behavioral description will always be accompanied by other ongoing mental processes, maintenance of stamina and motivation, underlying discomfort and confusion, distraction by aspects of the neuroimaging process, etc., and we cannot define and describe exactly what mental state is being measured by neuro-imaging although we can, and do, often use a "subtraction method" where two tasks or trials are described as differing only with respect to a particular task demand.

At a more fundamental level, another problematic aspect of neuroimaging is confusion regarding what underlying biological processes are being tapped. Logothetis (2007) describes the wide range of hemodynamic responses that are assessed in various neuroimaging techniques and are interpreted as surrogates for neural functioning, and this leads to the obvious concern that fMRI data reflect "a complex interplay of changes in cerebral blood flow, cerebral blood volume and blood oxygenation" (p. 1230). This also leads to unanswered questions regarding the types of neural activity that evoke the most metabolism, the types of cells that are being tapped, the link between neural activity and cell metabolism, and the processes that link energy supply and demand in brain tissue. Beck (2010) notes that all fMRI data contain radio waves and magnetic signals that require extensive processing to be converted into a configuration that is labeled an image. Even more problematic for developmental neuroscience is the necessity of harvesting fMRI data as a contrast over time. The fMRI data are not a brain image per se. Rather, they reflect how the brain changes during tasks or conditions rather than the brain's specific response to a stimulus. For example, an fMRI signal that emerges while a person is seeing a dog could be different if that signal is compared with the signal that emerges while the person is seeing a different dog, a different animal, a chair, or a design. From this perspective, data interpreted as a lack of brain activity as measured by fMRI is actually a lack of difference between two signals that could each have evoked strong activity.

Researchers who describe individual neurons when discussing fMRI results are ignoring the fact that the smallest unit of measurement in this technique is called a voxel, which is only a few millimeters on each side, but can be described as containing approximately 5.5 million neurons (Sanders, 2009). And, some researchers have used the simplistic strategy of computing multiple correlations between individual voxels and a behavioral measurement and then reporting only correlations that exceed a particular threshold. Vul, Harris, Winkielman, and Pashler (2009) surveyed authors of publications showing correlation between brain activation and personality measures and found that a majority of researchers had used an inappropriate statistical strategy that harvested and over-interpreted strong correlations. Based on this analysis, Vul et al. concluded that inappropriate analysis in many fMRI publications has caused inflated correlations and inappropriate scattergrams, thus leading to inappropriate conclusions. The fMRI research community has become aware of this concern, is now less vulnerable to presenting biased correlations, and has shifted to including appropriate disclaimers in their publications (Vul & Pashler, 2012). However, further progress is needed to determine the location of signals in fMRI data and to combine data across large numbers of participants. We will feel more comfortable reading results in this domain when developmental scientists in graduate school (and developmental scientists who are maintaining an effective statistical toolbox) are required to have completed a course on "spatial statistics."

Continuing the broader perspective, a final zone of difficulty in the measurement of brain function is contemporary media's obvious fascination with any research that uses the word "brain." I read a newspaper story recently claiming that "billions of neurons fire in the brains of stock market traders as they decide whether to buy or sell shares in a matter of seconds." I would offer the additional possibility that billions of neurons fire in the brains of stock market traders constantly and would be associated with every activity they perform, mental state they experience, stimulus they perceive, etc. An article in the *Harvard Business Review* (2012) warns us that managers who pester their staff "jack up everyone's anxiety level, which activates the portion of the brain that processes threats – the amygdala – and steals resources from the prefrontal cortex, which is responsible for effective problem solving" (p. 100). A similarly abstract image of the brain could be used to promote any advice being offered to managers. Finally, the cover-story of *National Geographic* in February 2014, entitled "The new science of the brain," describes a broad array of research and provides very interesting graphics including 67 more or less clothed images (i.e., not just faces) of celebrities Jennifer Aniston and Halle Berry to accompany the claim that researchers have found an individual nerve cell that fires only when subjects were shown pictures of Jennifer Aniston and another neuron that responded only to pictures of Halle Berry. The magazine publisher might have been less interested in publishing claims that one of our 100+ billion neurons only fires when someone is shown a specific unattractive image.

Beck (2010) explores various reasons why the popular press focuses on human neuroimaging and offers the explanation that brain references or images provide a relatively simple and concrete explanation of behavior and mental processes. Another problem with media reporting of neuroimaging is that people often interpret direct measurement of the brain as tapping something that is innate rather than something that is being learned or has been learned, which is particularly problematic because it can undermine the developmental perspective. And, many people fail to realize that every experience we encounter affects our brain in some way. From this perspective, although data that reflect direct measurement of the brain can be useful, the direct measurement of the brain is also extremely vulnerable to being interpreted incorrectly. We can blame the media for this problem, but the most effective strategy for repairing the problem will be to facilitate better data analysis and communication from scientists who report data based on neuroimaging of the brain.

2.5 Genetics, Genomics, and Epigenetics

Genes and heredity are another biologic topic that is relevant for developmental science and that many of us have seen evolve dramatically in recent decades based on advances in technology. We began with the Mendelian perspective in which the genetic configuration we received from our parents' sperm and egg was described as essentially a blueprint that would determine various aspects of our body, and we were taught to question the Lamarckian perspective in which individuals could inherit acquired characteristics. The Watson and Crick discovery of the double-helix structure of DNA was a major advance, and it has led to the complicated world of gene mapping, understanding of gene regulation, identification of gene mutations, development of medical genetics, and techniques for artificially manipulating genes.

My main progress in this domain has been to shift my metaphor from blueprint to recipe book. That is, our initial genetic structure is an extensive set of recipes that are available in our genes and get selected and implemented in various contexts. For example, the recipe that was used to generate hair on top of my head was very effective for several decades, but some developmental change in my body then evoked a different recipe that shifted me to being bald. From an epigenetic perspective, various influences can alter the recipes and thus have modified effects on me and on my progeny.

Given the profoundly potent influence that epigenetics has on almost all aspects of development, all developmental scientists should devote some resources toward monitoring our ongoing understanding of this domain. My most successful exercise was reading David Moore's recent book *The developing genome: An introduction to behavioral epigenetics* (Moore, 2015). I also recommend that any Department of Psychology that seeks to validate its scientific credibility by altering its name should consider adding Epigenetics to the name along with other equally relevant perspectives such as Nutrition, Mental Health, and possibly Neuroscience.

2.6 Moving Forward in Adopting an Appropriate Perspective on Biology

Philosophers often notice aspects of developmental science that lead them to ask us questions that they find interesting, and that we find confusing. For example, in the previous chapter, we discussed science as truth. In the present context, philosophical questions lead us to confront the relevance of various levels of the complex human system. Behavior and mental processing seem most salient to many developmental scientists, but we realize that these phenomena are being manifest by an organism composed of cells in a complex organization of conductivity, chemical interaction, electrical interaction, and change. The organism is also in a context that includes external physical factors, fellow organisms, and social traditions that have evolved. Marshall (2009) reviews the challenges that emerge in efforts to describe and understand this complex situation. Some researchers prefer viewing behavior and mental processing from an abstract perspective with no interest in the underlying biology (that is, mind without body). This leads to interest in computer models, parallel distributed processing, connectionism, artificial intelligence, and the movie "Her." In contrast, some researchers prefer to focus on the underlying biology as the only level that is necessary for support of a realistic concrete explanation, which leads to interest in coma, brain death, persistent vegetative states, etc. Finding an effective synergy linking biology and behavior is a burden that is shared by all broad-minded researchers with expertise in either domain. Marshall explores the advantages and disadvantages of each perspective and arrives at a well-reasoned and compelling advocacy of an embodied perspective in which neuroscience (and other underlying biological processes) are combined with behavior and mental processes to combine "internal and external aspects of representations through the sensory motor interface of an organism that is deeply embedded in the world" (p. 122). In other words, the brain implements the mind and the mind supervenes on the brain. Cacioppo and Decety (2009) evoke Descartes' historical distinction between body and mind, and they advocate for accurate definition and measurement of aspects of mind and linking this to relevant brain mechanisms. Barrett (2009) in the same journal and the same year advocates for better measurement of complex psychological states and linking them to the brain. This is obviously a perspective shared by many scientists and an important goal to pursue in developmental science.

Based on my interest in the early development of infant mind, contrasting the validity and relevance of various levels of analysis seems rather ridiculous in comparison to the advantage of integrating the levels. When an egg and a sperm are connected, they begin the process of expansion, differentiation, and reorganization that characterizes human beings. The moment of their initial connection can be seen as the beginning of life from a spiritualist perspective, but the conjecture that the fertilized egg has the underlying structure that could support a mind evokes a relatively unrealistic definition of mind. From a developmental science perspective, as the process of underlying expansion, differentiation, and reorganization continues, the underlying structure allows the organism to become capable of increasingly complex behaviors and mental processes that can be credibly labeled "mind" at some point. Prenatal neurobiological development has been studied for decades, and we have developed an intriguing description of how cells in the neural crest migrate and consolidate, leading to the structure that is eventually the brain and nerves. The interaction among the participants in the neurological system is extremely complex, involving neurotransmitters, electrical signals, cell migration, connection to other cells, etc. The neurologic system is also set up to receive signals from surfaces of the body that represent input from the external environment in the form of light, sound, touch, etc. and these inputs alter the neurologic system in ways that are described as representations. As these representations progress, the system also engages in internal processing that affects storage of the representations, interaction among representations, and various translations of representation into activities conducted by the muscles and tendons that are attached to the bones.

A physical description of this system is possible, and we recognize its incredible complexity. The neural system evolves into a brain that has 100+ billion cells that can be categorized into many types, more or less interconnected with other cells, and differentially responsive based on experience. Projecting forward from our ongoing understanding of the complexity of the brain, it seems virtually impossible that we will ever reach a point in which we can map and describe the configuration of an individual's entire neural system and how all aspects of the system change as a function of experience, environment, health, nutrition, etc. Will the schematic drawing include the shrub cell, first described in *Science*, November 27, 2015 (Xiaolong et al., 2015) in an exploration of connectivity among morphologically defined cell types? And, recent research shows that the nets of proteins and carbohydrates that blanket nerve cells form a pattern that create the representational experience we label long-term memory (Palida et al., 2015). These patterns last longer than the underlying nerve cells. Where will this fit in the diagram? The evolution of neural mapping will help developmental science make better use of the underlying infrastructure as an explanation of behavior. However, we will probably not have the exact mapping of this extremely complex system for several millennia. Instead, we should continue to focus on the behaviors and mental processes that we can experience in ourselves or observe in others.

From this perspective, even though our understanding of the underlying biological infrastructure is relatively primitive and is not developmental science per se, we are aware that it can be used in many ways to inform the questions we seek to answer in developmental science. One strategy is to use the underlying infrastructure to differentiate behaviors and mental processes that seem similar, are notably ambiguous, have no obvious behavioral manifestation, or are not necessarily available to an individual's insight or awareness. For example, it is easy for us to postulate that someone is stressed, curious, intentional, aware of something, or lying, but we have no obvious way to detect or measure these states. We also make inferences regarding cognitive phenomena like the nature of a representation, the components of information processing, recognition, or different types of imagery, but measurement of these phenomena is always relatively indirect and thus affected by various confounds. Several decades ago, I collaborated in an unpublished study in which we attempted to use EKG signals to differentiate words that infants did or did not understand. For over a century, scientists have collaborated with the judicial system to develop physiological methods for differentiating between honesty and deception, and progress toward this goal has continued with the addition of each new physiologic measure that has been developed. Marshall (2009) describes an inferential strategy labeled "forward inference" in which physiological measurement is used to discriminate between behaviors that have similar prototypic manifestations but are based on different underlying processes. If differences in brain activation patterns emerge for related tasks, this suggests that the tasks may utilize different cognitive processes (e.g., a guess versus a memory; a lie versus a sarcastic joke; an intentional act versus an accident).

Another strategy is to use physiologic measures as "biomarkers" to improve clinical diagnoses and to profile individuals for possible therapeutic interventions by exploring underlying dispositional tendencies such as easily evoked frustration, a tendency toward over-reaction to emotion-inducing situations, a strong potential to abuse a child, vulnerability to suicide, etc. The advantage here is not only the detection of a subtle or unconscious state but also the opportunity to predict something before it happens and possibly to identify potential interventions and prevent it from happening, and to monitor the efficiency of those interventions.

Finally, mapping underlying physiologic changes could help us monitor the timing of developmental change and improve our understanding of the processes associated with behavioral or mental processing changes at a micro level (e.g., the process of learning), or at a macro level (e.g., moving from concrete operations to formal operations in the Piagetian perspective). Perhaps most obvious from a developmental perspective, physiological measurements offer a wide range of responses that are useful for measuring aspects of participants who have limited capacity for communication. For example, electronic signals can be used to assess fetal heart rate or infant hearing. And, even more compelling, most of our current understanding of infant cognitive development is based on using visual preference techniques. Eye movements are the only component of the central nervous system that can be viewed directly from an external perspective, and ocular musculature is the first motor system that transcends reflex and becomes amenable to intentional control. Additional opportunities to use underlying physiologic changes to monitor or influence developmental change will emerge when various specific aspects of eye movements that are being monitored can be linked to contingencies such as the stimulus presentations that are being seen or the rewards that are received based on visual behavior.

A similar evolution of micro-level specialization appears to be occurring in all aspects of biological science. When I attended talks on genetics, genomics, epigenetics, neuroimaging, immunology, nutrition, etc., I frequently faced the uncomfortable chore of trying to comprehend what has become essentially a foreign language for me. This difficulty can be attributed to my own lack of training on biological topics. However, from my perspective, the specialists in the various aspects of biological science who speak to me in a language that I do not understand are not communicating very well, and more broadly, they are not seeing the difficulty and importance of linking the underlying biological science to the broader behavioral phenomena.

The evolution of technology in biological measurement has identified mechanisms that will be relevant for our understanding of behavioral development, but the path to that synergy is not easy, and we have some risk of being detoured through a Tower of Babel. For example, I remember attending a seminar in neuroscience many years ago and listening to a talk on the genetics/genomics of ASD. I was able to comprehend the general goals outlined in the introduction, but when the speaker began reporting specific findings, I floated along in the sea of jargon and only experienced one moment of insight. The speaker described a study in which extensive biochemical and statistical tools were used to identify specific genes related to language development in children with ASD. What was most salient to me was that language development was measured in this study using the incredibly crude technique of asking parents to indicate the date when their infant had said his or her first word and first phrase. Any expert in the field of language development would probably laugh at this primitive measure, point out various flaws in validity and reliability, and note that the variable will be a proxy for an array of factors such as the child's sex or the parent's level of education. The painful analogy that came to mind was imagining a comparable study in which a language development specialist conducted an extensive assessment of child language and explored correlations with genetics by examining chromosomes using a microscope to measure their length. It is highly unlikely that blindly linking sophistication with ignorance will ever attain viable conclusions, and I see the need for finding an effective synergy linking biology and behavior as a burden that is shared by all broad-minded researchers with expertise in either domain.

Another salient problem in this domain is that developmental scientists who attempt to measure the subtle intricacies of behavior are likely to be tempted by the robust flow of data that emerges from a simple gauge or meter, and by the respect that direct measurement of underlying biological processes evokes from our colleagues, funders, and the media. Also, new measurement instruments, testing protocols, and pharmacological interventions are often owned by entrepreneurs and thus are marketed aggressively. Will developmental science automatically attain its goals if advances in technology allow us to monitor the entire wiring diagram of the nervous system; the interplay of transmitters, hormones, and cells; the part of the brain that is most activated when we think about a particular topic; a gene that makes a protein that is associated with ASD, etc.? In my opinion, the obvious answer is "no." Biology, neuroscience, endocrinology, epigenetics, etc. are all relevant topics in developmental science, but a complete mechanical blueprint of all aspects of the human body will not automatically answer our focal questions regarding the development of psychological processes and our understanding of diseases. Biological variables can play important roles in our efforts to describe, control, predict, and explain development, and will do so if, and only if, we find ways to infuse biology into our research on behavioral development in a way that will help us attain our goals. To make best use of biological variables, we must articulate their roles carefully and monitor how we use them.

3 Defining Constructs and Variables

The difficulty of establishing operational definitions of appropriate constructs is another salient legacy from Logical Positivism that remains problematic for developmental scientists in their attempts to accrue knowledge. The approach to behavioral science adopted by early researchers Hull, Spence, and their colleagues led to cumulative knowledge that was based entirely on arbitrary and unrealistic definitions of constructs like learning and motivation, and to results that not only failed to generalize beyond rodents but also were sometimes limited to specific species of laboratory rats bred for laboratory research and reared in unnatural circumstances. The Logical Positivist preference for empirical verification also promoted B. F. Skinner's behaviorist perspective in which he focused on observable phenomena (e.g., Skinner, 1972). Most mental terms do not meet the Logical Positivist criterion of being verifiable through experience, so Skinnerian behaviorists adopted a stimulus-response level of description that eventually ran out of fuel because behavioral science needs complex constructs like anxiety, attention, curiosity, and memory to describe, predict, control, and explain behavior despite the fact that these constructs do not meet the Logical Positivism definitional criteria.

Trespassing again into the worlds of philosophy, history, and other domains of intellectual scholarship, I will revert once again to my strategy of offering simple definitions for relevant terms. Specifically, I will use the term "construct" to refer to an unobserved or unobservable dispositional phenomenon, and the term "variable" to refer to an observable phenomenon that can be measured more or less directly. A philosopher of science might ask me for more articulate definitions of these two terms, but I would defer the request because I am confident that my relatively loose definitions of these terms will be adequate to allow me to describe the process that I am advocating for developing constructs and variables that will allow us to accrue a cumulative developmental science. For additional credibility, I note that my definitions are consistent with the distinction described by MacCorquodale and Meehl (1948) when they noticed that the behaviorist bandwagon was becoming mired in mud. The extensive conversation/debate among Tolman, Hull, Skinner, and other behaviorists in the 1930s and 1940s regarding mathematical models, scientific laws, the relation between motivation and drive, theories of learning, etc. is an interesting topic, but to skip to MacCorquodale and Meehl's conclusion, they proposed a linguistic convention for psychological theorists that they hoped would clarify ongoing discussions. The term "intervening variable" was defined as a quantity obtained via an empirical variable that has no definitive link to broader non-observed entities or processes, and the term "hypothetical construct" was defined as a theoretical idea that is not implicitly reducible to direct observation and measurement.

The terms "construct" and "variable" work reasonably well when applied to both physical science and developmental science. Physical science accrues knowledge about constructs like gravity or fusion, and developmental science accrues knowledge about constructs like memory or attention. Physical science measures variables such as temperature and Richter magnitude, and developmental science measures variables such as recall of specific digits in a phone number or reaction time for shifting gaze toward a peripheral stimulus. My goal in this chapter is to explore the relationship between constructs and variables, and use this perspective to shift our consciousness away from our automatic use of scientific terms and move us toward a more creative, synthetic perspective in which we address important issues regarding where the constructs and variables in our language of science come from and how these terms could and should change as we use them to accrue knowledge.

3.1 Top-Down Constructs

It is sobering to note that after more than a century of empirical research in developmental science, the constructs that we explore often reflect the folk psychological explanatory ideas described long ago by William James, James Mark Baldwin, Sigmund Freud, and other ancestors. Moreover, many of our current constructs were constituent parts of medieval folklore, various ancient Greek and Roman philosophical traditions, and descriptions noted in the Bible, the Koran, and other worldview documents that reflect consensus human knowledge and understanding over the past millennia. This top-down approach to establishing a scientific vocabulary begins with large, broad ideas and thus is aligned with what philosophers label as "sense meaning" or "semantic meaning" in which a construct can have general meaning without being linked to a specific or exacting referent or definition. This generality of meaning has allowed humans to communicate with each other, to translate abstract ideas across different languages, and to maintain some degree of semantic continuity across dramatic changes in civilization and technology. For example, when we read in Genesis chapter 2 that the first man and woman were naked but not ashamed, we easily understand the relatively specific term naked and the relatively abstract term ashamed.

From this perspective, developmental science incorporates some constructs that have been relevant for discussing human social interactions for as long as humans have observed each other and have been capable of, and inclined to, verbalize and share their observations. Thus, most of these constructs refer to phenomena that are imbedded in our cultural traditions, salient in our perception of the world, and well-represented in our vocabulary. For example, it can be salient and useful to characterize our peers as having behavioral tendencies such as trustworthiness, intelligence, or greed. This affects how we interact with them and predict or understand what they will do in specific situations. Interpersonal observations can be criticized as being inexact, biased, or non-systematic, but these objections do not invalidate the utility of the overarching folk psychological constructs that our observations address. Indeed, an evolutionary epistemology perspective would suggest that constructs that are patently false are less likely to have been retained in our accumulated knowledge than constructs that generate and support useful predictions and explanations of the behavior of our fellow humans. The longevity of folk psychological constructs does not prove their validity, but it does enhance their salience, credibility, and potential for validity.

One strategy for exploring constructs is to compare intensional and extensional definitions. An intensional definition defines a construct through specification of all the properties that are both necessary and sufficient to be considered a member of the set that is being defined. For example, the intensional definition of the construct bachelor refers to a male who is not presently married. An extensional definition is simply a list of all of the members in the set that is being defined. For example, I could generate an extensional definition of the construct bachelor by generating a list of males who are not presently married. As the intensional versus extensional comparison continues, both definitions can evolve. For example, closer scrutiny of the list of males who are not presently married reveals that these males are men who are eligible to be married (i.e., an infant male who is not married would not be on the extensional list), and awareness of exceptions like this could lead to an alteration of the intensional definition of bachelor to be a male who is eligible to be married and is not presently married.

Another example of the interaction between intensional and extensional definitions is the music streaming Internet site Pandora, and although I am currently listening to Pandora on my Amazon Echo, this metaphor will probably be seen as ancient history when this chapter is read in subsequent decades. Pandora users select a particular song or a particular artist, and their selection launches a flow of comparable music. The Pandora database contains a wide array of dimensions that describe particular songs and particular artists, and this dimensional profile can be labeled an intensional definition. Pandora uses this intensional definition to select a customized sequence of songs that have a compatible descriptive pattern, and this flow could be considered an extensional definition. The listener then has the opportunity to give each song a "thumbs up" or a "thumbs down" via a keypress or a communication to Alexa, which Pandora uses to modify the operational definition that is being used to generate the broadcasted sequence. Listeners can also add new songs to the station seed to further alter the operational definition that is generating the broadcasted sequence. The process of rating songs and/or adding songs to the descriptive pattern is an example of the iterative relation between intensional and extensional definitions that can lead to an optimal construct (or a great Pandora playlist).

Evaluating constructs based on the evolutionary retention model has both positive and negative perspectives. From the positive perspective, the longevity of maxims, proverbs, or rules of thumb are likely to reflect salient underlying truths about human behavior. Additionally, although folk psychological constructs do not have the precise operational definitions that a cumulative science requires, these constructs are likely to reflect dimensions or aspects of behavior that warrant rigorous scientific examination. A blind acceptance of folk psychological constructs could undermine an objective description of behavioral development (see Churchland & Churchland, 1998), but a blind rejection of folk psychological constructs seems even more problematic. Thus, an effective developmental science needs an explicit process by which relevant folk psychological insights are incorporated as constructs, and appropriate attention is paid to establishing and refining operational definitions that link these constructs to variables, examine the relations among similar constructs, and allow constructs to evolve on the basis of cumulative empirical research, interpretation, and generalization. From a negative perspective, some elderly maxims, proverbs, or rules of thumb may have longevity despite reflecting no underlying truth about human behavior. For example, when we sneeze and we hear a chorus of peers saying "bless you," this could be viewed as support for the traditional theory that we say "bless you" because we believe that the person who sneezed has now lost his or her soul. A more credible explanation is that this phrase is a reflexive form of politeness and not based upon a theory about souls.

3.2 Bottom-Up Variables

Sense meaning or semantic meaning can be contrasted with a more or less opposite approach to establishing meaning. The bottom-up approach to establishing a vocabulary for developmental science is to apply a measurement operation that provides a specific value within a dimension of possible values, thereby creating what philosophers call reference meaning or empirical meaning. For example, we can easily measure a person's height in inches, their weight in pounds, and their chronological age in years, and each of these numbers would be a variable. Further, we could combine these operationalized variables by dividing weight (in ounces) by height (in inches), and multiplying this quotient by chronological age (in months), which would produce a more complex variable that can be measured quite reliably for any individual human who is willing to be measured, and also could be measured in any other organism or object that is shaped in a configuration that has measurable height, weight, and chronological age. A more realistic example is body mass index (BMI), a widely used variable calculated based on a person's mass (weight) and height. These numbers are combined by dividing mass by height and expressing the result is in units of kg/m^2.

These measurements would yield precise data, and the structured combinations of variables and patterns of association that can be detected in the data flow could have important implications. However, as with sense meaning, reference meaning has both positive and negative implications. The obvious advantage of the bottom-up approach is that this type of measurement is precise, essentially by definition: we can only label a variable as having reference meaning when it reflects a specific value based on measurements. From a less optimistic perspective, a specific measurement or a significant coherence in a flow of data does not necessarily have the social relevance and face validity that is inherent in the constructs that we encounter in folk psychology. It is possible that a bottom-up variable might have an obvious link to a construct or the variable might change how we conceive of a construct, but it is also possible that a bottom-up variable has no utility in the world of constructs. For example, the combination of weight, height, and age described above has no obvious link to a reference meaning. BMI is an effort to quantify tissue mass and identify various forms of abnormal weight. However, ongoing research has raised many questions about BMI's accuracy, and various other weight-related constructs have been identified.

From a developmental science perspective, a developmental scientist could ask a child a question and listen to the child's answer and also measure the number of words the child states within each sentence, the child's heart rate and level of salivary cortisol, quantitative EEG, or rate of eye blinks. These variables could be linked to constructs like motivation, anxiety, or aspects of information processing, but the linkage would be less obvious from a broad, theoretical top-down perspective and more obvious if based on a pattern of correlations or an association with other aspects of performance. Linking measurements with constructs can become even more problematic when the level of measurement is so molecular that we not only fail to see the forest for the trees but also fail to see the trees for the molecules. Human beings are constructed with their brain as the central control and monitor of behavior. Thus, virtually no human behavior could occur without some engagement of the brain. As technology shifts our focus toward increasingly low levels of measurement as described in the previous chapter, we also run the risk of failing to see the behavior for the brain.

3.3 The Interaction between Constructs and Variables

Cumulative science must be based on constructs and variables that balance the theoretical relevance of sense meaning with the objectivity of reference meaning. This balance can be viewed from a theoretical perspective (described below), and it can also be described from a more functional perspective as a process in which our vocabulary of constructs and our toolbox of variables interact in a format that can promote a synergistic balance between these two perspectives that eventually creates an optimal level of measurement. The process that leads us toward an optimal level of measurement is ongoing and will always reflect various influences on progress. Any research domain will encounter a phase in which multiple terms are used interchangeably, definitions are unique to specific perspectives and individual researchers, and no consensus has been reached. And, progress can include new technologies and levels of analysis that lead to a perspective in which constructs that seemed quite different have unexpected similarity when viewed at lower levels.

One aspect of the iterative interaction between constructs and variables is the differentiation of our broader constructs as needed. Differentiating a broad folk-psychological idea into more or less specific aspects is an obvious step, and the term memory is a good example. From a folk psychological perspective, a statement like "She has a good memory" has some meaning. However, William James noted over a century ago that memory can be subdivided into several distinctly different components (James, 1890/1981). One metric of initial progress in the field of memory research was the plethora of different components of memory that emerged over the ensuing century (e.g., short-term memory, long-term memory, semantic memory, episodic memory, working memory, prospective memory, etc.). In contrast, some behavioral constructs have not received much attention from researchers and thus remain undifferentiated. For example, it is obvious that some individuals have more curiosity than others, and closer scrutiny would probably reveal many separable components that could be considered aspects, forms, or dimensions of curiosity. An example in the physical sciences is the term neuron. Early descriptions of neurons implied a generic identity, and subsequent research revealed different types of neurons. Researchers who view neurons as a relatively homogeneous category will probably be surprised by recent research suggesting that neurons have extensive diversity along dimensions such as polarity (unipolar, bipolar, or multipolar), or among types of neurons such as the granule neurons that form memories, the large, feathery Purkinje neurons that control body movements, and the various interneurons that transmit visual signals (Sanders, 2011; Yuste, 2013).

A countervailing aspect of the iterative interaction between constructs and variables is the consolidation of constructs. This consolidation is evoked when researchers begin using an array of overlapping terms to describe similar constructs. For example, self-concept, self-respect, sense of self, identity, and related terms seem to differentiate our perception of our self. However, this differentiation will not be efficacious if the components are not defined within an organizational structure that establishes each separable component's unique range of reference or its overlap with related components (Staats, 1999). Components of memory such as short-term versus long-term retention or episodic versus semantic representation can support unique theoretical definitions and can be linked to distinct operational definitions. Using multiple undifferentiated labels to identify the same construct not only impedes progress toward a cumulative developmental science but also precludes consilience among different branches of behavioral science.

Autism is a salient example of problematic consilience and differentiation in the Diagnostic and Statistical Manual of Mental Disorders (DSM-5) Axis I classifications. The DSM-5 has combined a wide array of symptoms into the category labeled autism spectrum disorder (ASD). Diagnostic criteria for ASD include: persistent deficits in social communication and social interaction across multiple contexts including social-emotional reciprocity, nonverbal communicative behaviors and developing, maintaining, and understanding relationships; restricted, repetitive patterns of behavior, interests, or activities, such as stereotyped or repetitive motor movements; insistence on sameness, highly restricted, fixated interests that are abnormal in intensity or focus; and hyper- or hyporeactivity to sensory input or unusual interests in sensory aspects of the environment; and clinically significant impairment in social, occupational, or other important areas of current functioning. This new broad spectrum includes individuals who were previously labeled as having autistic disorder, Asperger's disorder, childhood disintegrative disorder, or the catch-all diagnosis of pervasive developmental disorder not otherwise specified (PDD-NOS). The new classification system might have some advantages from a clinical perspective, but from a research perspective, the consolidation is clearly forming a diverse grab bag that will not support accurate scientific generalizations. Indeed, taking the opposite approach and moving instead toward more distinct differentiation could be much better for science on this topic because separating people who are diagnosed with ASD into relatively homogeneous subsets will probably put us in a much better position to identify causes and to develop and implement effective interventions.

As differentiation and consolidation occur, how can we incorporate these changes into the vocabulary that we use to describe results, interpretations, and generalizations? A dictionary of developmental science could reflect these changes through modified definitions, but dictionaries of common word usage may or may not reflect these modifications. A more cumbersome, but productive, strategy would be to use neologisms to reflect refined constructs and to incorporate temporary constructs to reflect refinement that is ongoing. The scientific use of the terms gender and sex is a good example of how this would work. From the perspective of common word usage, gender and sex tend to be interchangeable. That is, most people would provide the same answers to the questions "What is your sex?" and "What is your gender?" From a scientific perspective however, the word gender is often used to refer to our behavioral repertoire and self-identity, and the word sex often refers to the configuration of our sex-dependent chromosomes. It is possible that this distinction between sex and gender will eventually become incorporated into common word usage, but for now, developmental scientists face a significant problem if they are attempting to discover and accrue knowledge that is built upon this distinction. For example, some developmental scientists would claim that the term gender would be inappropriate to describe infants.

In some contexts, the use of such ambiguous distinctions can reflect naïve or blind optimism. I have read many published articles in which results are described as reflecting aspects of being a parent, despite the limitation that almost all participants in the research are mothers. The description of parenting might be quite different if it also includes fathers and parents in families in which children have two mothers and/or two fathers in heterosexual and/or homosexual pairings, or two, three, or four parents in post-divorce reconfigurations. Our culture has evolved, and we must alter our traditional format for gathering information on parenting. Specifically, if a questionnaire asks for "mother" and "father," some participants will be offended because this format lacks appropriate sensitivity. A more appropriate format is to identify "parent 1," "parent 2," etc. and ask for relevant information about each parent's gender, parenting role, etc.

In contrast, the personality configurations that are labeled Type A and Type B have become relatively widely accepted, and the distinction between these configurations is reflected not only in science but also in common word usage. Another example: some people describe themselves using terms like ESTJ or INFP as defined by their scores on the Myers-Briggs Type Indicator, reflecting a Jungian perspective on personality. I disagree with the suggestion from eliminative materialists that we should abandon folk psychological wisdom, but from an evolutionary epistemology perspective, I do believe that folk psychological constructs need to evolve and that changes in terminology may be necessary to support the survival of these evolved constructs.

As a final perspective on the iterative relation between constructs and variables, it is important to realize that flexibility in the relation between constructs and variables presents some challenges. Philosopher and logician Willard Quine noted many years ago that flexibility of measurement can impede the process of testing specific hypotheses, and specifically of subjecting specific hypotheses to grave risk of refutation (e.g., Quine, 1951). For example, imagine that a colleague holds the hypothesis that humans have a unique ability to use language, and that colleague then becomes aware of new data that suggests that a chimpanzee can use language. Rather than reject the hypothesis, the colleague now alters the operational definition of language to refer to sounds with phonological or articulation constraints that chimpanzees are not capable of producing. From Quine's perspective, what seemed like an objective test of a hypothesis would now be devalued as subjective. From an evolutionary epistemology perspective, progress has occurred because the broad construct language has been differentiated, and behaviors that can be observed in human beings and in chimpanzees have been consolidated. This process also steers us away from the idea that the results of any particular experiment can totally confirm or falsify a scientific hypothesis. Some physical sciences have attained a level of articulation in which an empirical finding could contradict a theory and lead to its elimination. In contrast, developmental science seems too young to proclaim that any operational definitions are sufficiently absolute to allow the definitive evaluation of hypotheses. Our progress could be more accurately described as an ongoing modification of constructs and variables that is moving us toward a more definitive level of hypothesis formation and evaluation.

3.4 Reflective and Formative Approaches

Edwards and Bagozzi (2000) and many others have focused on a distinction between reflective constructs, which are defined based on a phenomenon of theoretical interest (i.e., top-down), versus formative constructs, which are defined based on a quantification of data (i.e., bottom-up). The distinction between these two types of constructs, the procedures by which they should be defined, and their relative values have been controversial and salient topics for many years.

For reflective constructs, a real construct is considered to be the cause of the relevant variables. For example, a person who exemplifies the construct "athletic" can run fast, jump high, and/or lift a notable amount of weight. These variables are derived from the reference meaning of the construct in the sense that the identifiable reflective construct causes these variables and thus they can be viewed as reflections of that construct. The covariance among the variables that are caused by a reflective construct has a predictable pattern: variables should be correlated, and variables that are imperfect measures of the construct will probably deviate from this pattern of strong correlation. This description will probably sound familiar to many statistically sophisticated readers because it is consistent with our traditional definition of latent variables. For example, if people answer an extensive set of questions about their personality (e.g., Are you creative? Do you make efficient plans? Do you learn from your mistakes? Do you enjoy social events? Do some people dislike you?), a statistical analysis is likely to divide the answers into five clusters that can be labeled with the terms openness, conscientiousness, extraversion, agreeableness, and neuroticism, which are known as the "Big Five personality traits" (e.g., Costa et al., 1992) that frequently emerge in statistical segregation of a wide array of aspects of personality.

In contrast, formative constructs are formed or induced or caused by their measurement. For example, a particular set of variables can be combined to create constructs like socioeconomic status (SES), stress, social support, exposure to discrimination, and healthy behavior. The critical aspect of the distinction between formative and reflective constructs is that the formative construct is real in the sense that it has emerged because of this combination of variables, but it did not exist before the variables were combined, and it would not exist if the variables had not been combined. From a statistical perspective, formative constructs are derived from a more or less arbitrary set of variables and thus the covariance among the variables is not predictable, although it might fit a reflective pattern. If the variables fit a reflective pattern, the distinction between a construct being reflective or formative becomes somewhat deductive: Did the combination of variables exist first or did the construct exist first?

Some researchers favor either the reflective or formative approach to measurement. For example, Howell, Breivik, and Wilcox (2007) suggest that formative measurement is problematic and should be avoided when possible. The problem from their perspective is that a formative-measured construct can differ among the statistical models within a single study and even more when individual studies compile unique formative measurements of the construct. The problem here is that accruing cumulative knowledge would be virtually impossible without formative approaches. Raising our awareness of this potential problem has some usefulness, but they also note that a particular set of indicators could be interpreted as both reflective and formative. I see the latter as a more useful perspective. For example, Bollen and Ting (2000) define a formative construct that reflects exposure to media violence based on a child's viewing of violent television programs, playing violent video games, and listening to music with violent themes. Howell et al. contrast this with the reflective construct that reflects propensity to seek violent entertainment, which would be based on the same measurements. This steers me toward the advantage of conducting developmental science using an interactive model in which all constructs can be explored and evaluated from a formative and reflective perspective.

From my perspective as a researcher (and a relatively unsophisticated data analyst), the pressure to label a construct as either reflective or formative seems counterproductive. I prefer to view reflective and formative as two dimensions that can be more or less relevant for defining any construct. Specifically, a construct can be described as more or less reflective based on the extent to which it is measured using a set of highly correlated variables. For example, a construct like obesity could be measured using weight, body-mass index, and physical appearance, and this set of variables would be highly inter-correlated. Identifying additional variables that are also correlated would give further strength to obesity's dimension of reflectiveness. In contrast, a construct can also be described as more or less formative based on the extent to which it is measured using a set of variables that are not expected to have any correlation. For example, a construct that reflects having a great day could be measured using variables such as comfort with cuisine consumed, ease of commute to and from work, feeling healthy, feeling optimistic, or other indicators of contentment or happiness. A day in which a person experiences all of these attributes would be considered a greater day than a day in which a person experiences none of them. A day in which a person experiences two of these attributes would be considered a greater day than a day in which a person experiences only one attribute, but there is no reason to expect any correlation among the attributes that co-occur on a particular day. Identifying additional variables that could be considered relevant for defining a great day and that do not correlate with the original variables would give further weight to the claim that having a great day is a formative construct.

Obesity and having a great day have been described here as constructs that are virtually one-dimensional, but this perspective is not very realistic. For obesity, a variable like overeating could correlate with the measures of obesity although the correlation might be low. Some people who overeat are obese, some have normal weight, and some could have bulimia leading to anorexia. For having a great day, some additional variables like the day's weather could be added to the set of formative variables, but the day's weather might correlate with the ease of commute to and from work, or a day scheduled for skiing would be better if it snows. A construct that seems totally limited to a set of formative variables is more formative than a construct that has variables that overlap. Another example of multiple perspectives would be to measure the quality of family life by having multiple members of a family provide a rating and combining these scores. One dimension of the construct would be the average rating across all family members. Another dimension of the construct would be the extent to which family members agree. And we could compare the ratings provided by children with the ratings provided by parents.

I have encountered the difficulties of the reflective versus formative competition most saliently in my ongoing research on the development of a parent-report measure that can be used to identify infants who are at-risk for an eventual diagnosis of ASD. As described in previous paragraphs, ASD is currently defined as a wide array of developmental disorders that are characterized by symptoms such as lack of social interaction, poor communication, and repetitive behaviors, among others. Current clinical tools are progressing toward offering a diagnosis at 2 years for some children, and most cases of ASD are diagnosed by 3 years. However, a massive and growing body of research is identifying many behaviors and underlying neural and behavioral structures and processes that are abnormal during infancy.

My colleagues and I implemented a relatively straightforward strategy to develop our First Years Inventory (FYI): we accrued an extensive list of phenomena that were observed in infants who could be considered at-risk for an eventual diagnosis of ASD. Items were added to this list based on various research strategies including retrospective analysis of archived videos for children diagnosed with ASD, retrospective interviews with parents of children with ASD, analysis of younger siblings of children with ASD, and others. We then developed a set of parent-report questions to assess the presence of these behaviors, with possible answers structured in an array that would identify one or more answers as being relatively infrequent in a normative sample. We then developed a scoring metric in which risk points were assigned based on the presence of relatively infrequent answers to the questions.

If every question on the FYI was completely independent of the other questions, we could have created a straightforward overall risk score by adding together (or averaging) risk points across all of the questions. However, given that some unusual behaviors are easier to see than others, the original version of the FYI had a relatively uneven distribution of topics. For example, questions about social-affective engagement are salient and straightforward, and the FYI 3.0 contained 14 of them. In contrast, questions about reactivity were difficult to formulate, and the FYI 3.0 contained only three of them.

Given this uneven distribution of questions, a simple sum/average of FYI risk points would have given constructs like social-affective engagement and repetitive behavior much stronger influence on the risk score than reactivity or regulatory patterns. To correct for this asymmetry, we conducted a factor analysis and used additional categorization techniques to define eight constructs (namely, social orienting, receptive communication, social-affective engagement, expressive communication, sensory processing, regulatory patterns, reactivity, and repetitive behavior) that could be divided into two broader domains (social-communication and sensory-regulatory functions). A complex scoring system was then developed that balanced the contribution of questions across the eight constructs into a combined risk score.

I have used the term construct in two different ways in the previous paragraphs. Terms like expressive communication, sensory processing, or reactivity refer to traditional constructs. Social-communication and sensory-regulatory functions refer to broader traditional constructs. However, the construct "at-risk for an eventual diagnosis of ASD" is notably different in comparison to these constructs. I would describe it as a medley, aggregation, conglomeration, or composite in the sense that it is a diverse mixture of various behaviors that would indicate risk for ASD. Almost all children are reported to have a few risk behaviors. Children who manifest an unusually large set of risk behaviors are definitely at-risk for ASD, but the subset of risk behaviors is not necessarily the same across the children who have high risk scores. I am confident that progress in this area of research will eventually identify profiles that could be viewed as relatively homogeneous categories of ASD and/or could be used as triage for identifying appropriate interventions. Generalizations based on the broad array of individuals with different configurations of symptoms can be useful, but this approach should be balanced with the value of recognizing and measuring patterns of individual difference.

3.5 Homotypic versus Heterotypic Constructs

Defining constructs in developmental science evokes a significant challenge that would not necessarily be as relevant or problematic for most other sciences. Given that a fundamental component of development is change over time, one obvious challenge in measuring stability or change over time is that the behavioral manifestations of almost all behaviors and mental abilities are affected by the participant's age when the construct is assessed. A construct that has a relatively similar behavioral manifestation over time could be labeled homotypic. For example, visual acuity is measured very differently in infants, toddlers, children, and adults, but these techniques provide a relatively homotypic measurement based on the 20/20 measurement scale. Height and weight are assessed in different contexts (e.g., a baby scale, the weight of a parent holding the baby minus the parent's weight, or a traditional stand-on scale), but pounds of weight and inches of height constitute homogeneous measurement at all time points. Despite having relatively homogeneous measurement, all constructs also have some degree of age specificity. For example, measures of height or weight can have the same meaning across time, but would have different implications across time when they are linked to constructs such as obesity that can have a very different meaning and different implications for a toddler, a teenager, or an octogenarian. Conversely, looking time, which is used frequently for measurement in infants, can have a different meaning across the early months and later years of life, with longer looking time indicating boredom, difficulty in understanding, or attractiveness. Also, the definition of continuity can imply the presence of something at more or less the same level over time or the preservation of an individual's status on something relative to the presence of that thing among same-aged peers. The later perspective seems notably reasonable. However, it also raises the additional complication of amount of variability among peers and how this variability might change over time.

In contrast, constructs assessing behavior and mental ability are inherently heterotypic from the perspective that they have notably different manifestations at different ages. Many constructs have such well-articulated definitions in our folk psychology vocabulary that it is relatively easy to identify specific behaviors that seem relevant for defining these constructs at various ages. However, the definitional behaviors do change over time. For example, a 4-year-old child who is excessively physical with other children, behaves impulsively, and ignores personal boundaries could be labeled excessively aggressive on most qualitative or quantitative measures of aggression. A 12-year-old child with similar behaviors could be viewed as exhibiting symptoms of antisocial personality disorder, and a different set of behaviors or use of different tools would be relevant for measuring a nonclinical temperamental tendency toward aggression in the older child. Some 4-year-olds who are extremely aggressive may continue to be aggressive at 12 years either behaviorally or emotionally, and some might become relatively peaceful.

Constructs that are less well defined by folk psychology, such as creativity or attachment, are much more vulnerable to the problems associated with heterotypic continuity. Some children seem more creative than others. We can assume that this dimension of individual difference could be detected in infants, but there is no obvious definition of what it means if we say that an infant is creative. An extensive longitudinal study assessing month-to-month changes in creative behaviors might allow researchers to map various manifestations of creativity and thus establish an empirical basis for measuring heterotypic continuity, but this sort of study would bring a notably different perspective on the definition of long-term change and continuity: we can assume continuity and determine how it is manifest, or we can assume change and interpret similar behaviors differently at different ages. A dense longitudinal study assessing month-to-month changes in creative behaviors might allow researchers to map the departure and arrival of various manifestations of creativity and thus establish an empirical basis for measuring continuity, but this sort of study would ignore the perspective of long-term change versus continuity and would also need to address questions of individual differences and typical versus atypical development.

3.6 Multifaceted Developmental Constructs

Our folk psychological history has evolved many constructs that are extremely relevant for developmental science, but are notably problematic due to their multifaceted nature. Intelligence is an example. Even though the underlying construct of intelligence is difficult to define precisely, intelligence has been a very important idea for over a century because it is an effective predictor of school-related outcomes. The first formal test of IQ was developed in 1904 by Alfred Binet, a French psychologist, who was attempting to identify children who were unlikely to be successful in a traditional classroom so that they could receive special education tailored to their unique needs. Binet designed tests to measure abilities that would be relevant in school such as reasoning or comprehension. His intelligence test was very effective at identifying children who needed special attention, and more broadly, it predicted the grades and other academic outcomes for a wide range of students. This success led to extremely prevalent use of intelligence tests by educators, particularly when they are trying to assign students to appropriate levels of educational challenge.

Binet recognized that ability and knowledge change profoundly over time, particularly during the first two decades of life. Because of this ongoing change, an index of a child's intelligence must be calculated relative to other children who are the same age. All intelligence tests consist of subtests that tap particular dimensions of behavior related to intelligence. Items on each subtest are arranged in order of difficulty that was determined initially by administering each item to a large number of individuals of various ages. A scoring system has been developed that reflects an individual child's performance score relative to the performance that would be expected at that age, with performance above the norm leading to higher scores and performance below the norm leading to lower scores. Adjustments have been made in the items and the scoring such that the expected distribution of IQ scores is a normal, bell-shaped curve with an average score of 100.

Certain key dimensions are represented in almost all Western-based IQ tests. In John Carroll's influential three-level theory of intelligence (Carroll, 1993), he recognized that the wide range of abilities that are tapped in traditional IQ tests can be organized into a set of eight abilities with wide enough range of diversity to be considered the prototypical example of a multifaceted developmental construct:

- Fluid intelligence – Flexible, ongoing mental processes in which one must think in the current context rather than rely on previous knowledge (e.g., our ability to assemble puzzles, predict the next item in a sequence, detect an item that is different from other items).

- Crystallized intelligence – Factual knowledge about the world (e.g., our knowledge of word definitions, rules of mathematics, facts derived from geography or science).
- General memory and learning – How we process information (e.g., how long we can hold arbitrary information in memory, how many pieces of information we can keep in mind at the same time, our ability to learn arbitrary associations).
- Broad visual perception – The ability to detect visual relations (e.g., find a specific shape in a visual array) or to visualize relationships on the basis of verbal information (e.g., listen to statements about the relative location of various points and then recognize the figure that has been described).
- Broad auditory perception – The ability to discriminate among sounds (e.g., to say which one of four sounds differs in tone from the other three or to predict which tone would come next in a sequence of tones that has a pattern).
- Broad retrieval ability – How easily we can access stored knowledge (e.g., generate a list of foods, name the Chinese dynasties or American presidents, recall the words of a national anthem).
- Broad cognitive speediness – How long it takes to perform various tasks reflecting the previously described abilities.
- Processing speed – The ability to respond quickly in a reaction time task (e.g., to press a button whenever a particular target appears in an ongoing stream of visual or auditory stimuli).

The recent evolution of intelligence within the world of developmental science has shifted into a construct called executive function. I participated in an interesting collaboration two decades ago in which we defined executive function as problem solving, which we saw as the common denominator among ongoing research that mentions this construct (Zelazo, Carter, Reznick, & Frye, 1997). The definition of executive function continues to evolve, but consensus is becoming much less obvious. One notable perspective is that an individual's level of executive function can be defined as a profile containing assessment of various relevant constructs, with a realization that each component in the profile could have further differentiation into variables such as working memory for location, identity, or timing, or retaining representations that are auditory or visual, and that are object or social, numerical or alphabetical, or familiar or novel. Further progress includes the National Institutes of Health Toolbox for the Assessment of Neurological and Behavioral Function (Bauer & Zelazo, 2014), a tool for developmental science that does something a bit different with executive function than has been done with IQ, treating it as a developmental phenomenon (as a skill) instead of as an individual differences phenomenon. Increasingly complex versions of the same task emerge. The whole project reflects the perceived need for some temporary (and evolving) consensus on definitions of constructs, variables, measures.

Parenting is a major influence on child development, and this construct has a relatively obvious definition. However, the multifaceted nature of parenting makes it one of the most poorly measured constructs in developmental science. One of the main problems here is the bandwagon effect. Baumrind's initial research (Baumrind, 1968), followed by modifications from Maccoby and Martin (1983), led to a self-report instrument that classifies parents into one of four distinct styles of parenting: Authoritative, Authoritarian, Permissive, and Unengaged. This tool has become the definitive measurement of parenting. Contemporary developmental psychology textbooks describe parenting using this taxonomy, and the textbooks state general descriptions of the effects of parenting that are almost all based on this strategy for assessing parenting.

If we examine this strategy for measuring parenting, we can see many obvious potential problems. For example, a child's mother and father might have notably different parenting styles, but the measurement of the child's parenting will be defined based on who provided the data. From a broader perspective, a child who has two parents with different styles is actually experiencing a blended form of parenting that could be measured. Additionally, and even broader, many children have parents who have separated and may or may not have reconnected with a new partner. In some families the parents are male and female, and in other families there are other combinations. And, from an even broader perspective, parents could be identified as the people who are legally responsible for child, the people whose sperm and egg created the child, or people in the child's environment who are managing the child. Another important aspect of the measurement of parenting is how the parenting is perceived by the child. One child might perceive authoritarian parenting as reflecting meanness, and another child might interpret the same parenting as an indication of appropriate concern. Alternatively, one child might interpret permissive parenting as an effort to help the child establish an independent identity, and another child might see it as a lack of interest. If we refresh our folk-psychological perspective on the measurement of parenting, several important concerns become quite obvious, and we realize that this "bandwagon" strategy for construct measurement may have slowed progress toward a cumulative developmental science of parenting.

3.7 Inventing New Constructs

Given the extensive catchment area that breeds constructs and the rich array of variables that developmental scientists have used to measure their constructs of interest, is there any reason to suggest that we should be attempting to identify additional constructs? I will say "yes" because the fact that a construct exists does not necessarily preclude the possibility that it could or should be replaced with something better.

One strategy for identifying useful new constructs is to explore potentially relevant metaphors. For example, many aspects of information processing emerged in the context of considering computers as a metaphor for human cognition. Those of us who often find ourselves thinking and speaking in metaphors learn that appropriate metaphors not only facilitate communication but also can help us identify a missing component or can lead us to a novel idea. For example, if Mark Twain is correct when he claims that "the human race has one really effective weapon, and that is laughter" (Grothe, 2008), we might ask if other emotions are also used as weapons or if laughter is often used aggressively. At a more narrow level, we can ask why aphorisms, proverbs, and rules of thumb have attained notable longevity. Some of the statements may be cute or funny, and some may be familiar rituals that we learn to recite at prescribed moments, but some may have attained this status because they express an underlying truth about behavior. Identifying these underlying truths can be a useful source of valuable constructs.

A second strategy for identifying new constructs is to look for correlational patterns in data. This approach is particularly relevant for data that are amenable to factor analysis and related statistical approaches. In my own experience, I collaborated with colleagues to develop the Infant Intentionality Questionnaire (IIQ) (Feldman & Reznick, 1996), a parent-report assessment of infant intentionality. We had several aspects of intentionality in mind when we constructed the IIQ questions, but we were not aware of a distinction between positive intentionality and negative intentionality until a factor analysis indicated a strong clustering of questions that asked about the infant's tendency to be intentional in contexts in which intentionality would be considered negative. Subsequent research identified socio-cultural aspects of parent perception of negative infant intentionality (Burchinal, Skinner, & Reznick, 2010), and this aspect of the IIQ has utility in predicting parents who are at-risk for abusing or neglecting a child (Berlin, Dodge, & Reznick, 2013).

Finally, constructs will emerge if we make more effort to notice behaviors. We do not have access to experiential engagement with our cellular interactions, our digestive system, subatomic particles, or ongoing activities in outer space, but we do see the behaviors of our fellow human beings and ourselves, and can also become more aware of our emotional reactions, self-directed speech, beliefs, and attitudes. This ongoing tradition of observation has yielded our current array of constructs, and we should use the context of discovery to continue expanding the list of interesting constructs. For example, I heard a student describing her roommate's tendency to continue talking to her even though the listening student had fallen asleep. It occurred to me that this tendency could be measured by programming mobile phones to calculate how long a person continues talking to their phone without realizing that the connection to the person they are talking to has been lost. This behavioral tendency could be linked to sense meaning constructs (e.g., narcissism), but this opportunity for a relatively objective measurement of self-orientation might surprise Sigmund Freud and his peers who were exploring narcissism in a previous century. Another new zone is the Internet and how we use it. Patterns of Internet usage that are defined based on various electronic parameters are reflective and/or formative measurements. Some aspects of how people are using Internet-based social networking can be linked to ideas like bravado, humility, privacy, or curiosity. Other aspects of Internet usage might eventually spawn new constructs about information processing, social development, and perception. If these novel aspects of Internet usage can be shown to be relevant in our effort to describe, predict, alter, or understand behavior, we will eventually name them and adopt them into our collection of constructs and our cumulative knowledge.

4 Validating Measurement

It seems virtually impossible for any measurement operation in closed or open systems in any domain of science to determine quantitative or qualitative indices of a construct with no possibility of error. The advanced technology that is used to measure well-defined physical phenomena in closed systems might seem likely to eliminate almost all possibility for error in the quantification of the focal phenomenon. However, even in that rigorous context there are many ways that error of measurement could occur. For example, an apparatus might have a defective component, a reagent might be mislabeled, or a research assistant might skip a step in the experiment's protocol or misread a gauge. What constitutes an improvement in measurement also has different connotations in different scientific domains. For example, in April 2014 the US National Institute of Standards and Technology (NIST) officially launched a new atomic clock, called NIST-F2, to serve as a new US civilian time and frequency standard. The NIST-F2 will be correct within one second for approximately 300 million years, which makes it three times more accurate than the atomic clock that has been the standard since 1999. Will a fine-tuned adjustment like that emerge someday for developmental science constructs like working memory, attachment, or self-concept? Probably not. When measurement is focused on behavioral phenomena, error is essentially unavoidable because behavioral constructs are inherently difficult to define precisely, and are volatile over time. Error also emerges because behavioral phenomena are often affected by the process of being measured and by interacting with other constructs.

4.1 Validity

The term "valid" has numerous definitions that vary by context, but consistent across each is the contention that validity refers to an aspect of the measurement's performance. When we apply the term valid to our scientific constructs and variables, we are usually referring to the extent to which our constructs and variables are accurately linked to the phenomenon that we claim to be measuring. Validity of measurement is a very central topic in all types of science, and it has received a tremendous amount of attention for a very long time.

Researchers who have explored the history of validity in psychological sciences have found some interesting perspectives on how validity has evolved. Newton and Shaw (2013) explored how standards of validity have changed since the late 1800s with a particular focus on how organizations like the American Psychological Association, the American Educational Research Association, and the National Council on Measurement in Education have attempted to develop standards for assessing measurement validation in educational and psychological contexts. In 1954, the American Psychological Association published a report (American Psychological Association et al., 1954) in which four types of validity were identified: content validity, predictive validity, concurrent validity, and construct validity. In subsequent years, various aspects of validity were added, subtracted, or re-defined. Reviewing the use of the term validity in journals, Newton and Shaw found several dozen definitions of validity that have been mentioned in publications in the three decades following 1975, with frequent use of forms of validity like predictive, construct, or concurrent, and less frequent use of other terms such as face, discriminative, or consensual.

The context in which measurement is occurring also has important implications for validity, with a distinction between validity in a limited scientific context in which a tool is being used to measure a particular construct in a laboratory, and validity in a broad translational context in which a tool is being used to attain goals relevant for domains such as education, human resources, or medicine. Focus on validity in the scientific context is relatively limited, with concern about how well a tool is producing data that are widely agreed upon. Focus on validity in the translational context is more about how a measurement tool is used, how its validity is monitored, and the implication of incorrect measurement as expressed explicitly in manuals or as legal stipulations. Cizek (2012) distinguishes between these two different perspectives and describes them as the "support for specified interpretations of test scores" and the "support for specified applications." This leads to a differentiation between the definitions of validity and validation. Cizek defines validity as "the degree to which scores on an appropriately administered instrument support inferences about variation in the characteristic that the instrument was developed to measure." Validation is defined as the "process of gathering, summarizing, and evaluating relevant evidence concerning the degree to which that evidence supports the intended meaning of scores yielded by an instrument and inferences about [reflecting] the characteristic it was designed to measure."

One overall generalization that often emerges based upon validity scrutiny is the consensus that developmental scientists should avoid using the term validity because its definition varies inconsistently across a wide range of contexts. For example, Krause (2012) views validity from what I would describe as an absolutist perspective. He notes many of the problems mentioned here and arrives at the conclusion that we should establish a consensually implemented process to rate our measurements as either valid or invalid with no zone of relative validity between these extremes. I agree that it would be valuable to attain the goal of conducting developmental science with totally valid measurement techniques, but I see the process of validation as likely to progress too slowly to ever attain a universally accepted metric that would declare measurements in developmental science as either valid or invalid.

Our inability to agree on a consensus definition of validity can be viewed as problematic, but I do not like the solution of simply skipping the problem by no longer using the term. Validity in developmental science is clearly important from the folk psychological perspective in which we are able to assess the extent to which we are measuring the construct and variables that we intend to measure. Moving forward into cumulative developmental science, I hesitate to say that any measurement technique could be perfectly valid. Rather, I suggest that researchers need to devote more attention to the relative validity of the measures that they use, and invest more effort in attempting to improve validity in their own research and the research conducted by their colleagues. Concretely, researchers should routinely describe and defend their measurements in all publications, include an open-minded disclaimer noting problems with their measurement and recommending ways that measurement of the construct of interest could be improved. And, when crafting a peer review, they should hold their colleagues to the same standards, thus making this an implicit standard in journals. I hope that maintaining this commitment for centuries will lead us to a time when Krause's Validation Committee will have the data they need to evaluate validity, but I would be very surprised if the phenomena of interest in developmental science are ever universally accepted as correctly measured with no room for additional improvement.

4.2 Reliability

Reliability, repeatability, or test–retest reliability are often cited as an aspect of validity in the sense that this describes the extent to which a measure dependably provides the same score across occasions of use. The obvious "best case" is a measure that is valid and reliable, and the "worst case" is a measure that is invalid and unreliable. From a broader and somewhat antithetical perspective, alignment between reliability and validity is not a guarantee: a measure that is invalid might have excellent test–retest reliability and a measure that is valid might have no test–retest reliability. For invalidity and reliability, a measurement could be dependably based on precise, reliable measurement, but be invalid because it has no linkage to a relevant construct. For example, an equation based on weight and height could be offered as a measurement of obesity. Repeated measurements of weight and height would probably be highly correlated and thus have strong test–retest reliability, but the calculation provides a score that many researchers would not consider to be a valid measurement of obesity. For validity and unreliability, many factors could undermine the test–retest reliability of a valid measurement depending upon the construct and the cohort. For example, listening to a joke multiple times would not necessarily elicit reliable laughter each time. Additionally, research with infants raises the challenge of being able to test them multiple times or in exactly the same state of emotionality, wakefulness, and motivation.

The closest I ever came to overcoming the challenge of testing infants in the same state more than once was in a study that I conducted in collaboration with Barbara Goldman and our students. Our laboratory located in the Frank Porter Graham Child Development Institute (FPG) was proximal to the preschool in the same building. Parents of infants agreed to let their infant participate in a longitudinal study of working memory in which we sought to assess each infant every 2–3 weeks using the following strategy: We would come to the classroom and ask the teacher "How is X feeling today?" If X was having a normal day, we would take him or her upstairs to our laboratory and conduct an assessment of working memory. If X was cranky, cutting a tooth, sleepy, etc., we would postpone the testing and return periodically until X was back to normal. Most infant research labs do not encounter this opportunity, and indeed, they encounter a much worse situation: they must test an infant after the infant has been sleeping in the car or strolling through uncomfortable cold or heat. Or, an infant is tested after arriving in a new location and thus facing the challenge of unfamiliarity. On a second visit to that same lab, the unfamiliarity can attenuate (if the infant has strong memory). An infant who is tested once can be contrasted with an infant who makes multiple visits to the same laboratory. Some infant labs identify families who are interested in participating and they make use of this resource by having those infants participate multiple times in various studies. In that context, the infant is a skilled research participant, and the results for that infant might not generalize to a broader population. Developmental science definitely evokes a wide array of challenges to validity and reliability!

4.3 Multiplicity

Given the difficulty of measuring behavioral phenomena in open systems, any claim about a construct that is assessed using a single measurement should evoke considerable scrutiny and skepticism. At a theoretical level, the skepticism is fueled by the ambiguity inherent in mapping constructs onto operations. The problematic implications of using a single measurement are even more obvious when viewed from a reliability/validity perspective. When a single procedure is used to measure a phenomenon, how could we determine that the measurement is reliable? Even if the measurement procedure is standardized and widely used, questions can arise regarding its implementation in a particular study conducted by a particular experimenter in a particular context. Any empirical report that makes a claim based on a single measurement should include some effort to assess the measurement technique's test–retest reliability, with a particular focus on the percentage of variance in the measurement that could be attributed to error. Error-related/induced variance is particularly important because a moderate test–retest correlation might be statistically significant but practically insignificant. For example, a test–retest reliability correlation of 0.33 might sound impressive to developmental scientists. However, a correlation of this magnitude indicates that one measurement accounts for only 10% of the variance in the other measurement. A metaphor that comes to mind for illustrating the limitations of accounting for only 10% of the variance is to what extent can we predict the sound that will emerge from a piano when we only know the key that will be touched by one of 10 possible fingers?

Some error of measurement is unavoidable in developmental science, and ignoring this reality seems unproductive, unrealistic, and futile. Our attempt to build a cumulative developmental science on the basis of constructs that have vague and fragile measurement is challenging, and our biggest mistake would be to avoid acknowledging and confronting this difficulty. For example, the description and conclusions of any behavioral study that reports only a single measurement should include an explicit acknowledgment of the limitations in interpretation and generalization that are inherent to this approach. The report should also address the need for subsequent research that incorporates improved measurement techniques.

The need for multiple measurement operations is not a new idea. Over 50 years ago, Campbell and Fiske (1959) recommended that behavioral researchers adopt a multitrait–multimethod model. For example, to explore a construct like creativity, Campbell and Fiske would have recommended placing the focal trait in the context of several other traits (e.g., Is this person creative? Is this person happy? Is this person liberal?) and to assess each of these traits using three independent measurement techniques (e.g., a structured interview, observation, and reports from an informant). Patterns of correlations within the multitrait–multimethod model have the advantage of assessing validity defined as comparable trait scores across different measurement techniques. The pattern of correlations could also reveal the influence of method variance (i.e., a systematic bias associated with a specific measurement technique).

A literature review conducted by Fiske and Campbell three decades later (Fiske & Campbell, 1992) indicated that their call for using the multitrait–multimethod model had been ignored. One problem was the lack of statistical procedures for conducting the relevant assessments, but statistical modeling has become much more sophisticated in recent decades and traditional procedures like factor analysis could be helpful. Also, the approach sometimes took researchers into topics that they did not consider interesting or worthwhile because of the need to measure some unrelated traits. The main message for us from Fiske and Campbell is that we need to be aware of these challenges and not let them undermine our efforts to incorporate multiple measurement procedures into our research. I will now describe various aspects of multiple measurements and how they can be incorporated to enhance the quality of developmental science.

The Campbell and Fiske approach implies combining existing measures to create an informative matrix that provides insight into the extent to which we are measuring what we claim to be measuring. Extending this into a more creative domain, we could consider strategies in which paradigms could be engineered to include assessment from multiple perspectives. For example, imagine a paradigm in which a 3-year-old child is being assessed for working memory capacity by viewing a screen on which a stimulus appears at a particular location and then disappears, thus making the screen blank. Then, after a specific delay the screen reactivates and shows an array of locations. The child's direction of gaze is observed, and focus on the location where the stimulus disappeared is defined as successful use of working memory. This scenario could then be repeated with various delays between the original stimulus and the test, with arrays of different size, and with more than one stimulus to assess the overall strength of the child's working memory. This would be a useful approach because it combines multiple methods for assessing working memory.

A similar configuration of this paradigm could then be used to assess recognition memory or other related traits. For example, the child sees a stimulus appear and disappear at a particular location, and a delay is imposed, but in this configuration the stimulus reappears either at the location where it disappeared or at an alternative location. Recognition memory could be defined as differentiation of these two possible outcomes with various manipulations to challenge the strength of the child's recognition memory. We are thus using the same context (i.e., computer-based experimental task) to assess a different type of memory that might correlate with working memory, but might be completely independent of it. The next step is to use this same paradigm to assess a different cognitive ability such as attention. In this configuration, the child could see two stimuli that are either identical or more or less different, with attention assessed based on how the child's visual response changes as a function of the difference between the two stimuli. Finally, to tap a different aspect of attention, the two stimuli could appear, disappear, and return with one of the stimuli in its original location and the other stimulus rotated slightly. Attention is a construct that is as complicated as memory, so details of the presentation and responses would require sophisticated adjustment to assess relevant aspects of attention. A child who does well on all four of these tasks is cooperative, has stamina, and is awake. Differences in performance across tasks could be used to measure particular aspects of cognition, but a correlation across all of the tasks evokes the concern that each task is measuring a more general aspect of performance. Moving further into our search for validity, we could also devise a different paradigm that utilizes hands-on experience with real objects rather than passive viewing of computer-generated stimuli. In this scenario, the child would observe and touch experimental stimuli, and delays would be imposed by distracting the child or removing the child from the room. Similar results on specific aspects of cognition assessed with a wide range of stimuli would be impressive. And, moving toward reliability, the multitrait–multimethod procedures could be repeated on subsequent days.

The details of this example have many flaws, but the general goal is to craft a procedure in which different constructs are measured in a context in which general factors such as motivation, compliance, and attentiveness can be assessed and differentiated from the specific aspects of cognitive, social, emotional, or other developmental domains that are being measured. I have reviewed many manuscripts that describe research in which the assessment that was used to measure an infant's specific cognitive ability could also reflect cooperation, stamina, understanding the paradigm or other peripheral influences. To improve developmental science, I always seek a revision that explores whether performance reflects the specific aspect of the infant's cognitive ability that is being investigated rather than the various other general aspects of the infant that could affect performance in that context. And, when that issue is raised in a review of my own manuscript, I appreciate this effort to help me improve my research.

Moving forward into the implementation of multiplicity, we notice that multiplicity can be applied to various aspects of measurement. As will be discussed in the sections below, multiplicity can refer to repeating the measurement procedure across multiple trials and multiple levels, conducting measurement using multiple procedures, or conducting measurement from multiple perspectives.

4.4 Multiple Measurement Trials and Levels

An obvious strategy for improving measurement quality is to conduct multiple assessments using a single measurement technique. In addition to being used to calculate test–retest reliability, multiple measurements can be combined to enhance the quality of measurement. For example, an infant's correct search on a single trial could indicate correct performance, and it could also indicate random search. Incorrect performance on a single trial could indicate a lack of some ability, and it could also indicate a lack of interest in procedure, general fatigue, or distraction caused by a peripheral stimulus. One obvious strategy that would minimize the salience of these alternative interpretations would be to present the infant with a series of trials in which various parameters are counterbalanced. The ratio of correct trials to total trials (i.e., percentage correct) in this context is a multiplistic variable that reflects the infant's general level of performance across trials. If a comparable series of trials could be administered more than once during a testing session or across successive testing sessions within a short span of time, an index of percentage correct would be reflective of the infant's general ability to perform correctly.

Research participants are often affected by the experience of being measured and thus would be expected to respond differently when measurements are repeated. Thus, combining data across multiple trials can have advantages and disadvantages. For example, measurement repetition can have an advantage if the repetitions are designed to evoke peak performance. However, the opposite effect must be considered: measurement repetition could evoke boredom and thus artificially depress performance. Another obvious disadvantage is that repeated trials can undermine test–retest reliability. For example, as previously mentioned, we can measure the construct "sense of humor" by observing a person's laughter in response to a joke, but laughing at a joke is most often a one-time occurrence, so we cannot assess this measurement by presenting the same joke on subsequent trials. In this context, multiple measurements must use alternative test items that are designed to evoke parallel responses.

Most psychological constructs are salient at the behavioral level, and some constructs have a theoretical connection to underlying biological processes and/or to overarching introspective processes such as the conscious experience associated with emotions, beliefs, memories, or knowledge. For example, a construct like obesity is usually linked to specific biological measurements such as weight, body-mass index, or skin-fold thickness. However, obesity can also be linked to subjective experiences like perceiving that one has a large body, detecting disapproval from peers, or feeling a sense of shame or victimization depending upon one's attitude toward the cause and implications of obesity. Another example of a multilevel construct is anxiety, which can be associated with fine-grained motor patterns such as twitching as well as underlying changes in hormones, heart rate, or galvanic skin response. Anxiety also affects cognitive variables related to how information is processed as reflected in reaction time patterns (Fox, Russo, Bowles, & Dutton, 2001). And, anxiety can be associated with self-reported thoughts and feelings regarding memories, expectations, etc. Coherence among responses that span various levels of measurement offers an important index of the extent to which broad constructs are being measured accurately and validly.

Measuring a construct at various levels can contribute to establishing a valid definition of that construct. For example, an underlying difference in neural functioning could be used to differentiate short-term memory from working memory. Or, differences in vagal tone could be used to differentiate general attention from more focused attention. Some constructs emerge as patterns across variables at different levels. For example, Kagan and Snidman (2004) report that children who are fearful at 14 months and have strong right frontal neural activity are qualitatively different in development when compared to children who are fearful at 14 months, but have relatively strong left frontal neural activity. This pattern would not emerge in an analysis focused entirely on either variable in isolation. Advances in all levels of measurement and the sophistication of statistical modeling will facilitate our efforts to create multiple measurement trials and levels.

4.5 Measurement Using Multiple Procedures and Perspectives

The Campbell and Fiske (1959) multitrait–multimethod model evokes the use of multiple procedures to measure a construct and enhance validity. For example, the weight of an object is commonly measured using a spring scale that detects the force of gravity, and weight can also be measured by comparing the object with calibrated objects that have specific weights. Multiple measurement procedures are less common for psychological constructs than they are for physical constructs such as weight or temperature, but this approach seems even more necessary when we are attempting to measure psychological constructs. For example, infant working memory can be assessed by having infants search for a hidden toy, gaze toward a location where a social target appeared and then disappeared, or observe an action and then try to perform it after a delay. Each measurement operation that is added to our tool kit for measuring infant working memory potentially improves the accuracy with which working memory is measured and reduces the influence of factors specific to each measurement operation (i.e., method variance). Multiple measurement operations also open opportunities to differentiate the focal construct from related constructs, and to attain a broader understanding of how measurement operations are linked to the focal construct.

Linking a construct to a single measurement operation has both positive and negative implications. For example, for several decades (and in a large number of publications) many researchers have relied on measurement of an infant's behavior in the Ainsworth Strange Situation (Ainsworth & Bell, 1970) as the definitive index of the infant's security of attachment. Thompson (2006) notes that reliance on this single procedure has allowed researchers to amass a large body of comparable research findings based on the same assessment technique, but this reliance on a single assessment technique has also limited the theoretical issues that can be addressed and has constrained researchers to focus on specific categories of attachment security. It is tempting to ponder how progress toward understanding this critical aspect of social development will be advanced if researchers devote more effort toward identifying alternative strategies for measuring attachment using multiple measurement procedures. For example, multiple representational measures of attachment have been used in toddlerhood, childhood, and adulthood. Measures (e.g., MCAST, family drawing task, story stems, etc.) generally align with the Strange Situation and could suggest alternative approaches. Developing alternative forms of measurement could allow us to use a multimethod approach to assess attachment and/or it could lead to the identification of other types of attachment classifications.

Another aspect of multiple measurement emerges when a measurement reflects one individual's subjective perspective on a phenomenon that can also be viewed from other perspectives. For example, some children have a single parent, but most have two or more parents who are of different genders or the same gender. The parents and the child often live together in a single household, and many children have parents who live in separate homes. In some families, parents share child-rearing duties. In other families, one parent is the primary caregiver and the other parent is secondary, and these roles can vary across contexts. In some families, both parents share the same parenting beliefs. In other families, parents have quite different views about child rearing. Finally, differing beliefs can lead to a differentiation of roles along the strict-lenient dimension, and either role can be played by the primary or secondary caregiver, in traditional households by the mother or the father, and in gay marriages by either partner. Given the complexity of family structure, it is hard to imagine how we could amass a cumulative developmental science on the basis of singular measurement, whether it is research that asks children to describe the overall parenting that they receive, or research that measures parent behavior or attitude without attempting to identify the role that is played by the parent who serves as the informant. This is also a domain in which observational data could have notable advantages.

4.6 Combining Across Measurements

The overarching theme of this chapter is to enhance validity through multiple measurements that can range from simple repetition of a single measurement procedure to combining measurements across multiple trials, multiple levels, ostensibly comparable procedures, or comparable perspectives. In combining measurements, it is critical to look at factors that might give one measure more weight than another. Differential weight should be theory based, not just a byproduct of structure (e.g., averaging a measure scaled 1–10 with a measure scaled 1–100).

From a positive perspective on multiplicity, we should always try to increase the number of measurements we are gathering to assess each construct, although this may cause us to reduce the number of constructs we are measuring. From a less positive perspective, a set of multiple measurements opens a wide array of opportunities and the difficult challenge of selecting the appropriate strategy for combining the measurements.

From a top-down perspective, if theory justifies the claim that a particular construct is best measured through the combination of a set of separate measurements, then various statistical techniques can be used to combine those measurements. The increasing sophistication of these statistical techniques could warrant an entire book that discusses strategies for combining across measurements. The present paragraph will present a shallow description of some general approaches. If we assume that each measurement contributes equally to the construct, and the variance among the multiple measures is simply error of measurement, then a mean that is calculated with appropriate standardization to equate magnitudes across measurements (e.g., by using z-scores) is one way to create the construct. Factor analysis is a strategy for testing this assumption and for recognizing the need to have multiple constructs.

Using similar assumptions and more sophisticated statistical techniques, modeling procedures can be used to calculate a latent variable that is posited to be the underlying construct that is reflected in the observed measurements. Many modern statisticians tend to focus on an Item Response Theory (IRT) perspective in which responses are combined to assess constructs and they balk at including items that do not have a statistical linkage with other items. From a bottom-up perspective, measurements can be combined if they are correlated, which from a more sophisticated view is essentially a principal component analysis or factor analysis.

Another decision with multiple measurements is whether to combine them in an average or to focus on the highest/best measurement. Following the example above of calculating weight using multiple scales or assessments of the same individual on the same scale, the variability across measurements would be considered error, and the obvious way to combine measurements would be to average and thus reduce the error. In some instances, variability across measurement is intrinsically relevant because it measures a person's consistency. Another perspective is that multiple measurements can give individuals multiple chances to demonstrate their maximum competence rather than their average performance. For example, if we give an individual multiple opportunities to perform a high jump, the highest jump reflects the individual's highest level of skill. Another example is that most universities evaluate undergraduate applicants on various parameters including the highest score that they have attained on an ACT or an SAT standardized test. Some students perform better on a standardized test when they have learned about appropriate strategies (e.g., whether or not it is wise to guess), have practiced working within the test's time limits, slept well the night before the test, or are feeling confident that they will do well. Thus, prioritizing the highest score is based on the implicit assumption that the higher score reflects the student's highest level of performance (personal best) and the lowest level of performance is caused by error of measurement. In this context, a multiple measurement approach is beneficial, but averaging across multiple measurements would be likely to create error of measurement rather than a more accurate estimate.

Using multiple measurements may seem like a panacea, but it is important to note that if multiple measurements are not combined into a unitary construct, the use of multiple measurements can be inimical to the goal of a cumulative developmental science. Specifically, obtaining multiple measurements of a construct and analyzing each measurement individually in search of statistically significant results violates the assumptions of most inferential statistics and is the operational definition of capitalizing on chance. For example, infant gaze toward a location can be quantified in various ways (e.g., total duration of gaze, number of gazes, average length of gaze, length of longest gaze, latency to gaze toward the focal location, etc.). Parameters of infant gaze can be linked to specific constructs (e.g., direction of first gaze may reflect memory, whereas direction of subsequent gazes may reflect strategy or sustained attention). (See Aslin (2007) for an intriguing and compelling discussion of how looking time can be linked to underlying constructs.) Analyzing each multiple measurement separately and interpreting measurements that produce statistically significant or theoretically interesting effects while ignoring measurements that do not attain this status capitalizes on chance and undermines a successful cumulative developmental science. This error seems particularly egregious because it indicates that the opportunity to combine related measurements to form a more robust construct has been missed.

Another alternative to the value of a combined construct is the value of a multifaceted profile. As I described in Chapter 3, my colleagues and I have conducted much research in which we use a parent-report instrument (the FYI) to detect infants who are at-risk for an eventual diagnosis of ASD. One strategy that we have used is to combine parent responses across a wide array of domains to calculate a broad index of risk. In contrast, when infants are profiled based on their risk in several specific domains, we find that some infants have unusual behaviors that are more likely to involve social and communication behaviors, while other infants are experiencing more problems in sensory and regulatory domains. Overall risk can be quantified based on a broad array of problematic behaviors, but as we move forward in search of effective interventions or predictions of long-term development, infant profiles based on specific domains are likely to be more informative than a unitary broad index of risk.

5   Designing Developmental Research

Previous chapters have helped us understand the difficulty of the questions that we are trying to answer in developmental science and the role that constructs and variables play in our effort to accrue a cumulative collection of knowledge. Moving forward into the implementation of research, our next step is to explore the research designs that allow us to deploy our research tools to attain our goals. We have established a virtual dictionary of potential measurable constructs, and we must now focus on how to conduct research that will help us learn more about these constructs.

As discussed in previous chapters, development is defined as change over time, and this important parameter makes developmental science notably complicated. Time measurement ranges from micro units to light years, and spans historical phases such as from prehistoric life to the Dark Ages, Renaissance, and Industrial Revolution. It includes events like empires, world wars, and the evolution of social climates passing through phases of totalitarianism, slavery, and democracy, and the introduction of new resources such as writing, printing, radio, telephone, computer, Internet, mobile phone, smart glasses and watches, and neuro-mobile implants. Most of these changes have different rates based on rural versus urban, country, and continent, and other factors.

There are many things that cause difficulty in developmental science, and one particularly salient difficulty is the temporal aspect inherent in development that is generally defined as change over time. The effect of time can be inferred on the basis of comparisons between participants of different ages, although some developmental scientists (e.g., Gottlieb, 2007; Kraemer, 2000) would view cross-sectional differences as less interesting than the changes that emerge over time within an individual. The highest quality of time-related research will become possible when physical scientists discover a technique that allows retrospective analysis via time travel and contemporary research via invisibility and mind hacking. At present, some aspects of retrospective analysis can be accomplished via detective work (e.g., inspecting medical and academic records, or borrowing family video recordings or photographs). However, critical events in a person's past are frequently inaccessible either because they were not observed or because they were experienced by the person internally and may or may not have been reported or represented. The difficulties inherent in temporal measurement will be a recurrent theme in subsequent chapters.

5.1 Measuring Age

Development includes both stability and change over time, and incorporating time as a construct in empirical research is a significant challenge. In the developmental sciences, time is usually defined as age, which leads to a perspective in which we focus on the behavioral capacities of individuals at specific ages and how these capacities change as a function of growth and experience from conception until death. The minutes, hours, days, weeks, months, or years of life are obvious metrics of age. However, despite our precise measurement of time, age is always complicated in the developmental sciences and sometimes complicated in the physical sciences. For example, what is the age of an automobile? Years-since-manufacture is relevant for the aging of various aspects of the car such as paint and the technological sophistication of the sound system. Mileage accrued is relevant for the aging of the engine, transmission, brakes, and tires.

One complication in the study of early development is the distinction between gestational age and date-of-birth age. A gestational age of 38–42 weeks is generally labeled normal, so infants with gestation of only 33–36 weeks are essentially 1 month younger than their date-of-birth age would suggest, and infants with a gestation of only 31–32 weeks are almost 2 months younger than their peers who have the same birthdate. These differences dissipate eventually for most children who are raised in a supportive environment, but some infants who are 6 months old based on their date-of-birth are essentially 16% younger than their peers. This topic became very salient for me when my colleagues and I were analyzing the data from 1,200 families who had completed the First Years Inventory Version 2.1, a questionnaire designed to identify infants at-risk for an eventual diagnosis of ASD, within 2 weeks of their infant's one-year birthday. We established a risk-point system on the basis of relatively infrequent answers that thus suggested atypical development. In my initial examination of the group of infants who had accrued high risk, it was obvious that a disproportionate number were born preterm and thus were likely to have lagged behind their same-aged peers on a wide variety of questions because they were actually younger.

Researchers who study later development do not need to draw a distinction between gestational age and date-of-birth age, but here too, the precise measurement of time is not always the best definition of age. The onset of adolescence is often defined based on menarche, but how do we adjust our definition of adolescence to reflect the recent changes whereby many young women begin their first menstrual cycle and accrue secondary sexual characteristics at 7–8 years? Also, some researchers claim that adolescence is associated with a phase of brain development that affords limited capacity for future-oriented thinking. If we align the offset of adolescence with the onset of future-oriented thinking, many of our children (and us) might be described as having retained our adolescence long past our second decade of life.

In midlife, there can be a notable difference between a person's chronological age, their physical age, their underlying biologic age, their cultural age, etc. For example, a 65-year-old who is retired, suffers health issues, does not have a mobile phone or an email address, and watches Fox News all day could be considered much older than a 65-year-old who works fulltime, plays tennis, owns a mobile phone, a sports car, and a vaporization pipe, and responds to emails and texts all day.

5.2 Selecting the Best Ages for Conducting Assessments

When age has been defined as appropriately as possible, another challenge in developmental science is to select the ages we should focus on in our research. From a broad perspective, months and years reflect a constant flow of time. However, when we focus on the development of individuals, we notice that the flow can have some differentiation. A study based on orthogonal chronology (orthochronology) might explore developmental progression by assessing infants at 6 months, 12 months, 18 months, 24 months, etc. and treat these intervals as equal. In contrast, a study based on semantic chronology and a strategically timed assessment range (STAR) would capture a richer array of milestone-relevant individual differences. For example, when I have input on a milestone based infant assessment timetable, I recommend assessment at 8 months rather than 6 months because 8 months is more definitive and interesting from a developmental perspective. Six-month-old infants are developing, but 8-month-old infants are more likely to display working memory, word comprehension, stranger anxiety, expectations, and many other phenomena that are very relevant for subsequent progress. The key thought here is to select the assessment ages based on the phase of life that will be most relevant for the hypotheses that are being explored rather than adherence to a traditional symmetric chronologic metric.

When research includes later childhood, entry into school and grade level become relevant. If initial recruitment is a continuous process, participants will be stratified across grades, but depending upon the actual calendar month when recruitment begins and ends, the distribution of children across grades in school could be relatively asymmetric. Also, the age range within grades can be problematic. For example, if recruitment continues for one year from October through September, most participants will eventually be in the same grade and will range from being the oldest to the youngest student in that grade. If recruitment continues for one year from April to March, some participants will be relatively old in a particular grade and other participants will be relatively young in the next highest grade, which could profoundly influence development in some domains. Finally, it is also important to realize that some school systems do not change grades based on age (or employ cutoffs) but structure their classrooms based on ability in various subjects. And some school systems are not based on age or ability and are thus even more ambiguous.

Adolph and Robinson (2011) challenge developmental scientists to sample development at a rate that will allow an accurate description of developmental change. Specifically, the actual timing that is selected for assessments can be more or less informative or misleading. Their primary zone of research is early motor development, and they provide various examples in which different conclusions emerge based on the rate of assessment. For example, they display some interesting data in which one infant appears to have a stepwise acquisition of a motoric ability in comparison to a second infant whose ability ebbs and flows on a daily basis. When the second infant is sampled less frequently, the stepwise acquisition emerges, and is clearly incorrect. This example reminds me of an insight reported by my friend, language development expert Elizabeth Bates. When her daughter began speaking, she noticed that a word appeared early in Julia's vocabulary and then disappeared for several months before reappearing.

Frequently repeated assessment has theoretical advantages and can also create operational problems. McKnight, McKnight, Sidani, and Figueredo (2007) note that frequent data collection and short intervals between collection can create problems for participants and research staff and thus promote missing data. From this perspective, rate of assessment must balance the theoretical advantages and operational problems, and we must incorporate strategies that balance these concerns. My own optimal experience with this issue was the study described in the previous chapter in which we tested working memory in infants on a biweekly schedule when the infant was available for optimal performance.

5.3 Time as the Historical Context of Research

History is another aspect of time that is often ignored. Time can be defined as historical context in the sense that individuals develop in the broader context of an environment and culture that changes more or less dramatically year-by-year, decade-by-decade, century-by-century, etc. It is hard to imagine any aspect of human development that would be identical in an urban context, a rural context, a technological society, an agrarian society, a literate society, a non-literate society, in 1924, 1957, 1982, 1993, 2005, 2009, etc. [What do these dates share? Go Heels!]

Environmental and cultural changes are usually viewed as relatively trivial in the short term, particularly in their relevance for fundamental psychological cognitive and social processes. It would be interesting to time-travel back through previous centuries and explore possible changes in human working memory, executive function, and social referencing, despite the fact that most researchers assume a relative stability in these fundamental processes and ignore the ongoing historic increase in IQ scores labeled as the Flynn effect. There is still some uncertainty regarding how to interpret it, but if the Flynn effect is real, many aspects of cognitive ability have made notable progress over the past century. If this is true, it would not be difficult to explain as due to changes in nutrition, education, media, and technological support, among others. However, this phenomenon leads to a concern that the results of studies of cognitive development are not only limited to generalizations on the specific sample of participants, but also to the year in which the study was conducted.

On a recent plane flight, I was seated next to a mother and her infant, which would be torture for some travelers, but it was fun for me. When our plane began its descent, the infant experienced some discomfort and her mother quickly launched a program on her mobile phone that displayed a colorful animated rattle. The infant stared at the image and calmed down, but I experienced some discomfort: Piaget's theory of cognitive development suggests that our capacity for accruing knowledge emerges on the basis of sensory motor repetitive behaviors. From a Piagetian perspective, was this infant living in an environment with relatively impoverished sensory motor stimulation? Piaget observed infants who played with toys, and he did not have access to technology that would have allowed him to compare the effects of visual and motor experience. Thus, history imposes limitations on the generalizations we can draw from Piagetian theory, and more important, on all research conducted in previous decades with less sophisticated equipment and possibly with less sophisticated participants. We can help future generations in their interpretation of our research by noting the limitations on our generalizations that we are aware of, and further, by including conditions that connect our advanced procedures to the procedures used by our relatively primitive ancestors.

In contrast to cognitive topics, social topics like the influence of racism, poverty, and family configuration on self-concept, interpersonal relations, or episodic memory are likely to be very different in contemporary research compared to research conducted in previous decades or centuries. For example, how does the effect of parental divorce differ for my elementary school classmate who faced the unique challenge of being the first member of our community who had parents who were divorced versus elementary school children today who are much more likely to experience this phenomenon? A finding that is offered as a general description of the effects of divorce is misleading at best. Each finding regarding the effect of divorce is relevant for a cumulative developmental science, but only if it is circumscribed within the boundaries imposed by historical, geographical, and cultural parameters.

When I think about research on discrimination, I compare contemporary contexts with my own experience of attending an elementary school that had no ethnic diversity, and living in a Southern community in which various minority groups (e.g., Jews, Blacks, Catholics, and Greeks) were not allowed to join (or visit) the country club that was a few blocks away from my home. Poverty is an example of a construct that is explored across time, but the definition and experience of poverty changes vastly across historical time. In recent news, issues of racial discrimination and the occurrence of hate crimes have become increasingly salient, and explanations can focus on specific aspects of recent history, such as the presence of an African American man as president of the United States, without noticing other historic correlations, such as the expanding presence of social media and the economic ramifications of climate change. Racial self-concept, academic motivation, and the perception of racial bias might be very different in African American youth who experience middle school and high school while an African American man is president of the United States or who are inundated with examples of racism, bullying, or inappropriate police behavior that go viral via social media.

Another problematic aspect of history is the ongoing change in how we measure many constructs. The measurement procedures that were used to identify various levels of joint attention in the 1960s could be completely different from the methods being used contemporaneously. This challenge also occurs in ongoing studies when a new version of a measurement tool emerges and the researcher must choose between the previously used older version and the improved newer version.

On the positive side of this perspective, developmental research conducted on some topics in previous decades can provide an informative perspective on historical influences on various aspects of development. These influences include obvious sociological and political changes and also changes in other aspects of the environment that are less obvious. Old films remind us that our previous environment was filled with tobacco smoke, canned vegetables, and various environmental toxins (e.g., my bicycle ride in the cloud behind the DDT spray truck). Our children will eventually be reminded of an environment filled with portable electronic devices, multiple streams of audio-visual stimulation, bisphenol-A (BPA) in plastics and cash register receipts, and the myriad of bad components in foods from factory farms. The most negative side of this perspective is the impact of historical influences on our cumulative developmental science. We are very vulnerable to drawing incorrect and misleading conclusions when we generalize across studies of parenting, self-concept, or social relations without categorizing the findings based on the historical epoch during which the data were collected. This blindness is present not only in our discussion sections but also in our time-blind literature reviews and meta-analyses. I recently used the term "chronologic conclusion" when I noticed an article in the newspaper showing a change in women's rate of exercise at two points in time. Were assessments of rate of exercise comparable at both times?

Historic context of assessment will be an important aspect of design when we have access to time travel. We can currently use archival data in some contexts, but too much focus on this would make us historians. For now, our main obligation is to acknowledge the role that historical context can play in our interpretation of results.

5.4 Cross-Sectional, Longitudinal, and Life-Span Design

There are two obvious research strategies that can be used to explore development over time. In a cross-sectional design, different individuals are measured at specific points in time. The cross-sectional design can thus characterize development at various time points, and it eliminates test–retest issues and puts less emphasis on the participant's long-term commitment to a research project. Cross-sectional research also has the advantage of being amenable to a regression discontinuity design in which an arbitrary cutoff (e.g., a state mandated birthday cutoff for enrollment in kindergarten) can be used to establish a control versus treatment group that approaches the random-assignment criterion required for demonstrating causal effects. However, these advantages in cross-sectional research are offset by acquiring data that are less relevant for exploring change and continuity.

Cross-sectional research in developmental science is usually conducted by recruiting groups of participants at specific ages that have been selected to provide insight into developmental change across a specific period of time. A variant of this is an age-range design in which participants are sampled across a specified range of ages, and age is analyzed as a continuous variable. For example, Pelphrey et al. (2004) assessed working memory (WM) in infants aged 6 to 12 months, and the primary focus of the analysis was on modeling the development of WM across this age range. A comparable approach using a longitudinal design is to test participants at more or less regular intervals across a focal age range. For example, in a previously described study of WM, we recruited a sample of infants who began participation at approximately 6 months, and we retested the infants every few weeks until they were 12 months.

The more common approach in cross-sectional studies of development is an age-group design in which participants are selected at a particular age, and results are compared among groups of participants at separate ages. If analyses are focused on measures of central tendency at each age, variance within each age group is regarded as error variance. This raises an issue of whether the same range of birthdates is appropriate for each group. For example, the variance in production vocabulary that would emerge in a sample of infants aged 12 months plus or minus 3 weeks is likely to be notably larger than the variance of production vocabulary in a sample of toddlers aged 24 months plus or minus 3 weeks. For analyses of central tendency, the resulting heterogeneity of variance would invalidate various statistical models. For analyses based on accounting for variance, the issue is more theoretical because the heterogeneity could indicate that the variance in each age group reflects a different aspect of language development. This concern becomes increasingly problematic when inferences are being drawn regarding developmental changes in the relations among variables.

In both the age-range and age-group designs, the other issue that must be considered is how the range of ages affects anchoring new knowledge with previous knowledge. The range is obvious in the age-range design, so anchoring would be relatively straightforward. The main problem would be if the distributions are not comparable (e.g., a Gaussian distribution around a central age versus a flat distribution across the age range). Anchoring is much more problematic in the age-group design because results can be influenced by seemingly subtle parameters such as the limits that are imposed on the range of birthdates at each time point.

Another parameter in longitudinal research is the duration of time that is covered. Most developmental science uses relatively short-term duration, but a much broader perspective is possible. Glen Elder is a developmental scientist who focuses on life-span development, which usually explores changes that occur across decades or years (e.g., Elder, Shanahan, & Jennings, 2015). Elder's research on life-span development has evolved to include a rich set of perspectives that help us understand that individuals are shaped by their choices and actions that occur within the range of opportunities and constraints that are present during their life, which are defined by the historical period in which they live, the geographic location where they live, their social world, their economic circumstances, their personal health, and their interpersonal relationships. From a scattered perspective, each individual life-span could be seen as unique. From a clustered perspective, various circumstances could have some similarity in their effect on individuals. For example, life-span research could detect common themes in how people in the United States were affected based on their phase of life during World War II or how people in Nepal were affected by an earthquake. In contrast, developmental science can also address changes that occur rapidly, such as how a person learns a specific skill such as writing a word, knowing a fact, or using a new app on their smart phone. The development of these changes could be assessed across seconds, minutes, hours, or days.

I have drawn a distinction between cross-sectional and longitudinal designs, but it is important for developmental scientists to realize that these two types of designs can be merged. Names such as sequential design or cross-sequential design are used to refer to these combinations. This topic is salient to me because this design led to interesting and unexpected conclusions in a study in which we tested one group longitudinally at 8, 10, and 12 months, a second group longitudinally at 10 and 12 months, and a third group at 12 months (Reznick & Schwartz, 2001). A parent-report measure of word comprehension revealed comparable scores for both groups at 10 months and for all three groups at 12 months. In contrast, a parent-report measure of perception of infant intentionality evoked higher scores at each age from parents who were not completing the measurement for the first time.

5.5 Methodological Difficulties in Longitudinal Research

In a longitudinal design, the same individual is measured at different points in time either over a short interval or with repeated measurements spread over days, weeks, months, years, or decades. The value of a longitudinal design is that it affords not only a view of the individual at various time points but also data that can be analyzed to explore the mechanisms and processes associated with change and continuity. Issues such as effects of repeated testing and missing data can cloud interpretation in longitudinal research, but many nuisance factors can be addressed with specific design strategies or analyses.

Most longitudinal research is prospective, which implies various problems such as attempting to study an outcome of interest that has not yet occurred and that might be relatively rare or be affected by the fact that it is being studied. Participants in longitudinal research are usually not only aware that they are being studied but also have given their explicit consent to participate, and there are usually some more or less systematic differences between participants who do or do not participate and among those who agree to participate but then discontinue their participation. Measurement over time entails many difficulties. Most obvious, the repetition of the same measurement technique can influence outcomes. Some participants may accrue better performance based on previous experience. Some may get bored. Some tools could be equivalent to telling the same joke twice, a metaphor I am using for the third time thus far.

A second challenge in longitudinal research is to incorporate a design that acknowledges both convergent and divergent causality (Meehl, 1978). Convergent causality, also called equifinality, refers to developmental phenomena that have an array of different starting places (X1, X2, and X3) that lead to a comparable outcome (Y1). For example, various teratogens can lead to hearing impairment as an outcome. Divergent causality, also called multifinality, refers to developmental phenomena in which an identical starting place (X1) leads to an array of different outcomes (Y1, Y2, and Y3). To extend the previous example, in utero exposure to a particular teratogen can lead to various outcomes. A longitudinal study that begins with a cohort that is relatively homogeneous can be used to explore divergent causality, but a longitudinal study that is focused on a specific outcome (i.e., convergent causality) must include a broad array of participants in order to identify the initial starting places that can lead to the focal outcome.

One of the most debilitating methodological errors committed by developmental researchers is to assume that the measurement techniques that are effective in a cross-sectional design will be equally effective in a longitudinal design. The most salient problem with this assumption is that measurement error in a cross-sectional design usually causes randomly distributed within-group error variance. If measurement error is small, group size is large, and a strong effect is present, group differences can overshadow measurement error, thus allowing a statistically significant effect to emerge in a cross-sectional design. In contrast, in a longitudinal design, the hypotheses of interest are directed toward individual differences on a particular variable and how these individual differences are changed or preserved over time. Thus, the primary analytic focus in a longitudinal design is on effects that influence within-group variance per se. Measurement error in a cross-sectional design can be ameliorated by adding more participants and thus giving the random errors more chance to create a distribution in which the central tendency is an accurate estimate of the focal variable. Adding participants to a longitudinal design does not ameliorate measurement error per se because each additional score can be yet another inaccurate estimate of an individual's status on the focal variable. Amelioration of measurement error in a longitudinal design requires better measurement of each participant.

Various modifications can facilitate the transfer of cross-sectional measurement techniques into a longitudinal study. For example, as described in a previous chapter, one strategy for improving the precision of measurement is to repeat measurement procedures several times within a session or across sessions at a particular time point. This can be seen as problematic if it undermines a participant's commitment to a study, but having multiple assessments of a construct also offers the advantage of providing more or less comparable substitutes if a measure is missing. Another strategy is to expand the measurement procedure to include a larger number of trials or a broader array of test stimuli. Finally, measurement procedures that evoke correct or incorrect responses and that have discrete trials that reflect ordinal levels of performance can be administered using a stair-step protocol. That is, easy trials are administered until a criterion is attained. Subsequent trials of increasing difficulty are administered until a criterion of failure indicates that the participant's level of competence has been exceeded (e.g., Reznick, Corley, & Robinson, 1997).

Longitudinal research is notably vulnerable to missing data, and various strategies can be used to minimize this problem. Research studies that include multiple surveys sent via traditional mail can encounter the following problem: when families move and file a change of address, the change of address has a finite tenure, which is currently 6 months in many locations. Based on this constraint, I wrote a grant in which we included this consideration in the timing of our mailed contacts with participants. In another study, we had mailed birthday greetings and other social communication as a strategy for contacting families and receiving notification if their address had changed. As we began implementing the project, we learned an important alternative strategy: professional printers have access to a database from the US Postal Service that allows them to perform a task they call "scrubbing" in which old addresses are scanned and updated with new addresses despite the expiration of the change of address procedure.

Another strategy for avoiding missing data is to use modern technology if participants are able to engage in this opportunity. Telephones have evolved to a new status in which effective apps make them a virtual laboratory. For example, in the early days of mobile telephones, I considered developing an app that would time the duration of continued expression a person manifests despite the loss of connection with the party to whom the person is speaking. Telephones can also be used for frequent assessments of current mood and activity and can provide reminders about upcoming appointments and can link participants to an online survey. Additionally, if participants permit it, modern telephones can provide data about use of time, sleep cycle, social communication, and much more.

Efforts to avoid missing data can be problematic if they alter the array of participants in a study. Individuals who are not able to attend all assessments as scheduled can reflect a group with special needs or who are facing unique challenges. To simply eliminate these participants or avoid them could bias the generalizations that emerge from longitudinal data. Reversing this theme, a final suggestion for avoiding missing data is to consider modifications that alter participation in ways that make it a more positive experience. Zones of improvement include the actual measurement technique, the context in which measurement takes place, the valence of having participated in research, and the interpersonal contact between participants and research administrators.

5.6 Design Challenges of Clinically Relevant Research

Developmental scientists can focus on typical, normal development, but many are also interested in translational aspects of research that can be used to identify atypical development and remediate problematic aspects of that development. Clinically relevant research evokes various complications that must be considered when designing this research. For example, the diathesis-stress model in clinically relevant research provides another perspective on the difficulty of an open system. Diathesis refers to the underlying vulnerability that puts a person at risk for a particular behavioral manifestation, usually with negative implications. The diathesis can be based on some aspect of a person's underlying infrastructure, cognitive tool kit, temperament or personality, life situation, or life experiences. Stress refers to something that happens to a person and causes an effect due to that person's diathesis. The diathesis-stress model has been used to describe, predict, explain, and modify various aspects of human development, but the precise description of each diathesis can be notably difficult.

Research on medically oriented interventions go through a regulated set of preclinical then clinical phases that could be seen as contexts of discovery then justification. Research studies begin in a preclinical context of discovery in which the experimental drug or treatment is administered in vitro or in vivo to nonhuman animals. Depending on the results, the next phases are clinical trials in which a small cohort of humans receive the experimental drug or treatment to evaluate its appropriate dosage, side effects, and overall safety. The next phase focuses more on the context of justification by administering the experimental treatment to a large enough human cohort to gather data that can be used to test specific hypotheses regarding its effectiveness and to further evaluate its safety. Further expansion of justification can include a much larger cohort who participate in research that is designed to confirm the treatment's effectiveness, explore a broader array of its side effects, and perhaps most important, compare the treatment with other treatments in the current standard of care. The implementation of these options will depend on whether or not a drug company is simply trying to boost sales versus a competitor or is trying to establish a novel treatment. The main challenge here is to create an experimental context that generalizes to the broader context of patients who will be receiving the medication or treatment. One strategy that can help attain that goal is to establish communication with patients that helps researchers understand the patient perspective.

Another broad perspective is the distinction between deficit and surplus. A frequently occurring theme in research on behavioral development is to identify a deficit and find ways to remediate it. For example, research might indicate that a child who is a poor reader in comparison to his or her peers benefits from supplemental exercises that facilitate an appropriate eye movement pattern or a more extensive comprehension of terms. Some interventions will be appropriate for a relatively wide range of children, but it seems highly unlikely that a single intervention would have universal applicability. Constraints on the appropriateness of a particular intervention would arise due to a wide array of factors including the child's cognitive style, temperament, motivation, family support, etc. It is important to note that an intervention that remediates a deficit does not necessarily help children who do not have a deficit. For example, children who suffer from anemia show significant increases in various aspects of cognitive development when they receive supplemental iron, but this does not imply that iron would provide a general enhancement of cognitive ability in normal children. Quite the contrary, iron becomes toxic relatively quickly and thus is a difficult deficiency to treat. Iron is also metabolized in complicated ways, causing ingestion to be ineffective for some people depending upon genetics and various aspects of lifestyle.

Research on clinically oriented interventions is very prominent in developmental science and evokes many of the challenges of open systems discussed previously. From a broad perspective, we can differentiate research that aims at remediation or compensation. Remediation involves addressing the underlying deficits that lead to difficulties with daily living skills. For example, a person may have difficulty learning new skills due to poor concentration. A remediation approach would mean that the person would engage in tasks to improve concentration. Compensation involves adapting around a skill deficit to still find a way that the task can be accomplished. It usually involves making changes in the way the task is done or to the environment in which it is done. For example, if a person does not feel like she can leave her apartment due to anxiety, a way of compensating would be to help her learn to order groceries online or by phone.

The variables that are used to detect the effects of interventions can be relatively straightforward, particularly when atypical development is associated with specific symptoms that would be ameliorated by an effective intervention. However, when the outcome that reflects the efficacy of the intervention is less obvious, researchers often presume that a general measure of developmental level or intelligence is a viable target. This can be contrasted with a research strategy in which the effects of an intervention are monitored in a set of relatively specific theoretically relevant constructs. A focus on specific outcomes is advantageous if the initial impact of the intervention is to induce improvement in a targeted component (e.g., attention), with an expectation that general effects will emerge peripherally.

When a typical child's response pattern is being compared to an atypical child's responses, it is important to determine whether or not instructions and task demands are comparable. For example, Leevers and Harris (2000) report that instructions encouraging imagery improve logical reasoning by typical preschool children and children with learning disabilities, but the same instructions cause children with ASD to develop a response bias and perform at chance levels. From this perspective, it is important to anchor seemingly comparable variables. Consider a study in which children hear a string of words and are asked to say "yes" if the words form a grammatically correct sentence and "no" if the words do not form a grammatically correct sentence. It is reasonable to assume that typical children will use the terms yes and no as requested. In contrast, atypical children in this context might respond with yes and no, but their responses could be based on a preference for a particular response and not on grammar per se. To anchor the responses from atypical children, a simpler task could be included in which the yes or no is evoked but both groups of children would be expected to respond correctly (e.g., say "yes" if the string is words and "no" if the string is numbers). A more difficult task could be included to determine whether both groups of children respond randomly when they do not know the correct response.

One overarching barrier to the goal of developing optimal interventions is the likelihood that the efficacy of an intervention will be affected by aspects of the individual, the family, and the broader social context. Possible influences include the individual's age, temperament, physiologic constraints, and cognitive ability, or the family's resources, stability, and beliefs, and various aspects of the broader social context. From this perspective, optimal research on interventions should be designed to identify the characteristics of individuals for whom an intervention is effective rather than a more general determination of whether an intervention works.

Another challenge in intervention research is handling partially nested designs. Some clinical interventions can be administered individually, but some interventions are efficiently and effectively administered to groups. For example, Cognitive Behavioral Therapy can be administered face-to-face with a therapist, via an interactive computer interface, through published guides, or in a group educational course. Participants can be randomly assigned to receive treatment or a placebo in any of these contexts, but from a statistical perspective, participants who receive their treatment in a group context can have strong correlational effects influenced by the skills or personality of the person who administers the treatment, aspects of their shared experience, or the composition of their group. Researchers can investigate these potential confounding influences via simple exploratory data analysis or by using sophisticated statistical models.

A placebo is a harmless medicine or procedure that is likely to provide some psychological benefit to the recipient and can be used as a comparison to explore the effect of a potent medicine or procedure. I once participated in a clinical trial in which I assumed I had received a medicine rather than a placebo because I felt some immediate effects. This led me to the insight that an effective clinical trial could use a placebo that does have an effect, but an effect that is irrelevant for the focal outcome of the study. This would prevent patients like me from initially discriminating a placebo compared to a medicine, and would thus boost the credibility of a statistically significant treatment effect.

Finally, as mentioned earlier in the case of anemia and cognitive impairment, the design of intervention research sometimes fails to acknowledge the possibility that interventions that ameliorate problems for individuals who are at risk or who are developing atypically do not necessarily enhance the development of individuals who are developing typically. For example, a nutritional intervention that accelerates growth and promotes intellectual development in children who are failing to thrive does not necessarily enhance the development of typical children, and worse, might have an iatrogenic effect and lead to obesity and other problems. The possibility of iatrogenic intervention effects is particularly salient in a social rehabilitation context. For example, Poulin, Dishion, and Burraston (2001) report that a preventive intervention in which high-risk youth are placed in cognitive-behavioral groups contributed to higher rates of self-reported smoking and teacher-reported delinquency. From a broad perspective, most intervention research is conducted within a more or less instantiated 2 x 2 x 2 design: participants are at risk for a problematic outcome or they are not at risk, participants receive a focal intervention or they do not receive the intervention, and participants experience a bad outcome or they do not experience a bad outcome. The cell that reflects being not at risk, receiving intervention, and having a bad outcome is sufficiently problematic to warrant appropriate scrutiny.

6   Selecting a Sample

Decisions regarding who participates in developmental science research will have an enormous impact on the validity and quality of the data that are gathered and on the generalizations that can be asserted based on these data. This chapter will explore various aspects of sample-selection that can affect the quality of developmental science. It is important to keep in mind that not only is it virtually impossible to produce a universal generalization but this is also usually not our goal. The accrual of a cumulative developmental science will require targeted generalizations based on identifying and reporting the relevant characteristics of the research participants that determine the range of generalization that is supported by their data. Most developmental science research recruits a sample of human beings, but the present chapter will also address the evolution of traditional nonhuman animal behavior models and their relevance for investigating diseases.

6.1 Competence of Participants

One obvious consideration in the selection of research participants is that they must have the knowledge, skills, stamina, availability, motivation, and other attributes that will allow them to be competently engaged in the data-gathering process. For example, it would be virtually impossible to attain valid data from a participant who cannot perform the task, read the questionnaire, or use the mathematical skills that would allow accurate completion of a rating scale. Some participants may have relatively low motivation because they feel obliged to participate due to academic requirements, fiscal necessity, or other pressures. And, some participants might be less honest because they view research as an intrusion on their privacy, a possible trigger for an unwanted diagnosis, or the possible cause of a sanction for inappropriate thoughts or behaviors. Various techniques can be used to assess relevant parameters such as participants' competence, motivation, and honesty, and any study that ignores this issue has undermined its credibility. *Voir dire* is the legal term referring to the selection of jurors who have no obvious bias or incompetence that would reduce their likelihood of providing a fair judgment. From a research perspective, an experiment that has not explored the *voir dire* of participants could suffer the same fate as a mistrial.

An additional consideration related to the competence of the participants within developmental science may arise when participants are too familiar or comfortable with a research endeavor. For example, an active research laboratory that draws on a small catchment area might engage the same families so frequently that children become semi-professional research participants whose behavior in an assessment context is notably different from the behavior that would be evoked from amateur naïve children who have not learned to interact with researchers and with laboratory-based stimuli and activities. Or, in a metropolitan area that has many colleges and universities, the convenience sample may have participated in similar research in other laboratories, and their previous participation may affect their current performance. Research conducted in metropolitan areas should always include screening for potentially problematic influences based on participation in other studies, and reviewers of grants and empirical reports should be aware of this potential problem.

A wide array of variables affect how an infant or child will perform in a data-gathering context, and many studies of infants and children report that a relatively large percentage of participants did not provide data. Various factors could cause this lack of participation, but it is important to consider possible systematic variations that would influence the distribution of participants and generalizations based on those participants. For example, assessment of any aspect of intellectual development based on a child's performance on a long series of tasks administered by a tester will be affected by the child's motivation, stamina, and relationship with the tester. In some studies, the sample of participants will only include children who have relatively strong motivation or stamina, and who are comfortable in an unfamiliar environment interacting with an unfamiliar person. This constraint was very salient to me in a collaborative study in which we performed psychological assessments on infants following their participation in a brain scan at a hospital. Infants who completed the brain scan, who were transported to our laboratory, and who were able to be psychologically assessed were probably systematically different when compared to infants who were not cooperative after the brain scanning and the travel. Unfortunately, we did not have an opportunity to retest the latter group and compare them to the other participants.

6.2 Demographics of Participants

A second obvious consideration in the selection of research participants is that the extent to which findings can be generalized from the data will be profoundly affected by the demographic characteristics of the sample. Research based on a randomly selected sample of human beings could be used to support a broad generalization about people, but even if participants represented every location on the planet and every age between infancy and elderly, and every human being on the planet had an equal probability of participating, the generalization would still be limited to human beings who are alive at the time that the research is conducted, and therefore the conclusions may or may not generalize to all humans who have ever lived in the past or all humans who will ever live in the future. Even though universal generalizations about human beings are obviously impossible, many empirical reports describe their conclusions as being about people with no explicit attention to the more or less obvious limitations on generalizations that should be stated explicitly.

When developmental science is viewed from a more translational perspective, it is important to recognize that universal generalizations are sometimes not developmental science's primary goal. We always hope that our findings will generalize to studies that use nearly-exact or as-close-as-possible sampling procedures. However, a contrasting strategy is to explore aspects of a relatively narrow sample and develop a theoretical or translational understanding of that sample that is relevant for theory or treatment. For example, research could focus on theory and intervention that is relevant for a particular cultural group, or for individuals with a particular background, experiential history, temperament, or set of cognitive abilities and particularly salient for developmental science, a specific range of age. The focused generalization perspective will affect how a sample is recruited and described, and how the results from this sample are discussed.

Henrich, Heine, and Norenzayan (2010) have written an extremely valuable analysis that demonstrates the remarkable (and disappointing) presence of broad claims about human psychology and behavior that are based on samples that they label WEIRD (Western, Educated, Industrialized, Rich, and Democratic). Their analysis suggests that 96% of the samples in recently published behavioral research come from countries that represent 12% of the world's population. And, even within that relatively limited cohort of research participants, a randomly selected American undergraduate is approximately 4,000 times more likely to be a research participant in published empirical studies than a randomly selected person from outside of the West. Their extensive analysis of a broad array of data make it quite clear that many of the conclusions that textbooks offer as truth may be true for the WEIRD people, but are not necessarily true for the rest of the world. Influences of culture, economics, geography, etc. affect human behavior at all levels. From a developmental science perspective, children acquire cognitive, emotional, and social skills in different contexts that influence these skills. Even phenomena that seem basic such as visual acuity, perceptual tendencies, motor development, etc. can be affected by culture and geography. It is important to note that the WEIRD analysis provided by Henrich et al. is followed by several dozen pages of Open Peer Commentary in which colleagues offer perspectives on this topic as viewed by anthropologists, neurologists, philosophers, and other specialties; raise similar concerns regarding animal models and other subdomains; and note other concerns such as research paradigms, and diversity of researchers.

Research conducted on WEIRD people has obvious limitations. However, it is important to realize that almost all developmental science research will have constraints on who can participate that will set limitations on the conclusions and generalizations that can be drawn from the research. For example, political polling based on random-digit dialing of landline phone numbers in the early 2000s precluded participation by individuals who used mobile phones exclusively and thus provided a description of the political opinions of a specific segment of voters. Service assessment that is based on responses from service receivers who agree to provide feedback could bias the report to be either extremely negative or extremely positive depending upon the motivation and characteristics of the service receivers who agree to participate. A study that explores development of children who participate in high quality educational experiences must recognize that these children live in families with ample resources and motivation to promote education. A study that looks at the effects of full day kindergarten on children's academic achievement and well-being will reflect the characteristics of children who have family resources that allow them continued access to full-day kindergarten.

6.3 Assessing Demographic Differences

A further complication in developmental science is that race/culture is never a straightforward construct to measure. Official surveys offer a choice between white and non-white and then various other options. For example, a birth certificate in North Carolina asks if the mother and father are: White, Black or African American, American Indian or Alaska Native, Asian Indian, Chinese, Filipino, Japanese, Korean, Vietnamese, Other Asian, Native Hawaiian, Guamanian or Chamorro, Samoan, Other Pacific Islander, or Other. And, for "Hispanic

Origin of parent" the birth certificate also includes the options Mexican, Puerto Rican, Cuban, Other, or Other literal. Other forms might code race using different options. Another example of complicated demographic differences is the recent news that mentioned a civil rights activist who labels herself black, in contrast to her parents, both of European descent with some Native American roots. The parents described their daughter as being a Caucasian who had altered her appearance over time to look black and be more linked to her four younger adopted black siblings and her black spouse.

Focusing more on culture, the East–West difference between individualism and collectivism has attained some salience in developmental science and has been linked to phenomena such as attachment. Moving beyond geography, Cohen (2010) explores various dimensions that are relevant for defining culture such as religion, socioeconomic status, and region within a country, a topic that has been salient in developmental science for several decades (Tudge, Putnam, & Valsiner, 1996). Students in my research methods class had an interesting engagement with this problem when I asked each of them to describe their cultural background. From this perspective, we noticed that all parameters of cultural difference can be complicated. For example, religion was sometimes a simple label, but it could also tap descriptions of spirituality and how parental expectations in this domain were handled. Descriptions of region of birth had various parameters including urban versus rural, northern versus southern, college town versus other specialty, etc. Socioeconomic descriptions were sometimes expressed in parental income/wealth and sometimes in how comfortably and generously parental money was deployed.

From an evolutionary perspective, the entities we currently label as Homo sapiens evolved across time based on crossbreeding of various ancestors. Segregated geographic domains promoted interbreeding of specific subsets of Homo sapiens, but recent advances in travel and openness to self-selected interbreeding are promoting the generic crossbreeding that could someday lead to a population of similar Homo sapiens across the world. At the present time, we face various challenges in identifying a particular person's race. Someday, a biomarker might be used to classify the racial profile of each individual. For now, race is based on self-report, which can be interpreted differently by individual self-reporters. One obvious challenge is to incorporate information about racial diversity among predecessors, and also the situation in which an individual is not aware of racial diversity among predecessors. I also remember hearing a presentation by a sociologist who was conducting longitudinal research on a large sample of adolescents with race as a critical independent variable. A problem that emerged was surprisingly frequent change over time in the race reported by an individual.

From a broader perspective, even if we establish reasonably accurate boundaries among racial groups, it becomes useless to attribute effects to groups without identifying an underlying mechanism. For example, in the contemporary United States, randomly sampled African Americans are likely to have less education, lower SES, and various other differences in comparison to European Americans. Thus, it would be short-sighted to describe differences between these groups as African Americans versus European Americans, which would be more accurately viewed as a proxy for the underlying differences. When we identify effects that are associated with differences between ethnic/racial groups, we need to transcend obvious surface-level differences and attempt to identify the underlying constructs that are most likely to affect behavior. One strategy for solving this problem is cross-participant matching, but this can be a misleading strategy because matching individuals on one variable can force a mismatch on other variables. For example, matching groups of African Americans and European Americans on annual income could create a mismatch on wealth because individuals who have a relatively high income but are from a lower SES are likely to have an extended family that has relatively low income and thus they would be sharing more of their high annual income with family members than the matched European Americans whose extended family members are more likely to have relatively high income. A more sophisticated approach for identifying the array of differences among groups is to use statistical techniques like propensity score matching (PSM) to identify the covariates that are linked to receiving the treatment.

6.4 Number of Participants

One obvious question is how many participants must be tested in order to obtain reliable, valid, and generalizable results? When a study has too few participants (i.e., is under-powered), statistically insignificant findings are ambiguous because it is impossible to know if an effect was not observed because the effect does not exist or because the study lacked the power to detect the effect. Cohen and others identified problematic under-powered behavioral research half a century ago (Cohen, 1962) and developed techniques to determine the number of participants needed to attain adequate statistical power to detect an effect if it is present (e.g., Cohen, 1977). Maxwell (2004) updated us with bad news that despite ample attention to this problem, under-powered studies remained prominent in the research literature because researchers often analyze a single study greedily and use it to test multiple hypotheses, thus potentially reducing the study's credibility.

Testing multiple hypotheses with the same sample seems efficient and practical, but if effects are defined on the basis of statistical significance, this type of multiplicity is a strategy for identifying statistically significant results and it thus undermines the potential for our research to contribute to cumulative scientific knowledge (Wilkinson & the Task Force on Statistical Inference, 1999).

In contrast, a study that has too many participants (i.e., is over-powered) wastes resources and can support trivial or bogus results. Maxwell (2004) describes some multi-researcher, multi-site collaborative projects in which a large sample is recruited and assessment time is divided among research questions. This space shuttle model in which an array of separate studies are crammed into a single, costly vehicle has the appeal of allowing research to attain impressive levels of sample size and diversity among participants, but as noted in previous chapters, most psychological constructs are not easy to measure and thus would receive very shallow measurement in this context and would be uninterpretable despite having a large number of participants. Yes, we should be concerned about a study's power, but we should be even more concerned about its wiring and architecture! Boosting power with better measurement has notable advantages over boosting power by engaging more participants.

I experienced an interesting perspective on the balance between power and measurement while serving on the Cognitive Assessment Team of the NIH National Children's Study (NCS). Our team was developing the measures of cognitive skills that we assumed would eventually be implemented for a cohort of 100,000 participants in the United States who would be tested during infancy and followed longitudinally until they are 21 years old. The sample was expected to have broad diversity and to be tested in a wide array of domains relevant for health and general success in life. The obvious trade-off in our planning was the balance between shallow assessments of a wide range of variables versus deep assessments of a limited number of variables. Given the broad NCS collaboration, the plans were strongly oriented towards breadth rather than depth. The more the merrier but sometimes less is more! Perhaps this is why the NCS was canceled.

6.5 Recruiting an Optimal Sample

Efforts to recruit an appropriate sample are vital to support generalizations to a wide or narrow population and to effectively measure the focal construct. Recruitment opportunities will depend upon various details about the targeted individuals, the geographic constraints of the data measurement process, and the resources that are available to support the research. A convenience sample is convenient but almost always imposes very strict limitations on the generalizations that are supported by our research. Broad generalizations and specific generalizations both require replacing convenience with diligence and creativity in recruitment.

My own efforts to recruit families for participation in research on infants have been notably different at different locations and in different decades. During one phase, a local newspaper printed a list of families who had recently given birth to a child, and we used this information to send them an invitation to participate in research. During another phase, birth certificates were a public record, so we sent research assistants to City Hall to prepare a mailing list. During another phase, I regularly obtained birth certificates in an electronic format for all infants born in this state. During another phase, research assistants visited families in the maternity ward of the hospital or spoke to them in the lobby of a medical clinic and invited them to participate in our research. My colleagues have used other strategies such as posting a research participation invitation in a campus-wide informational email, publishing a research participation invitation in a local newspaper or family-oriented magazine, or purchasing names of possible research participant families from marketing firms that have attained birth information using various strategies. It would be difficult to link limitations and other problems to specific recruitment strategies particularly given our tendency to not explicitly address this topic in our publications. However, given possible limitations based on research participants, a description of our recruitment strategy should definitely be included in publications.

The definition of an optimal sample in developmental science is also affected by the design of the experiment. Many developmental scientists are notably biased toward the efficacy of longitudinal research, and as discussed in the previous chapter, longitudinal research is associated with many difficulties. In the present context, if reduction of missing data is viewed as the criterion for obtaining an optimal sample in a longitudinal study, this could introduce some characteristics of the sample that would not generalize to a broader range of participants. For example, individuals with higher SES are more likely to retain their current address, remain available for participation over a long period of time, and maintain their commitment to completion of a longitudinal study. Selecting these participants would reduce missing data and would also reduce the potential breadth of generalizations. One compromise between these two approaches is to explore factors that can cause attrition and make adjustments to accommodate the needs of participants who are less likely to complete the study but are needed because their participation would contribute to broader generalization. For example, some participants need facilitated transportation, some need home visits rather than laboratory assessments, and some need more reminders when they have failed to provide data.

Another aspect of recruitment is the location of the data collection. If a developmental scientist's goal is to recruit a broad income level sample, one obvious strategy is to test participants at a location that will be convenient for them rather than limiting participation to families who have the resources and motivation to visit a laboratory that is cloistered within a college campus. For example, research can be conducted in a storefront, an urban neighborhood, or a health center or other institution that caters to a low-SES clientele. I once conducted a study in New Haven Connecticut in which I obtained access to low-SES participants by renting a room at a health care clinic located in an impoverished neighborhood (Reznick, 2008).

Another strategy for obtaining an optimal sample is to collect data in the participant's home rather than in a laboratory, although this can be problematic if the home is chaotic or unsafe, or if a home visit is viewed as intrusive from a cultural perspective (e.g., I consulted with colleagues in Japan who were designing a replication of one of my studies and they indicated that home visits would not be feasible in their country because at that time families did not accept this intrusion). Collecting data in classrooms also introduces constraints based on availability. Urban classrooms in cities that have major universities can be inundated with requests from researchers. This can introduce various constraints on who gets access to the classroom, what topics educational administrators are most interested in, and how far away some researchers have to travel to get access to classrooms.

As discussed previously in the Henrich et al. description of WEIRD participants, a large percentage of data in psychology is accrued from undergraduate students who are participating in research as a course obligation and this configuration introduces obvious constraints on generalizations. Some research includes volunteers, and other research offers participants a monetary compensation. And, compensation can be hourly pay, a large sum, entry in a lottery, etc. The effect of these parameters deserves scrutiny, and will probably be complicated by other factors such as the demography of the participants and the nature of the research. I cannot offer a definitive recommendation on which strategy is best.

Researchers who conduct research in the United States late in the 20th century and early in the 21st century face an increasingly salient need to identify and recruit representatives from the rapidly growing population of Latino families. Language is an obvious concern, although simply translating a recruitment letter into Spanish is not very effective in North Carolina and probably in all other states. Broader issues affecting research participation by immigrant Latino families include hesitancy to engage in activities that could challenge one's status as an illegal immigrant, cultural differences in accepting the rationale for research participation, or simply a lack of transportation and time. The most successful strategy that I have observed for recruiting Latino families is to set up an information table at a community center or a popular event, and attempt to recruit participants through direct interaction with them (e.g., Ratto, 2013).

Research in developmental science is often conducted in laboratories in which researchers can create a carefully structured environment. In contrast, some research in developmental science is conducted in real-world contexts such as classrooms or homes. The recently evolving Internet is positioned between these two extremes: It is amenable to mechanized assessment and is also currently a somewhat real-world environment that is occupied by a broad array of people. This context now offers a very contemporary strategy for recruiting a broad or specific sample of research participants. Specifically, a website called Amazon's Mechanical Turk is an online marketplace where people can do various work for pay, including participation in research. Buhrmester, Kwang, and Gosling (2011) conducted research on the participants in Mechanical Turk and found a large, diverse workforce reflecting people from over 50 different countries and all 50 US states. The gender split followed the traditional Internet participation of a slightly larger female sample, 36% non-white, and somewhat older than average Internet users. Other limitations could include the rationale for participation, the willingness to share personal information in a context in which identity can be hacked, Internet access and a level of sophistication that allows cognizance of Mechanical Turk, and a relatively limited age range that does not include children. However, compared to the typical American college student sample, Mechanical Turk can be adjusted to generate a much broader range or a relatively specific range. Mechanical Turk appears to offer the opportunity for improving the set of participants in some research studies, but it is not a total cure for all problems in this domain.

From the perspective of attempting to improve developmental science, my primary suggestion is that we be aware of recruitment's possible influences, we make efforts to detect recruitment's effect, and we provide appropriate description of recruitment in our manuscripts. Hopefully, this will eventually lead to a better understanding of effects caused by recruitment, better strategies for optimal recruitment, and better awareness of limitations on generalizations due to recruitment.

6.6 Implications of Range of Individual Differences in Sample

Many statistical tools use the variance in a set of numbers as the basis for detecting differences among parameters, measuring the relationship among potentially independent variables, or testing the causal relationships among components of a process. Given that generalizations in this research are based upon the variance that characterizes the sample, it is important to consider how aspects of the sampling strategy may affect the variance that is present and detectable.

One possible problem is that a lack of variance might lead to unrealistic conclusions. For example, a research strategy that was typical in the early days of behavioral genetics compared correlations between fraternal twins and identical twins on the assumption that both types of twins share the same environment. Thus, a larger correlation among identical twins than among fraternal twins was interpreted as reflecting the magnitude of genetic effects in the sense that genetic similarity caused identical twins to attain similar scores on a dependent variable (DeFries & Fulker, 1988). However, if participants were selected from a wide range of genetic backgrounds and a limited range of environments (e.g., all twins in the sample are from middle class families living in suburban neighborhoods) then the nature of the sample could cause environmental variance to be relatively low and genetic effects might be artificially enhanced. In contrast, if the participants were selected from the same range of genetic backgrounds but from a wide range of environments extending from luxurious royalty to abject poverty then environmental variance could be much higher and the same genetic influence would now account for a much smaller percentage of the overall variance. In either of these unusual environmental contexts, conclusions about genetic and environmental effects should not be automatically generalized to a broader population. Most contemporary research is less extreme, but this issue should not be ignored.

Another problem emerges when the source of within-group variance differs across groups. For example, consider a study that attempts to account for variance in the early development of reading ability. In a classroom with children from a low-income neighborhood but a wide array of ethnic backgrounds, variance in reading within that classroom is likely to be influenced by the language ability of the parents and the specific language exposure the child has at home. In a classroom that is composed of children who have the same ethnic background but who come from a wide array of socioeconomic statuses, variance in reading is likely to be influenced by variables such as parental education or the availability of reading materials in the home.

Finally, in a classroom in which the children are all from the same ethnic background and relatively high socioeconomic status, variance in reading ability is likely to be affected by the child's level of cognitive development and other aspects of the child such as gender, motivation, or temperament. Research that focuses on a single type of classroom is likely to detect some influence on the early development of reading ability, but this influence would not necessarily generalize to all children. And, if data from these different types of classrooms are pooled, a model that accounts for the amalgamated variance will identify an overall effect size that reflects the relative presence of each particular type of classroom in the total sample. The appropriate generalization of these results will depend upon the degree to which the distribution of sampled classrooms aligns with the distribution of classrooms in the population that is the target for generalization.

Issues related to sampling across different types of classrooms can be viewed as the tip of the iceberg. Comparable concerns emerge when samples are drawn from different neighborhoods to generalize to a city, different municipalities and rural areas to generalize to a state, different states or providences to generalize to a country, and different countries to generalize to the world at a particular point in time. As noted earlier, totally broad generalization is virtually impossible, and this does not imply that research is inherently flawed. The problem is that researchers seldom address the question of generalizability in their empirical reports, and worse, they often implicitly assume universal generalization when that claim would be ludicrous at best.

Variance in the sample can also become particularly relevant when a researcher attempts to link new results to previous discoveries and the new results are based on accounting for variance. For example, some research has found an interesting negative correlation between a parent's SES and the parent's estimate of an infant's vocabulary. That is, parents who had lower SES tended to indicate a larger comprehension vocabulary than did parents who had higher SES. This phenomenon evoked various explanations and, clearly, more research is needed. However, if a subsequent study fails to replicate the relation between SES and parent-reported vocabulary, variance in SES is a critical anchor between the two studies. If the subsequent study has a relatively narrow range of levels of SES or less variance in SES among participants, this reduces the possibility of a correlation between SES and any other variable. And, from the perspective of anchoring, any inferences regarding replication or extension of previous findings would require explicit examination and reporting of the comparability of variance across relevant studies.

6.7 Identifying and Interpreting Homogeneous Subsets

A researcher who has accrued a large enough sample, a broad enough range of participants, and a representative array of variance should be proud but not complacent because even with appropriate variance, one additional aspect of the sample needs thorough attention. To the extent that the sample can be construed as reflecting a more or less continuous distribution of individual difference, analysis of the amalgamated data leads to conclusions that can be generalized to the broader population that the sample represents. However, if the sample can be divided into separate homogeneous subsets, which is highly likely, the conclusions will be more accurate and valid if they are linked to these specific homogeneous subsets.

At an extreme, the issue I am raising here connects to Magnusson's (1998) distinction between variable-oriented versus person-oriented approaches to developmental science. Behavioral phenomena emerge in an open system, and thus are complex. As discussed in previous chapters, each individual's neural and physical structure, environment, history, accrued experience, cognitive and emotional abilities, etc. leads to the obvious perspective that there is a level of description at which no two human beings are identical. From this extreme perspective, we could question whether it is possible to defend any generalization based on behavioral data amalgamated across a collection of unique individuals. From an alternative perspective, the fact that developmental science has accrued an impressive set of research projects that can be used to describe, predict, control, and explain human behaviors indicates that some more or less accurate generalizations are possible.

The compromise between these two extremes evokes the need to identify specific subsets that contain humans who have sufficient homogeneity and then to use these homogeneous groups as the basis for limited but accurate generalizations. For example, if we randomly select individual children to receive either a pep talk or a relaxation exercise before taking an academic achievement test, would all children be equally affected by each treatment? Probably not, because it seems likely that the pep talk could enhance motivation in some children but heighten anxiety in others. And, the relaxation exercise would probably reduce anxiety in some children, thus enhancing performance, but reduce motivation in others, thus undermining performance. To carry this example a step further, what would happen if these two types of children were equally likely to participate in a study designed to compare the effect of a pep talk versus a relaxation exercise? If the effects of these two interventions were equally strong and we did not separate the two types of children, a broad statistical analysis would indicate that the treatments have no effect. In contrast, if we identified the two homogeneous subsets and analyzed each group separately, our analysis would reveal strong effects for each treatment that would each generalize to a particular population. The bottom line is that research can be simplified to focus on a specific homogeneous subset but any simplification of a complex phenomenon is likely to lead to random conclusions that will not contribute to a cumulative developmental science.

Various approaches have emerged for identifying homogeneous subsets within a heterogeneous sample. Some groups can be defined on the basis of an intensional metric or biomarker with specific indication of the properties that define the sample. For example, most humans who have a pair of identical sex chromosomes have bodies that are similar to other humans who have a pair of identical sex chromosomes and are notably less similar to the bodies of humans who have a combination of two different sex chromosomes. In contrast, research literature tends toward gender similarities and gender variation that is primarily age dependent (Hyde, 2005). Humans whose genetic heritage can be traced to Africa tend to have darker skin and be more vulnerable to sickle cell anemia than are humans whose genetic heritage can be traced to China. An extensional metric is based on a broader construct that can be linked to individuals but not to an underlying set of properties. For example, human beings named Steve have one aspect of homogeneity, but they have nothing in common. Humans who are affiliated with Christianity are likely to have beliefs about abortion that would contrast with humans who regard themselves as atheists. The primary challenge here for developmental science is to find appropriate properties that define homogeneous subsets that generalize to broader groups.

For variables that have a continuous distribution, the challenge is identifying a range of normal individual differences and a range that reflects a homogeneous subset. For example, consider a study in which various measurements are used to define level of stress. The index of stress might be in a normal distribution, and dividing children into groups would form arbitrary, meaningless boundaries and ignore meaningful individual differences. Or, a subset of children who have high stress might have unique responses to treatments or performance in various procedures.

Statistical techniques can be used for analyzing variance and looking for coherence within the variance as an identity of groups, and also the general examination of variance to determine whether there is heterogeneity in the effect of the treatment. All approaches to identifying homogeneous subsets offer possible insights into behavioral development, but must also be evaluated with appropriate caution. A statistical approach used with appropriate power can be expected to always identify a group that could be considered to be a homogeneous subset. However, the contribution that this finding makes to the accrual of knowledge will depend upon whether or not the group can be described in a way that helps us predict, control, or explain behavior. The homogeneous subset identified statistically might also reflect a chance co-occurrence of variance or a decision to focus on a particular subset of variables or the presence of measurement error. You should definitely discuss this topic with a statistician.

The use of existing classifications can also lead to misleading or ineffective generalizations. For example, research that is currently being conducted in the United States is likely to have some participants who can be labeled European American, some African American, and some Latino or Hispanic. These labels are not only obvious, but also particularly salient in efforts to conduct research with a diverse sample that will support broader generalizations. However, it is important to draw a distinction between using ethnic/racial categorization to insure diverse sampling and assuming that ethnic/racial categorizations should be used as the basis for identifying homogeneous subsets that can be used as the basis for statistical analysis.

The bottom line here is that we should monitor every study in developmental science to evaluate the accuracy of generalizations based on the sample of individuals who have been tested. The list of potentially inaccurate generalizations is infinite, but here are some frequently occurring examples in developmental science: Research studies that refer to parents and have only tested mothers; that explore relationships among siblings and ignore the varied age gaps, gender configuration, family structure, etc.; that generalize to adopted children without recognizing issues such as age at adoption, pre-adoption maltreatment, demographics of parents who can afford an adoption, etc.; that generalize to bilingual samples and do not explore the particular languages that are involved, the age of exposure to each language, the linguistic proficiency of parents in each language, if the child has the role of being family spokesperson, demographic variables that are correlated with bilingualism in various countries, etc.; that compare males and females without considering differences in genes, bodies, socialization, environment, cognitive style, brain laterality, hormones, etc.; or that examine infants who are at risk for an eventual diagnosis of ASD and only have data from infants who have an older sibling with ASD. The quality of developmental science will be improved when we become more diligent and reduce our use of convenient samples to support broad generalizations.

6.8 Participants in Clinical Research

Research on atypical development and the efficacy of interventions are affected by each of the topics discussed thus far, and some additional concerns should be noted for this difficult domain of research. One consideration is recruiting an appropriate sample. Limits on generalizations based on an atypical sample are constrained by the demographic factors described previously, and with additional constraints that emerge in a clinical context such as co-morbidity, relative functional ability, family history of comparable problems, or family beliefs and attitudes about the dysfunction. More subtle, results from an atypical sample accrued on the basis of a formal diagnosis may generalize to other atypical children with that diagnosis but not necessarily to the broader group of children who have the disorder but who have not received a diagnosis. For example, young children are more likely to receive a diagnosis of attention deficit hyperactivity disorder (ADHD) if they have extremely salient symptoms, parents who are actively monitoring their child and are knowledgeable, or are in classrooms with teachers who are sensitive to ADHD symptoms. Research on diagnosed children may or may not generalize to undiagnosed children who have fewer symptoms or a less sensitive family or educational context.

In some clinical research, it is necessary to distinguish between illness and diagnosis. This leads to a 2 x 2 table: YY and NN are straightforward: Illness-Y and Diagnosis-Y or Illness-N and Diagnosis-N. Two other combinations are possible and are much less straightforward: Illness-Y and Diagnosis-N is a missed case, and this could have a profound effect on generalization. Illness-N and Diagnosis-Y is sometimes a false alarm, but in a world with performance enhancing drugs for ADHD or medical marijuana for some diagnoses, one possibility is heterogeneous groups.

One strategy for recruiting participants in clinical intervention research is to use a screening tool to identify potential participants who are considered at-risk. The exact definition of at-risk would depend upon the particular topic being investigated, but the generic definition would be based on the assumption that participants can be identified who have a relatively high probability of eventually being diagnosed with a focal disorder. Screening tools can be evaluated on various obvious dimensions, but the bottom line is often an analysis of how well the tool predicts its target outcome.

In the lingo of prediction, the term sensitivity refers to the probability that the screening tool identifies each person who will eventually succumb to the outcome. The term specificity addresses the possibility that a person will be incorrectly identified. From many research perspectives, the primary goal in screening is sensitivity rather than specificity. For example, one strategy for conducting research on ASD would be to recruit a sample of typical children, randomly assign participants to receive the intervention or a control condition, and evaluate efficacy of the intervention by comparing outcomes for the two groups. Given that ASD has a prevalence of approximately 1 per 75 and that an effective intervention would involve extensive resources, this strategy is obviously flawed. A more efficacious strategy would be to identify children who are at-risk for ASD and randomly assign these children to receive the intervention or the control. From this perspective, the specificity of the screener is not critical because from a research perspective the problem that emerges is that a child who is actually at-risk for ASD and not flagged will not participate in the study. Given the uncertainty of the efficacy of the intervention, this mistake does relatively little harm. In contrast, the sensitivity of the screener is the most important aspect of the screening because heightened sensitivity increases the chance that some children who are not at-risk for ASD will participate in the study. Parents who are invited to participate in a study like this must understand that being flagged by a highly sensitive screener indicates a possibility of risk but not a definite problem, and parents who accept the invitation should realize that the intervention might be helpful but the researchers will not know the efficacy of the intervention until they have conducted basic research.

Much research on ASD uses a different strategy for recruiting participants. ASD is linked to an underlying genetic dialysis that increases the risk rate for siblings of children who have been diagnosed with ASD. A cohort of children who are identified as at-risk because they have an older sibling with a diagnosis of ASD have a relatively high risk of eventually having a diagnosis of ASD, so this recruitment strategy is obviously more efficient than monitoring a typically developing sample. However, generalizations are limited because these infants might differ from a broader sample of infants who eventually develop ASD because the ASD-siblings have many unique characteristics including having parents who are currently interacting with an older sibling with ASD, living in the context of an older sibling who is manifesting symptomatic behaviors, and possibly having a particularly strong epigenetic endowment toward ASD.

When an appropriate sample of potential participants has been identified, clinical research also faces the challenge of how well these potential participants can participate. Any assessment in developmental science can be affected by how well the participants understand the assessment task, how motivated they are to perform well, how their stamina is affected by their illness, etc. These parameters are generally ignored in research on typical participants but deserve explicit attention in clinical research. For example, if a hypothesis about a specific aspect of memory is being tested, credibility of results will be enhanced if a comparable procedure is used to assess a different aspect of memory, and results for the two aspects of memory are different.

Finally, clinical research faces some additional challenges in long-term participation. An intervention that is administered to a control group could be relatively uncomfortable for some participants and increase their probability of discontinuing their participation. The experimental group might drop out because the intervention is being effective and they feel that they no longer need to participate. Given both of these challenges, intervention research needs a strong incentive for long-term participation.

6.9 The Evolution of Traditional Animal Behavioral Models

Animal models have an extensive history in behavioral science. At the beginning of the 20th century, Ivan Pavlov explored learning using an animal model in which dogs heard a buzzer, metronome, or other sound when food was being presented and would eventually salivate when they heard that sound. Pavlov identified this reflexive behavior as a form of learning that was initially called the conditioned reflex and was eventually labeled classical conditioning. As Pavlov's research progressed, other animal models evolved for exploring learning and other aspects of behavior. In the 1930s, B. F. Skinner developed an operant conditioning chamber (eventually labeled a Skinner box) in which the behavior of rodents and pigeons was linked to systematic contingencies (e.g., press the bar twice to activate the food hopper). Research conducted in the Skinner box paradigm led to an extensive array of theories and models that explained aspects of learning, stimulus discrimination, memory, etc. This behaviorist perspective continued until researchers realized that their conclusions about these phenomena not only failed to generalize to humans but also failed to generalize across different species of nonhuman animals.

When developmental scientists viewed animal models from a broader perspective, animal models evolved into a much more useful tool to help us describe, predict, alter, and explain behavior and mental processing. Robert Cairns, the founding director of the Center for Developmental Science at UNC-Chapel Hill in 1993, integrated ideas from biology, sociology, anthropology, and psychiatry and explored these topics using various strategies including the development of social attachments in animals. Combining his expertise in behavior genetics and social interactions in animals, Cairns created a multigenerational rodent community to investigate social, biological, and genetic factors that influence the development of aggression, thus augmenting naturalistic longitudinal research in humans with parallel experimental investigations in behavior genetics using an animal model.

Another well-known developmental scientist, Gilbert Gottlieb, also affiliated with the Center for Developmental Science, used animal models to investigate bird development, and as his research progressed he discovered that it is unrealistic to assume that trait development always follows a predetermined path. For example, he explored the claim that ducks have genes that cause them to be imprinted during a critical period; he found instead that imprinting is controlled by complex and subtle feedback that ducks receive pre-birth. This led to Gottlieb's epigenetic perspective (Gottlieb, 2007) in which no aspects of behavioral development are completely predetermined rather than being influenced by aspects of the environment. Gottlieb played a major role in the Center for Developmental Science by helping developmental scientists understand the importance of multilevel, multidirectional models.

I have experienced an interesting perspective on the evolution of animal behavioral models. In my days as an undergraduate student at UNC-Chapel Hill, my introductory psychology courses evoked my interest, and I began working in Dr. Vincent LoLordo's research laboratory in the Experimental Psychology Program. His research focused on how pigeons learn various responses, with the goal of discovering the general mechanisms that presumably explain learning in all species (e.g., how learning is affected by the schedule of reinforcement). When I returned to UNC-Chapel Hill several decades later, the Experimental Psychology Program had become the Biological Psychology Program. Animal models were still being used, but the research had shifted toward more focus on the exploration of biological mechanisms that would be relevant for understanding behavior. The program changed its name again a few years later and became the Behavioral Neuroscience Program with its focus on the neurological mechanisms involved in phenomena such as addiction and pain in rodents, and the Psychology Department was pushed to rename itself the Department of Psychology and Neuroscience. Understanding neurologic mechanisms could be relevant for answering questions like: What causes alcoholism? How does alcoholism emerge in adolescence? Why are some treatments for alcoholism more effective than others? However, I often hear much more discussion of the underlying biological mechanisms per se than of these more behavioral, translational questions that would traditionally be viewed as topics of interest in psychology and developmental science. And, neuroscience is relevant for understanding behavior and mental processing but other biologic perspectives such as genetics, physiology, health, etc. are also relevant.

6.10 The Pros and Cons of Using Modern Animal Models to Investigate Diseases

Early use of animal models was primarily focused on cognitive topics, but even the earliest animal model can be used for understanding aspects of psychopathology. For example, Laborda and colleagues (2012) review the various uses of animal models to investigate psychopathology including phenomena like the clinical implications of Pavlovian conditioning. A major technological advance that is influencing contemporary animal model research is the ability to manipulate genes and thus create an organism with a predetermined profile. For example, Babineau, Yang, and Crawley (2012) summarize research on an inbred strain of mice who manifest unusual behaviors that can be considered similar to symptoms in ASD. Specifically, mice in this strain have low sociability on multiple social tasks, reduced ultrasonic vocalizations, and behavioral responses to olfactory social cues, and high-repetitive self-grooming. These mice were treated with interventions that have been tested with children with ASD and the effects were similar. Babineau et al. note the important constraint that "Animal models of autism will need to meet the standard criteria of face validity (analogous symptoms, such as social deficits), construct validity (analogous causes, such as genetic mutations), and predictive validity (analogous responses to treatments)," and they interpret the efficacy of their behavioral intervention as providing credence to the mouse model of ASD. Wöhr and Scattoni (2013) describe how additional behaviors such as social facilitation and empathy can be incorporated into a useful autism severity score, and highlight the potential advantage of using a rat knockout model of autism. Schwartzer, Koenig, and Berman (2013) focus more on genetic animal modeling of ASD and the opportunity to directly test the role of exposure to environmental toxicants, which many researchers see as a potential explanation for the ongoing increase in the occurrence rate of ASD worldwide.

From a broader perspective, genetic manipulations in animal models can create novel creatures who have some aspects of human disease, but the animals are not humans, are not embedded in the human culture, probably do not have the human consciousness experience, definitely receive and represent different dimensions of sensory input, have differential self-control, etc. Thus, generalization from these synthetic animal models is always open to question. Some research focuses on behavior, and other research uses advanced measurement techniques to examine animal models at a cellular level and lower, including assessment of neuronal development, presence of neurotransmitters, and the structure of genetic information. A detailed description of the underlying biologic structures could lead to possible cures and treatments for various disorders, the identification of biomarkers, and an understanding of the underlying structure that influences various aspects of behavior and mental processes. What remains to be determined is the extent to which traditional animal models generalize to human beings.

A notably salient topic here for me is ALS. Approximately 85% of the studies that I see in my daily review of published research on ALS are based on animal models and/or are focused specifically on genes. From a demographic or epidemiologic perspective, the gene encoding superoxide dismutase 1 (SOD1) is definitely associated with what has been labeled familial ALS, but this label is applied to a very small percentage of diagnosed cases. Mice carrying multiple copies of this gene are currently being used as the model for research on ALS. van der Worp and colleagues (2010) list several problems with this model including being relevant only for patients with SOD1 mutations, creating mice whose behavior may be atypical due to having multiple copies of the gene, and also mice who are more susceptible to infections and other non-ALS related illnesses, which might be the locus for efficacious treatments. Another problem is that these rodents have progressive muscular deterioration, but their symptoms do not align well with most forms of ALS. It is also problematic that the only pharmacological intervention that has been proven to affect ALS (riluzole) has not been shown to affect these mice. This research could eventually identify a large portfolio of genes that are altered in ALS, but for now the mouse models and other animal models could be viewed as convenient for researchers but not necessarily optimally informative.

Many advocates suggest that disorders such as ALS that have no cure should evoke different research than disorders that have some treatments. Patients with ALS would encounter some risk when participating in the clinical trial of a medicine that has not been approved, but their only alternative is a relatively fast demise. From that perspective, animal models could be seen as less valuable for patients with ALS, although they are valuable for some entrepreneurs: I recently received an email offering me the opportunity to have a transgenic rat created with a cost from $10,200 and the promise that rats, in comparison with mice, have greater physiological and behavioral similarity to humans.

The review of research using animal models by van der Worp et al. (2010) offers many perspectives that can improve the quality of developmental science. One perspective is the aspects of animal model research that can reduce the credibility of generalizations to human patients. Most obvious is the assumption that the symptoms manifested by the animal have sufficient similarity to the symptoms manifested by humans and thus that the disease is the same. Other difficulties are more subtle: Most animals who participate in research are young and healthy, which undermines generalizations to humans who are elderly and have co-morbidities. They also may have life spans and developmental changes with no similarity to humans. The cohort of animals will be much more homogeneous than a cohort of human patients, thus amplifying the strength of effects. Many studies use either male or female animals only, thus not generalizing to diseases that affect males and females. The dosage that animals receive may be too strong for humans or have side effects that human patients could not tolerate. Finally, the outcome measures that are administered to animals may have no relevance for human patients. Would experimenter-induced exposure to cocaine be comparable to the effect of cocaine on a human being who chooses to consume cocaine? Researchers who explore cocaine addiction using animal models should address this question before offering a broad generalization based on their research.

7   Collecting Behavioral Data

Research in the physical sciences is usually conducted with phenomena that are the same in a wide variety of contexts (e.g., chemists combine assorted chemicals and obtain the same reaction in laboratories around the world). Research in the social sciences has a wider range of phenomena (e.g., a sociologist observes configurations of people walking by and what they are wearing, or an economist studies income levels and educational attainment). Experiments in developmental science are more difficult because the experiment in general and the measurement in specific are affected by aspects of the participant in addition to what is being measured and where it is being measured. And, the measurement process per se can have explicit or implicit effects on participants. The experiments we conduct in developmental science are therefore vulnerable to a wide array of concerns.

From a scientific perspective, the phenomena that most developmental scientists are attempting to describe, predict, control, and understand are aspects of human behavior, and from a developmental perspective, how and why human behaviors change over time. From a linguistic perspective, the term "behavior" can be interpreted in various ways. At a relatively shallow level, behavior refers to our actions and our responses to specific stimuli (e.g., specific responses include speaking, shivering, smiling, etc.). At a higher level, the definition of behavior goes beyond a simple action and incorporates a broader functionality that underlies specific responses, including descriptions such as sacrificing, summarizing, supervising, etc. Linking the specific action aspect of behavior to the broader functionality aspect is always somewhat ambiguous because any specific action could imply various broader functionalities (e.g., smiling could indicate joy, embarrassment, or an attempt at coercion). And, any broadly functional aspect of behavior could be manifest in multiple specific behaviors (e.g., to supervise could indicate monitoring performance, inspecting deliverables, or issuing specific commands). Another problem that developmental scientists face is scrutiny by the IRB that leads to potential problems, such as providing participants with information that could affect their performance.

Baumeister, Vohs, and Funder (2007) drew an interesting, comparable distinction in social psychology, contrasting research based on specific actions, which they refer to as "actual behaviors," and research based on peripheral measures, such as answers to introspective questions or reaction time to respond to stimuli, which they refer to as the measurement of "inner processes" that mediate and produce specific actions. From a historical perspective, they noticed that since the mid-1970s social psychologists have drifted away from eliciting, observing, and measuring actual behavior and have become more committed to measuring inner processes. However, they also noticed that the inner processes are usually being measured by asking introspective questions that can have limited credibility and by assessing low-level behaviors (e.g., reaction time) that can have a remote connection to a hypothesized inner process. This led Baumeister et al. to a strong complaint: "Social psychologists cannot claim that attitudes or personality predict behavior if by *behavior* they do not really mean behavior" (p. 401). They adopted a more optimistic view of developmental psychology, suggesting that developmental psychologists have consistently focused on behavior because participants "cannot fill out questionnaires or read prompts on a computer screen."

Developmental scientists can take some pride in this compliment, but my goal in the present chapter is to explore our commitment to measuring behavior and to point out aspects of the measurement of behavior that could be improved. It is also important to note that although developmental scientists often evoke and measure behaviors, we also gather data from parents who can fill out questionnaires and read prompts on computer screens. A child who is participating in a well-structured experiment and a trained observer who is working within the context of a well-defined scoring metric are likely to generate data that are specific and reliable. However, this measurement context can be difficult for a child, and a professional observer may have limited access to the child and may be coding observations that occur in an artificial context. In contrast, most parents have extensive contact with their child in a wide array of contexts, but are unlikely to have the training or motivation that allows observations to be specific and reliable. Further, it is well documented that parent-report can be strongly influenced by personality characteristics of the parent (e.g., Feldman & Reznick, 1996; Vaughn, Taraldson, Crichton, & Egeland, 1981). One strategy for tapping the extensive observations made by parents in a wide variety of contexts is to develop parent-report instruments that harvest this rich source of data, but these instruments can vary in their effectiveness.

Some human behaviors can be described as the more or less constant ongoing integral components of human life. For example, our hearts are pumping blood at a particular pressure level, our lungs are transporting oxygen and carbon dioxide, and our eyes are coordinating and adjusting their focus. The measurement of these low-level behaviors is relatively straightforward and can be useful to the extent that these low-level behaviors are relevant for describing, predicting, controlling, or understanding the development of higher-level human behaviors. Indeed, recent technological advances in monitoring heart rate and eye movement have fueled an interesting stream of research on infant cognitive development and other topics. However, from a broader perspective, most of the human behaviors that we seek to measure do not have constant ongoing low-level aspects. For example, a total mapping of the ongoing status, interaction, and change of all neurons in my brain would not necessarily indicate my definition of the word "flag," a description of the most recent flag I noticed, or how I will feel when I see a flag at half-mast. The sine qua non and difficult challenge in measuring higher-level behaviors is to find or create a context in which they are likely to be evoked. And, given that many of our most relevant and interesting constructs refer to a person's capacity to do something, the behavioral manifestations of these constructs are less obvious. The physical sciences posit some variables that refer to an entity's capacity (e.g., flammability, buoyancy), and physical scientists then measure these variables by evoking the capacity (e.g., attempting to burn the substance or placing it in a liquid). In contrast, developmental scientists often face the challenge of measuring potential capacity without increasing its probability of occurring or actually evoking it (e.g., a child's potential for experiencing a tantrum, attacking a peer, or becoming anorexic or obese).

7.1 General Approaches for Collecting Behavioral Data

Our opportunities for collecting behavioral data in developmental science can be separated into three different zones: innovative novel assessment, established paradigms, and standardized testing. Each zone offers advantages and disadvantages and evokes some concerns that must be addressed if we seek to improve developmental science. I will provide brief general descriptions of innovative novel assessment and established paradigms, and a more detailed description of standardized testing. Subsequent sections of this chapter will explore general topics that are more or less relevant for each zone.

Innovative novel assessment refers to the development of new procedures for assessing a construct. Advantages include movement toward improved measurement of a construct, incorporation of useful advances in technology, and creativity in assessment. Disadvantages include difficulty linking the new measurement to traditional measurements, and specification of measurement in sufficient detail to allow replication in other laboratories.

Established paradigms are specific measurement protocols that have become widely accepted by researchers. For example, infant cognitive development is often assessed using variations of the A-not-B search task based on Piaget's observations of his children (Piaget, 1952/1936). Infant attachment is often assessed using the Ainsworth Strange situation (Ainsworth & Bell, 1970). Advantages of established paradigms include relatively similar assessments of a construct across multiple studies. Disadvantages include ossification of construct definition and lack of attention to potentially relevant parameters of the procedure.

Standardized tests contain a set of specific questions or tasks, are administered using an established format in a more or less constrained context, and are scored using a specific metric that often contextualizes outcome measures based on a broad, normative sample. The advantages of standardized tests are that they are expected to measure a more or less specific construct in all participants and that the measurements of this construct should be comparable across different studies conducted in different laboratories and at different times. One major disadvantage of standardized tests is their tendency to claim measurement of a broad construct and to become the relatively ossified operational definition of that construct. When this process evolves, some popular constructs become associated with an array of standardized tests that have notable differences among them. Another disadvantage of standardized tests is the extensive array of items, and thus the amount of time that is required to derive a measurement of individual performance that can be positioned within the broad range of all individuals who have participated in the standardized test.

One obvious example of standardized tests relevant for developmental science is measurement of the intelligence quotient (IQ). Items on an IQ test are chosen to reflect the test maker's theory of how intelligence should be defined. When IQ became a scientific topic in the 1800s, the primary definition of intelligence was related to success in school, so it included abilities like vocabulary, arithmetic skills, and knowledge of the world. A second approach to defining intelligence is to base the definition on popular traditions regarding what it means to be labeled intelligent, smart, or a genius. From this perspective, intelligence reflects mental abilities like problem solving, logic, or creativity, or personal characteristics like hard work, motivation, or collaboration. From either perspective, intelligence would be related to success in various domains of life including school, social life, or occupation. Finally, intelligence can be defined on the basis of mental abilities that psychologists have discovered in their research on how people process information. From this perspective, intelligence would reflect abilities like memory span, focused attention, imagery, etc. These components might ensure general success in life, but their primary relevance would be success in academic or intellectual pursuits. Recent standardized tests of early intelligence are referring to another relatively broad cognitive construct: executive function. The subcomponents in this domain are more obvious, and many of them can be measured in specific ways. However, from the broader perspective, there is no specific recipe for combining the subcomponents of executive function in the most appropriate configuration.

One complication in the world of standardized tests is the role of the authors and publishers who own copyrights and accrue financial profit by marketing the tests. This activity steers developmental science out of its prominent academic world and into the world of business. Marketing can lead to improvements in products and to broad distribution. However, marketing can also steer standardized tests more toward profitability than toward criteria that would improve the quality of developmental science. The transition from paper forms to electronic forms evokes another challenge. The original rationale for the cost of standardized tests included parameters like paper, printing, and shipping. Online versions of tests include some parameters like programming and website maintenance, but the cost trajectory is much different. Hopefully, publishers will adjust their policies to reflect this transition and make tools more easily available to scientists who are attempting to accrue a cumulative developmental science by improving measurement.

Another complication is that standardized tests can be affected by cultural differences. For example, in some cultures, definitions of intelligence emphasize individual academic and cognitive accomplishment, while in other cultures these definitions put equal emphasis on collective accomplishments, creativity, social sensitivity, or athletic ability. Or, some cultures view an infant's active exploration of the environment as an indicator of secure attachment, and other cultures view an infant's cohesion to a parent as indicating secure attachment. However the construct is defined, standardized tests can be affected by various cultural factors.

If a standardized test uses language or examples that are more familiar to a particular subgroup of the population, that group will have an advantage. If a standardized test is administered by an individual from one culture to a child from a different culture, that child might feel uncomfortable and perform less well. Finally, if the norms that are used for calculating the score on a standardized test reflect a narrower range of performance than would be expected in the broader population, scores from children at the low end of the distribution could be inaccurate.

7.2 Where Should We Conduct Our Measurements?

Developmental scientists have a long history of conducting their research in two very different domains. The emergence of psychology as a science was primarily based on laboratory paradigms that were designed to measure various aspects of learning. These paradigms had the notable advantage of allowing developmental scientists throughout the world to conduct research that contributed to an ongoing accrual of knowledge. As mentioned in previous chapters, behaviorists developed models to reflect various parameters that affect learning and moved forward with research that fueled debates about our understanding of learning. In recent decades, paradigms have continued to evolve based on increasingly sophisticated technology and increasingly sophisticated models of cognitive and social development.

From a broader perspective, although laboratory-based paradigms can be associated with these positive attributes, they can also be associated with some negative attributes. The primary negative perspective on laboratory-based paradigms is concern that they do not accurately tap phenomena that occur in the real world. For example, does a child learn and interact in a laboratory in the same way that the child would learn and interact in a classroom or at home? Does the game that has been constructed to challenge aspects of the child's intellectual ability accurately tap how the child's intellectual ability would be evoked in a more realistic context? These concerns are increasingly salient in social situations in which a laboratory-based context would not necessarily tap the child's social behavior in various real-world contexts.

Concerns about the artificial context of laboratory paradigms should be considered, addressed through efforts to improve the paradigms, and acknowledged in descriptions of generalizations based on laboratory paradigms. Mitchell (2012) used published meta-analyses to explore lab-field comparisons in hundreds of studies. It is difficult to generalize across areas of research, but Mitchell found strong symmetry in some domains and notable asymmetry in others. Researchers have also noticed advantages in laboratory paradigms from a more theoretical perspective. For example, Mook (1983) published an interesting essay comparing the problem of failures to generalize to the real world with various advantages of laboratory paradigms. From his perspective, research that confirms a predicted effect in an artificial laboratory context could be seen as a strong indicator that the effect would be even more apparent in the real world. Comparisons of laboratory versus field research can be notably difficult in developmental science. A laboratory setting can be unfamiliar and uncomfortable for children, and, as noted in previous chapters, retention of participants in longitudinal studies tends to be stronger when data are collected in locations that are convenient for participants. The ongoing evolution of technology is offering an interesting hybrid of laboratory and real world that is emerging in research conducted online. This new context allows us to set up the structure in a very laboratory-like way, but in a context that has emerged recently as an environment that is a major component of life for many people. For example, an electronic game could be created with parameters that measure aspects of memory, attention, or motivation, and this game could be administered as an app on a phone, a tablet, or another electronic device. There are positive and negative aspects of this new electronic environment, with the overall realization that using it to gather data could be notably successful.

Behavior that is observed in a context that is extremely artificial or that is short in duration is also unlikely to support broad generalizations. For example, researchers often conveniently assess parent–child interactions on the basis of a short observation of behavior that occurs in an unfamiliar laboratory context. The parent–child interaction that occurs in this context can be coded and recoded to assess reliability, but additional data would be needed to support the claim that the brief slice of parent–child interaction that occurs in an artificial context can be generalized to the broader context of this dyad's typical relationship. This issue is also salient when data are collected across contexts that are similar but that differ on minor parameters that might affect responses. For example, a social interaction between a research participant and an examiner could be affected by their location relative to each other, the color and decoration of the room, or the proximity of the observer or an audio-visual recording device.

Measuring behaviors that are rare or infrequent is a very difficult task, and the quality of cumulative developmental science could improve if researchers face this challenge directly rather than ignore it. Assessment of behavior in a brief, artificial context is unlikely to provide an accurate robust measurement. Because the measurement of behavior is inherently difficult, we should always consider the need for a relatively long period of observation and a wide array of contexts to increase the probability that we are evoking the behavior that we seek to measure.

7.3 Evoking Behaviors Appropriately

Another well-established zone of concern about laboratory research is the possibility of influencing participant behaviors via experimenter bias and the more or less intentional imposition of various demand characteristics that create an implicit demand for participants to behave in a particular way. The "Rosenthal effect" and "clever Hans" are classic examples of this problem. The Rosenthal effect refers to an experiment conducted by Rosenthal and Jacobson (1968) in which teachers who were led to expect enhanced performance from a randomly selected set of children taught and evaluated the children in ways that led to enhancement of the children's performance. Clever Hans was a horse who was described as understanding arithmetic based on his foot taps in response to questions until further scrutiny revealed that correct answers only emerged when the test administrator knew the answer and adjusted his posture and facial expression in a way that provided a cue for the horse to stop tapping. One of my earliest publications (Richman, Mitchell, & Reznick, 1979) explored how expectations influenced results in a cognitive paradigm in which participants were asked to memorize a map of a fictitious island containing several landmarks and then scan from one landmark to another using their mental image of the island. Previous interpretations had viewed this as evidence of pictorial representations in the brain, but our research showed comparable results when the distances between landmarks were introduced verbally or when participants were given a description of the image-scanning procedure and were asked to predict their reaction times. The publication also received an award for my clever title: "Mental travel: Some reservations."

Experimenter bias and demand characteristics are aspects of research that are very salient in social psychology but have received much less attention in developmental science. Based on advice from social scientists, we can improve developmental science by attempting to minimize demand characteristics and experimenter bias by using control conditions and outcome variables to assess their effects. Another strategy is to do a thorough debriefing in which participants (or their parents) are asked to describe their research experience. We should also be aware of other factors that affect the evocation of behavior, such as nap time, hunger, parent in the room, experimenter's tolerance for challenging child behaviors, etc. Given that demand characteristics and experimenter bias can affect the evocation of behavior and thus influence results, the general recommendation is that we must make more effort to describe potential problems in this domain and include them in our publications (Klein et al., 2012).

Despite the expectation that standardized procedures imply an inherent reliability, administration must be monitored because minor details can have a large impact. For example, the A-not-B paradigm based on Piaget's observation of object permanence became a widely used experimental procedure. The instruction "cover the toy" seems straightforward, but research revealed different performance if the toy is placed under a cover versus a cover being placed on top of the toy. Other studies also noticed effects of parameters such as having the infant reach for a toy versus look toward the location where the toy is hidden. If parameters that affect performance are ignored, the value of accrued knowledge that emerges from multiple studies using what is viewed as the same paradigm is undermined.

It is reasonable to have appropriate confidence in well-established measurement procedures, and it is also reasonable to monitor implementations for potential problems. The more salient concerns regarding experimenter effects in developmental science emerge due to the common situation in which the experimenter is essentially evoking data from participants. I once advised a graduate student who measured joint attention using the Early Social Communication Scales (ESCS) in which an examiner sits across the table from a child and administers various cues that provide opportunities to observe and code aspects of the child's social communication. I distinctly remember our surprise and disappointment when the strongest effect that our analysis revealed was a difference between two examiners in the amount of joint attention they evoked. A review of videotapes revealed an obvious cause: one research assistant was much more engaging and thus evoked more joint attention. Interactive measures like ESCS can have very strong experimenter effects and thus must be monitored throughout an experiment to ensure correct administration.

One strategy that can control for experimenter effects is to have one examiner administer all tasks. This strategy can reduce variability in treatment instantiation, but it can also undermine validity. A more effective strategy is to explore comparable administration among testers, longitudinally, or at multiple sites. Given the vulnerability associated with single measurements, an important strategy for improved measurement is to enhance test–retest reliability. The specific step toward this goal will depend upon the specific measurement procedure, but some steps seem broadly relevant. For example, if an experimenter is administering the procedure, the experimenter's training is a vital component in reliability, and administration ability should be tested and confirmed before data acquisition begins. And, as data acquisition continues, a well-trained experimenter can begin modifying administration intentionally or unintentionally. Any ongoing modification in how a procedure is administered is an obvious source of error that should be constrained by ongoing monitoring. Any equipment or stimulus materials that are used as part of a measurement technique are likely to be affected by use and must be monitored and assessed regularly to ensure reliability. Finally, if measurement entails interaction with a person, the relationship between the experimenter and the person being tested will affect reliability.

The verbal description of the task that is implemented in an experiment will be reviewed by readers who are evaluating a grant, members of a dissertation committee, editors evaluating an article for publication, and other audiences. This review is important, but it can be superseded by a more important form of evaluation; specifically, participating in a task can be a very different experience than reading about the task. Whenever one of my students was implementing a new study, I would often volunteer to be a participant. Sometimes this meant pretending to be an infant or toddler, and the experience always helped me understand the task and often led to important suggestions. I also recommend that each person who is involved in an experiment attempt to administer the task and be a participant who is tested in the task. An additional level of participation that I recommend is that students presenting a prospectus to their committee should either demonstrate the procedures that will be used or show a videotape of the procedures being implemented so that their committee members will have an intimate understanding of the tasks.

Another aspect of successful implementation of a task is to establish criteria to measure the extent to which each participant understands it. This will help differentiate the meaning of various levels of performance, which would generally be interpreted as levels within some dependent variable, and could also reflect the extent to which the participant understood the task and was engaged in the task. Establishing a training criterion is a useful strategy. If participants are dropped for non-compliance, etc., particularly if they are infants or toddlers, administering a baseline test of cognitive ability and personality is an important strategy to determine the extent to which participants who drop out have systematic differences when compared with participants who complete the study.

A related issue is whether the participant was within the range of his or her normal behavior. For adults, this is simply asking if they have been having a typical day/week. If they mention that they were in the emergency room until 2 a.m. the night before, they received a speeding ticket on their way to the laboratory, or they are currently experiencing a migraine headache, this information is relevant for determining the validity of their data. When participants are young children, it is relevant to ask the parent if the child exhibited typical behavior during the laboratory visit or was manifesting notable anxiety or discomfort.

In some contexts, the participant's understanding of the task is the phenomenon that is being measured. For example, when an infant is familiarized with a stimulus, subsequent behavior could reflect seeking that stimulus or avoiding it depending on aspects of representation and motivation. Also, when an infant is familiarized with a stimulus, the representation of that stimulus can be tapped by various aspects of memory. If subsequent behavior is monitored in a context in which the stimulus reappears, this could be considered an evocation of recognition memory or working memory. Another example is my own experience with the Miller Analogy Test (MAT) when I was applying to graduate school. My first score on the MAT was surprisingly low. Before taking the test a second time, I purchased a book that offered advice on the MAT, and I was amazed to learn that semantic analogies were not always the correct answer. Other analogies were based on structure, phonetics, or other parameters, and even though semantic analogies were present, they were not necessarily the correct answer.

Behaviors that are evoked by using a single incentive or context are unlikely to support broad generalizations. For example, one strategy for assessing a toddler's level of empathy is to observe the toddler's behavior in a situation that could evoke empathy (e.g., What does the toddler do when he/she sees a person pretend to experience a painful injury?). If a toddler manifests empathic behavior in this situation, the presence of this behavior supports the inference that this toddler is capable of experiencing empathy. However, we do not know if this toddler would display empathy across a broad range of contexts and thus could be considered more or less empathic relative to peers. And, we do not know if a younger toddler would experience empathy in this or a different situation. Given that most research in developmental science is oriented toward understanding age-related changes in ability or the stability of individual differences, data derived from behavioral observation based on a single incentive or in a single context offers very limited support for generalizations in either domain. A broad generalization about empathy would require behavioral observations in a wide array of empathy-eliciting situations involving a wide array of empathy-eliciting people (e.g., male or female; old or young; familiar or unfamiliar, etc.).

The importance of a broad array of appropriate stimulus conditions is relevant in almost any study. Meehl (1978) noted that "the problems of characterizing the stimulus side, even though often neglected by the profession or dealt with superficially, are about as intractable as the characterization of the response class" (p. 808). It is important to select test materials that allow appropriate generalizations. For example, in many studies participants are responding to a stimulus that could be a face or an object, and thus could evoke notably different responses. Stimuli that are designated as animate or social could also encompass an array of possibilities, such as pictures of animals, videos of dynamic faces, cartoon characters, etc., and some stimuli that are animate might not be social, such as trees blowing in the wind. The range of stimuli in any research project must represent the extension and variability of the focal category and differentiate it from related categories. The major guideline here is to always use more than one exemplar to generalize to a category. This applies to participants, independent variables, and outcomes.

7.4 Measuring Relevant Behaviors

Returning to our roots in logical positivism, philosopher of science Norwood Hanson noted an obvious challenge for developmental science: human observation of the behaviors of fellow humans is inherently tainted by subjectivity. What we perceive is influenced by what we know, believe, or have perceived previously, and thus is often inaccurate. One simple but salient example comes from the various visual illusions that we perceive as being something other than what they really are. Another favorite example is to ask "What color is a yield sign?" I predict that many readers will be surprised when they observe their next yield sign. Hanson's point regarding the subjectivity of perception is salient and is something that we must keep in mind. Developmental science is built upon inferences about behavior, and thus our goals must include finding valid and reliable ways to measure relevant behaviors.

At a very gross level, our ongoing interactions with our fellow human beings are fueled by our implicit behavioral coding, which lets us make claims such as "he was very impolite"; "the gift definitely pleased her"; "they were confused," etc. From this perspective, complex behaviors can be coded at a qualitative level that has an implicit validity that cannot be tested. Our challenge here is to establish a reliable taxonomy of well-defined qualitative variables.

Behaviors can also be coded at a more specific level. The overarching challenge at this level is to establish validity by linking the behavior to a construct. The underlying challenge is to develop a coding scheme that has acceptable reliability. This challenge can seem less problematic than establishing the reliability of complex, qualitative codes, but issues do emerge. For example, to determine the frequency of a discrete behavior we need a precise definition of the behavior. To determine the duration of a behavior, the measure must include a metric for establishing the behavior's onset and offset.

Advances in technology increase the quantity and quality of behavior that can be recorded and the context in which it can be viewed. We are approaching an asymptote at which observing recorded behavior becomes very much like being there, but with the added resources of being able to observe a focal behavior repeatedly, in slow motion, from different perspectives, and with an overlay of specific physical parameters. The fundamental issues related to coding recorded behavior are too extensive to be covered here. From a cumulative developmental science perspective, two broader issues are particularly salient.

The variables that emerge from the coding of recorded behavior may boost the validity and reliability of measurement, but a cumulative developmental science requires that these new variables be anchored in coordination with the traditional variables harvested from decades of research based on more primitive tools such as analysis of videotapes using stopwatches and roughly calculated variables such as direction of gaze, facial expression, or level of distress. The frontier of electronic coding offers an increasingly micro-analytic level of detail, which can be a dangerous path if followed blindly. From a practical perspective, the traditional rule of thumb has been to code variables at the most microscopic level possible because it is much easier to aggregate across low levels than it is to recode raw data to acquire a more fine-grained dimension. For example, an infant's gaze at a stimulus could be coded as a total amount of time or as the actual duration of individual glances at the stimulus. With the latter format, a distinction could be drawn between infants who stare continuously versus those who vacillate but attain a comparable total. Further refinement could detect patterns of vacillation that are faster or slower. If advances in techniques for coding behavior lead toward a bottomless pit of behavioral microscopy, researchers will need to find a more effective strategy for defining the optimal level of analysis. From a theoretical perspective, blind acceptance of the micro path also devalues broader folk psychological variables that are less specific but are also based on observation. As noted earlier, the vitality of psychological constructs depends upon an ongoing dialogue between top-down and bottom-up meaning.

One useful strategy is to always code behavior at the lowest feasible level of detail and to create a database that contains this lowest level. We usually need to aggregate across low levels of behavior to create relevant constructs and revisit the lowest level to establish the reliability and validity of the constructs. A suggestion from a reviewer that entails ignoring distinctions within a database or creating a different combination of components is relatively painless in comparison to a suggestion than entails recoding (or reentering) data at a finer level. Creating a database that contains the lowest level of feasible coding is a wise strategy for avoiding this pain. Furthermore, the trial-by-trial data of individual participants can lead to additional variables based on change over time.

Many aspects of empirical research have become increasingly mechanized. However, it is still virtually impossible to conduct a research study that does not include some reliance on human beings who play roles as investigators. The roles might be relatively mechanical (e.g., clicking on an appropriate selection in a computer program, setting switches, reading numbers from a gauge). However, human beings are not robots, so the probability of an error occurring is thus always greater than zero. Errors of this type can introduce variance that masks effects, or worse, causes a systematic erroneous pattern that is incorrectly interpreted as a true effect.

The most obvious (and probably prevalent) strategy to avoid human error is to institute a confirmation process. However, a simple replication is not always successful. I remember helping a friend install new carpeting in his wife's office. He measured the dimensions carefully, and we laid out a pattern on the carpet that would fit the office floor space. Before we cut the pattern, I suggested that he confirm his original measurements. He measured the dimensions again, confirmed his previous numbers on the pattern, and we cut the carpet. When we installed the carpet in the office, we were very surprised and disappointed to find that it did not fit. Upon subsequent investigation, we discovered that my colleague had misread "16 feet, 5 ¼ inches" twice, seeing it both times as "16 feet, ¼ inch." We cut an additional strip of rug to solve the problem, and we learned an important lesson: A valid replication of a measurement requires a truly independent assessment. Without an independent assessment, a replication can easily reflect multiple renditions of the same mistake and thus become an unfortunate form of reliable incorrectness.

Another form of reliable incorrectness can emerge when reliability is defined as a correlation between independent measurements with no attention to absolute difference. Many procedures in developmental science define preference based on a participant's visual attention to stimulus A versus stimulus B. Modern laboratories often assess visual preference by using technologically sophisticated gaze monitoring equipment, and traditional laboratories often use an observer's coding of live or videotaped views of the participant's eyes. A frequently used strategy to confirm the reliability of gaze measurement is to have an independent observer code the same sequence, and the reliability of measurement is then quantified as the correlation of the two measurements. What would happen if one of the observers adopted a more conservative perspective and only coded gaze when it was very obvious? The correlation in this context could be very high, but the absolute difference between the measurements would indicate a systematic difference. Correlations are inherently vulnerable to reliable incorrectness and should always be supplemented with calculations based on the absolute difference between the two measurements.

The general conclusion here is that simply stating that there is a correlation between observations does not define reliability. It is important to always expect a more articulated description of how reliability has been monitored and assessed. It can also be useful to calculate reliability early enough in an experiment to use this information as a context of discovery to not only improve reliability but also improve validity by adjusting the linkage between observations and the underlying constructs that are being measured. When I review a manuscript that assesses reliability using a simple correlation, I always request additional information about how reliability is being defined and measured.

7.5 Metrics of Measurement

Behaviors and mental processes seldom have obvious dimensions or inherent units of measurement. Behavioral dimensions can be as simple and artificial as the number of times a rat presses a button in a Skinner box. However, if we focus on significant aspects of behavior like shyness, aggression, or verbal communication, we find that these constructs can be measured using an extensive array of dimensions that seldom yield converging assessments, ratio measurement, or linear dimensions. The dimensions for measuring processes such as intelligence, anxiety, or hunger are even less obvious. Measuring these complex phenomena contrasts sharply with measuring phenomena in physical science, such as temperature, that can be assessed on a ratio scale using multiple independent and comparable assessment techniques.

For example, when we measure complicated constructs such as shame, we may need to ask "What is more shame?" I remember asking this question at a colloquium presented by a researcher who was investigating emotional development, and the answer was "experiencing shame in more situations." I accepted this answer, but it occurred to me that more shame could also be reflected by an individual experiencing shame more easily in a particular situation, experiencing shame more saliently, remembering shame in a particular situation for a longer period of time, and more; the list of possible measurements is very long. We can make the optimistic assumption that an advanced developmental science will have an underlying infrastructure that links these various aspects of shame. To make progress toward that cumulative knowledge, it is important that we recognize the need to examine and make explicit our assumptions regarding metrics of measurement.

A higher score on an outcome variable usually reflects a larger amount of a measured construct. For example, a person who weighs 160 pounds at assessment 1 and then weighs 200 pounds at assessment 2 is manifesting a 25% increase in weight. Or, success on 95% of the items in an achievement test versus 90% could be viewed as comparable to the difference between success on 85% of the items versus 80%. However, there are also contexts in which the implicit assumption that more is better should be examined and evaluated. For example, a large body of developmental research on infant cognitive development is based on the phenomenon labeled novelty preference. When an infant has become familiar with a particular stimulus, attention to that stimulus tends to habituate (i.e., decline). When a novel stimulus is presented in the context of this habituation, the infant's attention tends to dishabituate (i.e., recover). This habituation/dishabituation model has been used to explore a wide array of infant abilities. For example, when an infant habituates to a series of different exemplars from the same perceptual category and then dishabituates when presented with an exemplar from a novel category, we infer that the infant has an internal representation of the category. Or, when an infant habituates to a particular stimulus and then after a delay shows a preference for a novel stimulus paired with the habituated stimulus, we infer that the infant retained a representation of the habituated stimulus during the delay interval.

When dishabituation is defined as an increase in duration of fixations to the target stimulus, this opens an implicit question: Does a greater increase in fixations indicate a stronger representation of the category, greater working memory, etc.? Researchers who use the habituation/dishabituation paradigm often calculate descriptive and inferential statistics on the basis of this assumption, but in my opinion, this assumption has little support. From a theoretical and parsimonious perspective, dishabituation is more amenable to a categorical interpretation: if a stimulus is perceived as novel (i.e., it is seen as a member of a less familiar category or as not present in working memory), it will cause a recovery of attention. However, the magnitude of the recovery has no relation to the articulation of the category or the longevity of the memory. Given this lack of linearity, dishabituation should be viewed as a categorical state defined by an increase in attention that exceeds a pre-established criterion. If multiple criteria are set at varying levels, such that a stronger response is needed in order to meet a higher criterion, the relative difference might affect the researcher's confidence that an infant has dishabituated, but the performance at relative criteria does not reflect an interpretation of what the infant knows. Alternative interpretations include the possibility that the increase in fixation could indicate more motivation, stamina, etc. The metric that could most accurately measure the infant's ability to categorize or strength of working memory would be the percentage of trials on which the infant habituates across a set of different categorization tests or dishabituates to working memory tests across various levels of challenge.

Here is another example suggesting that more can mean less. The construct whistleblower generally refers to making statements that will expose alleged misconduct that is a threat to a public interest. But, after the whistle has been blown and the institution has made efforts to understand the misconduct and incorporate changes that will avoid or prevent repetition of the problem, additional whistleblowing becomes counterproductive and possibly reflects the self-interests of the whistleblower (e.g., she might be promoting interest in a book she is writing on the topic). In this phase, the term whistleblower becomes a less accurate description and other terms such as self-promoter would be more appropriate. Whistleblowing should be encouraged and protected, but it should also be examined to determine its accuracy. And, when the whistleblowing continues well beyond its productive phase, it should be redefined as self-promotion and used in a more appropriate context such as blowing whistles while serving as a crossing guard.

A comparable problem emerges when behavior is being indexed based on the presence of symptoms. For example, the Child Behavior Checklist (CBCL – Achenbach & Rescorla, 2000) is a parent or teacher symptom checklist used to identify behavioral problems in children (e.g., attention deficit hyperactive disorder, childhood depression, separation anxiety, etc.). The responses 0 = Not True, 1 = Somewhat or Sometimes True, 2 = Very True or Often True are grouped into subsets to measure syndromes, and a table is provided to classify scores as normal, borderline, or clinical based on quantiles from a normative sample. The CBCL has efficiency, and it also has some simplicity. For some disorders, severity would be measured by the relative level across a set of symptoms; for others, severity would be measured by the total number of symptoms. For some disorders, having any two or three symptoms could be considered diagnosable; for others, some symptoms could be considered much more problematic than others.

Finally, academic grading is an example of multiple metric measurements that became increasingly salient to me during my years in university administration. Developmental science research might use grades in particular courses or grade point average (GPA) across a wide range of courses as a measurement of academic success that can be used to explore efficacy of educational interventions, influence of ethnicity and social support, etc. From a general perspective, a grade of "A" can be interpreted as excellent, a grade of "D" can be interpreted as bad, and a grade of "F" can be interpreted as a total failure. However, when we look at the distribution of grades in classes, we see patterns that reflect different interpretations of grades. One frequently seen distribution is an inverted U, with a small number of A's, a large number of B's or C's, and a small number of D's or F's. This can be described as performance grading, in which the instructor seeks to identify the most stellar students, the most underachieving students, and those in the middle. Another frequently seen pattern is a large number of A's, a slightly smaller number of B's, and very few C's, D's, or F's. This can be described as competence grading, in which the instructor has established a goal, and gives a strong grade to all students who have attained that goal. For example, the goal in my First Year Seminar on human infancy was to have students "learn about the psychological development of human infants, evaluate the research procedures that inform this topic, and explore creative new procedures for assessing infant psychological development." Most students attained this goal and received a grade of A, with some minor adjustments to reflect parameters such as effective communication, creativity, and timeliness.

Given that performance and competence grading both have some validity, any use of GPA as a measurement in research needs to recognize this potential difference across courses. One obvious strategy is to evaluate course grades based on the distribution of grades within that course. This is an obvious improvement, and I am pleased that UNC-Chapel Hill is moving toward including this information in each student's transcript. Another improvement that will be more difficult to achieve is to mandate that instructors provide two grades for each student in each course: a grade reflecting performance and a grade reflecting competence. When this policy is instituted, the differentiation can lead to better use of grades. For example, eligibility for Honors, recognition on the Dean's List, competition for graduate programs, and other performance-oriented topics can use a GPA based on performance. In contrast, having attained prerequisite knowledge, being eligible to participate in an extracurricular activity or other competence-oriented topics can use a GPA based on competence.

7.6 Qualitative versus Quantitative Measurement

From a broad perspective, quantitative data are numeric measurements that can be analyzed using traditional statistical techniques. Qualitative data are verbal descriptions that emerge in conversations, descriptions, answers to questions, etc., and are analyzed using various techniques that describe or measure the relevant parameters. The distinction between scientific use of quality and quantity can be traced historically back to Aristotle and a debate that has been ongoing since then (Neuenschwander, 2013). Many developmental scientists are familiar with (and skeptical of) the qualitative research techniques that are prominent in anthropology and other social sciences and with the qualitative data we obtain when attempting to assess complicated constructs like love, depression, attachment, optimism, conservative politics, etc. They notice that qualitative data from small samples do not provide the opportunity for rigorous statistical hypothesis testing. However, they fail to notice that qualitative research can provide valuable opportunities for generating hypotheses, exploring possible explanations of effects, and identifying strategies for measuring constructs of interest. All these activities facilitate our effort to answer our question of interest by helping us understand the relevant mechanisms and develop ways to operationalize the measurement of focal constructs. Developmental scientists also sometimes fail to notice that qualitative data can be analyzed using sophisticated statistical techniques that have been developed for this purpose (e.g., see Rennie, 2012) and that qualitative and quantitative measurement can form a productive partnership (e.g., Madill & Gough, 2008).

Yoshikawa and colleagues (2013) provide an impressive description of various research challenges in developmental science that could be addressed more effectively with a combination of quantitative and qualitative measures. As I have noted repeatedly, constructs are difficult to measure in developmental science. From the present perspective, some constructs seem most amenable to either type of measurement, and it is difficult to gather data that efficiently reflect both perspectives. I remember an experience I had in graduate school when I was using a rule-learning paradigm to explore strategies used to learn rules of logic (e.g., conjunction, disjunction, etc.). I was recording a participant's responses across a series of trials, and I noticed an unusual pattern. When he completed the study, my curiosity motivated me to ask him a qualitative question: "What strategy did you use to learn the rules?" He chuckled, and confessed that he had heard me clear my throat after he made a particular response, so he assumed that this response was inappropriate and he no longer used it. Extrapolating from this valuable qualitative assessment, an informal conversation or a formal qualitative tool can often help us understand and validate our quantitative data.

Another zone of potential value in combining quantitative and qualitative data is the situation in which we have implemented a treatment or manipulation that we assume has had a specific effect, and our research is focused on the outcome of that effect. Various qualitative approaches can be used to explore how the treatment or manipulation was perceived by the participant, and thus how we should interpret whether or not the treatment or manipulation had an effect.

Our discussion of data analytic techniques will include the importance of exploratory data analysis as a strategy for exploring individual differences within the broader context of group effects. This type of analysis often identifies individuals who behaved uniquely in comparison to other members of a group. Outliers are often manicured from data, but to simply remove them without attempting to understand their uniqueness could cause a loss of insight. In some circumstances, the only materials for investigation are original questionnaires. However, from a qualitative data perspective, interviews might contain notes, videotaped data might reveal interesting characteristics, and other aspects of data can be explored. And, from a combined quantitative and qualitative perspective, we should explore ways to incorporate potentially valuable qualitative data that are not necessarily coded for all individuals, but can possibly help us understand why a particular participant had a unique profile.

Yoshikawa et al. (2013) note that the general occurrence that emerges when we combine qualitative and quantitative data is a set of common problems. One problem is the potential difficulty in finding publications that are comfortable with both qualitative and quantitative methods, and their mixture. I am confident that this pitfall can be avoided because in Burchinal et al. (2010) we were able to publish an article in a major journal in which we used qualitative and quantitative data to explore parent perception of infant intentionality. Another pitfall is that qualitative data are almost always more time-consuming for participants and more difficult for administration. Finally, a combination of sophisticated qualitative and quantitative data could require a collaboration of researchers from notably different scientific backgrounds. I can see some potential problems here; however, these problems can dissipate when we focus on the potential value of collaborations among researchers interested in behavior, neurologic development, epigenetics, social context, economic environment, etc.

On the positive side, notable advantages can emerge in a hybrid design in which a small qualitative sample is embedded within the context of the larger quantitative sample. Measurement in the two components of the design could overlap to some extent, with the primary goal being to use the qualitative sample to add depth and insight into various aspects of the research. It is important to have breadth in a research study and to combine it with depth, a situation that Gough and Madill (2012) label "reflexive scientific attitude" and define as viewing subjective or qualitative data as "a resource that can be tapped in order to contextualize and enrich the psychological research process and its products."

8 Interviews and Surveys

One approach developmental scientists use to assess constructs is to evoke, observe, and measure behaviors believed to reflect that construct. Another approach is to collect responses to questions from interviews or surveys. In previous decades, the distinction between interviews and surveys was relatively simple. Interviews were conversations with a participant in which an examiner either recited a formal set of questions or engaged in a flexible conversation. Surveys were written questions that participants answered in various formats such as yes-no, multiple-choice, or open-ended text. Recent advances in technology have merged interviews and surveys, and developmental scientists can now use electronics to recite questions, code verbal responses, administer written questions, follow up on questions that were not answered, and much more.

The data accrued from interviews and surveys in all formats have potential vulnerabilities that are important to keep in mind. For example, if a participant is asked questions about an aspect of behavior that the participant had not noticed previously (e.g., infant intentional behaviors), the participant can become more aware of these behaviors. A positive aspect of this awareness is that if the assessment is repeated in the future, the participant will have more accurate information about this aspect of behavior. A negative aspect of this awareness is that test–retest reliability can be reduced because the information that is being assessed has changed. The relevance of these vulnerabilities will depend upon many factors, including the topic being explored.

Another issue is that participation in a survey/interview can be profoundly affected by the topic that is being assessed. When I am asked to rate my experience on an airline, in a hotel, with a help desk, etc., I can see my own bias: I am much more likely to complete the survey if I had a great or horrible experience. Other factors that influence my participation include the length of the assessment and its format. Further, I always stop answering questions when I detect a flaw that will invalidate the data that are being collected, for example, not allowing me to leave a response blank or revise a previous answer. Any survey/ interview can be converted into data that can be analyzed and interpreted as the measurement of a construct. However, the data from all surveys/interviews must be scrutinized carefully to determine what is being measured and whether the measurement should be considered valid and reliable.

Multiple measurement is a perennial concern in developmental science, and this issue is notably salient in interviews and surveys. An individual who is interviewed or surveyed is providing their perspective on some aspect of their self or of someone they know. This information could be labeled as objective, subjective, or projective and in almost all circumstances could and should be compared with other perspectives on this phenomenon. For example, a child's problematic behaviors could be assessed using the child's report, reports from multiple parents, and reports from multiple teachers. The similarities or differences across these reports could provide some insight into the problematic behaviors.

Finally, as we have discussed for all aspects of development, potential assessments are different at different ages. As children get older, they become better able to read and understand questions and to provide accurate answers. From this perspective, change over time could indicate development of a construct or of the child's ability to participate in an interview or survey.

8.1 Creating Effective Questions and Answers

Gehlbach and Brinkworth (2011) describe a specific series of steps that could enhance the relative validity of any set of questions being used to measure a construct. An obvious first step for developing an efficacious survey is to conduct an expansive review of the previous publications that describe the tools that have been used to measure the construct of interest. A less obvious second step is to interact with potential participants to explore the vocabulary they use when discussing the construct of interest and the aspects of the construct they find interesting, boring, or distressing. The information gathered in these two steps can then be integrated to produce a list of specific indicators that are relevant for assessing the construct.

The third step is to use the information gathered in steps 1 and 2 to develop questions that could potentially measure all of the indicators that have been linked to the focal construct. The content of each question should be screened for lack of clarity and other potential problems. The goals of this screening are to ensure that words and phrasing will be easily understood by participants and to limit ambiguous figures of speech and other features that could preclude translation of the questions to other languages. An additional goal is to develop questions that can be answered objectively rather than by comparison with other experiences that some participants might not have access to. I recently completed a food survey that manifested a large number of these challenges. The survey asked about my consumption of specific foods in the previous 6 months, which was a challenge for my memory, and also would be notably different if the 6 months included summer. Each answer was based on some metric of consumption mentioning servings or ounces, neither of which would be obvious to me while eating. Finally, some questions in the survey referred to foods with unfamiliar brand names.

Gehlbach and Brinkworth (2011) offer two additional steps that survey developers should consider. One step is to seek feedback from experts, such as colleagues in the research community and others who would have a relevant perspective. In my own research on identifying infants at risk for an eventual diagnosis of autism spectrum disorder (ASD), feedback was helpful not only from fellow researchers, but also from clinicians who do diagnostic work with children and from pediatricians who see children in a health-care context. Gehlbach and Brinkworth's second step is relatively unusual but potentially very productive. They recommend a practice called cognitive pretesting or cognitive interviewing in which potential participants are asked to read each question, repeat it in their own words, and report the thoughts they consider as they attempt to answer the question. This step provides a valuable context of discovery to help researchers detect potential problems and notice additional opportunities to enhance measurement of relevant constructs. One final step is obvious: administer the final version of the survey to a pilot sample before beginning a major data collection endeavor.

Another important aspect of surveys is to select appropriate responses for all questions. Authors sometimes adopt a scale of responses (e.g., never, sometimes, often, always) that is appropriate for some questions but unrealistic or irrelevant for others. An inappropriate alignment of question and response not only leads to invalid and unreliable data, but also can frustrate participants and undermine their motivation to provide information. Some questions can be linked to a specific metric of frequency, while others are more appropriately linked to metrics of probability of occurrence. It is more important to match each question to an optimal rating scale rather than to use the same scale for all questions.

The range of responses is another zone of uncertainty. From one perspective, a wider scale could allow for greater precision and the magnification that would be needed to detect a subtle effect. However, although a broader range of responses can increase precision, it can also evoke some problems with measurement. For example, some participants may suffer from mathematical disabilities that make it difficult for them to conceptualize and use a Likert-like scale. Or, educational or cultural differences might influence the respondent's willingness to ponder and make use of subtle steps within the scale.

In contrast, a narrow scale can reduce error of measurement and evoke more confident answers from the observer. It can also be linked to relatively specific terms, but the level of response can become relatively insensitive. Although a broader range allows for more precision, the terms that define levels in a broader range can become increasingly ambiguous. One strategy for combining the two perspectives is to include specific terms that define clear steps within the scale and to use nonspecific indicators that reflect the gaps between them. I experienced this challenge with a scale that had previously defined four steps of relative frequency using the terms never, seldom, sometimes, and always. I searched for a fifth word that would expand the range, but found no term that fit well. Instead, I used the strategy of defining a five-step scale that had never at one extreme, always at the other extreme, and sometimes in the middle. Response 2 was an untitled column between always and sometimes, and response 4 was an untitled column between sometimes and never. This solution obviously expanded the range to include five steps, but additional research is needed to determine whether it is better to have all response columns labeled with more or less ambiguous terms or to label some columns with relatively unambiguous terms and leave others unlabeled to allow intermediate responses.

There are also important implications for choosing between an even and odd number of response alternatives for each question. When the participant must select a point along a dimension with an odd number of responses, the response in the middle might be an accurate assessment, but might also reflect an unwillingness to select an answer that has some alignment with either dimension. In contrast, an even number of alternatives requires that the participant express some alignment with either extreme, which can force an answer that may or may not be accurate.

When the questions and answers have been completed and the survey/interview has been implemented, there is one important final step that should be included. Before formal data collection begins, it is important to collect pilot data and develop an initial strategy for how the survey will be scored. Printed or electronic surveys can accrue data in an inconvenient format, and some information that is needed for scoring will not be obvious until some data analysis has occurred. Processing and exploring pilot data can allow for important modifications and avoid the need for time travel to correct mistakes.

8.2 Parent-Report and Cross-Cultural Challenges

A large percentage of the data we use in developmental science is based upon questions that parents answer in interviews or surveys. Most parents have had extensive experience with their children in a wide array of contexts, which gives these data potentially strong validity. However, it is important to be aware of potential influences and problems that can undermine the validity of parent-report data. Also, as mentioned previously, our culture has evolved, and we must alter our traditional format for gathering information on parenting. Specifically, if a questionnaire asks for "mother" and "father," some participants will be offended because this format lacks appropriate sensitivity. A more appropriate format is to identify "parent 1," "parent 2," etc. and ask for relevant information about each parent's gender, parenting role, etc.

One obvious zone of vulnerability is the context in which parents make the observations that are being harvested. A stay-at-home parent will probably have much more information to report on his or her child's development than a parent who has delegated child care to someone else. A parent who has had previous children can have a much different awareness of infant behavior than a first-time parent. Finally, a parent who has one child may be accruing a more accurate set of observations than a parent who is raising twins. For example, the words produced and comprehended by a singleton child will be notably salient. Confusion is possible when parental memory includes previous children, and much more likely when parents are observing twins, triplets, etc.

Another zone of vulnerability is the phrasing of the questions. Parent report is most likely to be accurate when it is based on relatively specific and straightforward questions about behaviors that are observable. For example, "Does your baby stare at lights?" is a more effective question than "Is your baby uncomfortable in new situations?" because the phrase "stare at lights" has a more specific referent than the phrase "uncomfortable in new situations." Questions that require positioning the focal child within the broader context of how other children behave will be strongly affected by the parent's range of experience with other children. An observer who has had ample experience with children in the relevant age range (e.g., a teacher, daycare provider, or pediatrician) is better prepared to answer peer-comparison questions than a parent who knows one child, albeit very well.

When parent-report questions ask for comparisons along a dimension that could be perceived as having a desirable or undesirable extreme, parents may be more committed to promoting their child than to accuracy. For example, I have seen data in which lower socioeconomic status parents tend to overestimate parameters of their child's cognitive ability. In contrast, parents who are seeking an intervention for their child might overestimate problematic behaviors with the goal of attaining clinical assistance.

As mentioned in previous chapters, all observations conducted by human beings have a potential subjectivity. I noticed an interesting implication of this when an experiment was conducted in my laboratory in which we measured infant language development using the MacArthur-Bates Communicative Development Inventory (CDI) (Fenson, Marchman, Thal, Dale, Reznick, & Bates, 2007) and parent perception of infant intentionality using the Infant Intentionality Questionnaire (IIQ) (Reznick & Schwartz, 2001). We used a cohort-sequential design that included one group of parents who completed both measurements when their infants were 8, 10, and 12 months old; another group who completed both measurements when their infants were 10 and 12 months old; and a third group who completed both measurements when their infants were 12 months old. Both measures showed developmental change over time, but an interesting phenomenon emerged when we compared the three groups on their scores at 12 months. For the CDI, there was no difference among the groups, but for the IIQ, parents who completed it for the third time had significantly higher scores than parents who were completing it for the second time, and their scores were higher than parents who completed it for the first time. From this perspective, parent report of child language is relatively accurate and not affected by previous assessments. In contrast, parent report of infant intentionality may be altered when parents become more aware of infant intentionality after answering questions about this topic. This difference could lead to the conclusion that parents can report infant language more accurately than infant intentionality. Or, that becoming aware of infant intentionality affects how parents interact with their infant or what they notice.

Measures in developmental science can evoke a wide array of challenges when administered cross-culturally. At a broad, theoretical level, one challenge is what Medin, Bennis, and Chandler (2010) describe as the "home-field disadvantage." Their point is that cross-cultural research is at risk for low validity when it uses one cultural group as the starting point for its cultural perspective. One problem with this strategy is that the original culture, or home field, will be seen as the appropriate normative level, and any cross-cultural variation will probably be seen as suboptimal. Another problem is that the measurement technique that is most effective in the home field might be less effective in other cultures, and thus may underestimate measurements. For example, pride assessed using an interview could produce higher scores in an individualist culture and lower scores in a collectivist culture.

Simply translating a survey or an interview from the home field language can raise issues. Possible problems include the content of questions and the dimensions for answers, because it is very difficult to translate a sequence of words like never, seldom, sometimes, and always into different languages and expect both sets of words to span the same dimension with equal spacing. Erkut (2010) notes various problems that emerge when surveys are translated and recommends several strategies that can be helpful. One strategy is to institute a horizontal collaboration in which researchers from multiple cultures and languages work together to identify a construct to measure, and strategies for measuring it. When potential questions have been developed, one obvious tool is back translation in which the previously translated questions are translated into the original language, and this is more effective with multiple iterations of the language-to-language re-translation. It is also advantageous to have multiple translators translate independently and to use various metrics to assess the accuracy of translation. Erkut also describes a novel tool-focus approach in which members of the research team are involved in all aspects of creating versions in different languages and selecting appropriate wording. By focusing on multiple relevant languages simultaneously, constructs are more likely to be identified and queried equivalently in every language. Finally, despite diligent efforts to create a multicultural assessment, we must recognize that some constructs are too abstract and culture-specific to be generalized. For example, I remember attending a symposium that explored questions about our description of our souls from a cross-cultural perspective, and I found it hard to imagine that this extremely abstract construct could attain comparable definition and measurement in notably different cultures.

8.3 Optimal Survey Format

A printed survey can range from simple text to an extensively decorative format. The optimal goal is a midpoint between these extremes in which the questions and answers are easy to read and well aligned. Multiple pages versus a fan-fold format affect the cost of mailing the survey and the probability of missing data. The most predictable implication of formatting is that any questions that are on the back side of a survey are less likely to be completed than questions that are on the front side of the survey.

The popular phrase "less is more" has direct relevance for surveys. Most researchers know (or eventually learn) the importance of assembling a battery of tests that fit within the constraints of the child's endurance, and the child's performance is monitored so that testing can be stopped or postponed when the child is no longer interested or motivated. In contrast, researchers seldom monitor the duration of interest and motivated performance that can be evoked from parents. Incomplete questionnaires are also a symptom of lack of compliance, and if respondents lose interest but continue answering questions while in a suboptimal state, the data they provide may be compromised. Some researchers add lie scales such as more or less identical variations of the same question or other measures that tap compliance such as a question that says "Please select never as your answer to this question." These additional questions can increase confidence in the answers provided on a questionnaire, but they also add length to the assessment protocol and thus can reduce the quality of answers. A more effective strategy is to adopt realistic limits for the time commitment entailed by a set of surveys and allow options for survey completion to be suspended temporarily. Other strategies can be used to help identify careless responses: For example, Meade and Craig (2012) recommend strategies such as tracking response time, and asking specific questions regarding diligence of response.

Within the survey, it is important to distribute questions in a pattern that optimizes appropriate responses. There is no one pattern of questions that could be labeled "correct," and the challenge is to examine the distribution of questions within each new study to determine its appropriateness. In some surveys, each section focuses on a specific theme, and the questions in each section will have some redundancy with the goal of having the respondent remain focused on the relevant theme. This format also allows for the efficient strategy of beginning each section with a broad question to assess the relevance of the section to the responder, and then instructing the responder to either answer each of the questions in the section or to skip the section. I recently participated in a survey that asked about various manifestations of an intervention. All of the answers were "no" because the intervention had no effect. An initial question asking if the intervention had any effect would have been much more efficient.

In other surveys, questions are distributed in a pattern that avoids redundancy with the goal of maintaining respondent interest. Some surveys arrange the array of answers to have similarity across the questions. For example, each answer that indicates no problem is on the left side of the grid or has a low number, and each answer that indicates a problem is on the right side of the grid or has a high number. One advantage here is that parents can leverage this pattern to help them interpret questions, and another advantage is that the surveyor can easily identify surveys that indicate a problem by scanning for excessive answers on the side of the survey that indicates problems. However, a better strategy may be to arrange questions such that answers are expected to be randomly distributed. Avoiding redundancy can keep the survey interesting, and in this configuration a redundant pattern of answers would indicate invalid data.

Modern technology offers an opportunity to implement surveys electronically rather than as paper documents, and an initial concern is the extent to which paper-and-pencil surveys are equivalent to Internet data collection methods. Investigating this concern is difficult because, as always happens in an open system, results can be affected by why a person is participating, the context in which they are completing the survey, and the operational definition of equivalence. Fortunately, recent research on this topic suggests that survey data gathered in these two contexts are generally equivalent (e.g., Weigold, Weigold, & Russell, 2013).

Electronic administration can obviously enhance surveys in several ways. For example, computer-based administration invites an approach called computer adaptive testing (CAT) in which questions are administered in an order that is determined by the responses to previous questions (Wainer, 2000). When assessing a child's language ability, on the basis of knowledge of words in comparison to a normative sample, the paper-and-pencil approach is to give the parent a list of words stratified to capture the range of word knowledge that would be expected on the basis of a normative sample and to have the parent rate the child's language ability in comparison to same-aged peers (e.g., the MacArthur-Bates Communicative Development Inventories; Fenson et al., 2007). The CAT approach uses a computer-based algorithm to evaluate the parent's response to a particular word and then administers subsequent words that are chosen to arrive at the child's level of word knowledge. This automated format to surveying is fast and efficient, and thus can facilitate gathering accurate reporting.

Another advantage of modern technology is that it allows us to provide options for responders who encounter a question lacking an answer they view as correct. When a survey does not offer specific instructions or response options for situations in which the observer does not have a basis for providing an answer, answers are less likely to be valid. From my perspective as a scientist, when a survey forces me to choose a response when I do not see an answer that I would consider correct, I usually discontinue my participation (and send feedback to the surveyor) rather than choose an answer I view as invalid. My recent online Qualtrics surveys make use of several sophisticated techniques that can remediate this problem. One technique is to detect questions that have not been answered. When a responder moves forward, they are informed that they have skipped questions X, Y, Z and are given an opportunity to complete them or to leave them incomplete and continue. I also recommend ending every online survey with two text boxes: one that allows participants to submit anonymous comments and suggestions, and one that allows them to ask non-anonymous questions that will receive an answer. These questions could be included in a paper survey, but being anonymous would have less credibility.

8.4 Administering Interviews

Face-to-face or mouth-to-ear interviews have the advantage of allowing the interviewer to create a comfortable context in which aspects of a construct are discussed and information is evoked that is useful for measuring relevant dimensions of the construct. The primary concern regarding cumulative developmental science is that an interviewer will attain less valid and reliable administration of the interview when the interview context is less comfortable. For example, participants can withhold honest information if they fear possible embarrassment or sanctions based on that information. Other participants might feel uncomfortable based on demographic differences. These concerns could affect surveys, but they seem more salient for interviews. Various procedures can be implemented to improve data based on interviews. One example is to have each interviewer be interviewed by a fellow interviewer to attain an understanding of what the interviewee will experience and how the interviewer will be perceived. This quality control is useful as preliminary training and should also be incorporated during ongoing data collection to avoid changes in how the interview is administered based on interviewer's experiences.

Telephone interviewers face various challenges in remotely managing participants who are more or less sophisticated, motivated, and attentive. One important tool that interviewers use is their voices. The tone and enunciation of the voice can influence how the participant reacts to questions. It is also important for researchers who manage interviewers to have each consult with a language assessor to make adjustments in their tone of voice and possibly use rehabilitative exercises to preserve voice quality.

Member checking is the term used to describe any tool that researchers use to explore a study's validity and accuracy. One type of member checking that is relevant for interviews is to repeat information provided by the interviewee during the interview and ask the interviewee if the information has been heard accurately. Another type of member checking is to repeat coded data after the interview and verify with the interviewee that responses have been coded correctly. We own the data, but it is provided by the participants, and their perspective on its quality is potentially very important.

9 Analyzing Data

The art and science of data analysis has progressed steadily for centuries, with a marked influx of new tools and techniques when Alan Turing developed creative technology to crack Nazi codes and we entered the modern world of computer technology (see the film "The Imitation Game" if you want to learn more about how Turing did this). The relatively primitive hands-on approach to data analysis that was prevalent in previous decades had some advantages, and the modern tools such as multiple imputation and modeling also have some advantages. I am not anachronistic, but I do see some potential value in promoting the art and science of data analysis by seeking an appropriate balance of old tools and new tools. Please note that I am not a statistician, so this chapter should definitely be consumed "with a grain of salt." My main goal here is to highlight some aspects of the data analysis process that we should be aware of when conducting our own data analysis or when collaborating with statisticians. Additionally, I seek to help us realize that the ongoing influx of new tools and techniques for data analysis creates a world in which mature (elderly?) developmental scientists must not only retain some of their relevant statistical knowledge but also make an explicit effort to become familiar with the innovative statistical procedures that began emerging after we completed our graduate training in previous decades or in a previous century. To enhance my credibility, I recommend that everyone who reads this chapter also read an article by Joseph Rodgers titled "The epistemology of mathematical and statistical modeling" (Rodgers, 2010), and if any discrepancies are detected, Rodgers is much more likely to be correct than I am. A recent book by Alex Reinhart titled *Statistics done wrong* (Reinhart, 2015) has been labeled a "succinct, accessible, and accurate assessment" of statistical flaws that are relevant for all scientists.

9.1 Exploratory Data Analysis

Data analysis can be seen from two broad perspectives: exploratory and confirmatory. The exploratory phase is the search for interesting patterns in our complete. This accomplishment could evoke a standing ovation from some reviewers, particularly if the results are interesting, and it could also evoke some concern because it is extremely unusual to conduct research in which 100% of invitees participate diligently and administrators and data coders make no mistakes. As discussed in previous chapters, research can be implemented using strategies that increase the likelihood of acquiring accurate data. However, it is virtually impossible to implement a research project that accommodates the idiosyncrasies of all participants, and some participants will view their participation in research as an incursion on their privacy, an insult to their intelligence, or a waste of their time. They will accommodate to this challenge by using a strategy such as answering randomly or checking all the boxes under the "sometimes" column to complete their participation. All measurements are data, but not all data are measurements. Identifying bogus data is an important step toward successful developmental science because even a well-intentioned participant might adopt a strategy that creates data that are misleading.

One strategy for identifying bogus data is to look for outliers. A traditional statistical approach defines outliers based on data points that are too far above or below the mean defined by the standard deviation of the unit of measurement. This approach has some appeal in the confirmatory phase and would have enhanced credibility if it was consistent with the exploratory phase. Inspection of a distribution of scores will confirm the extent to which a standard deviation (in a sample that includes outliers) is an appropriate metric for outliers. Additionally, from a broader perspective, the distribution could be skewed or bipolar, which would completely change the identification of outliers. Using this perspective, I have often defined outliers based on their distance from their nearest neighbor in units of standard deviation. If the outlier is one of many scores in a neighborhood that is notably separate from the other scores, this could lead to the identification of a small but homogeneous outlying group.

EDA also allows us to detect bogus data based on individual patterns. For example, an infant who is coded as looking continually at one of two screens in a randomly distributed set of trials in which one screen is designated as correct will receive a percentage correct score of 50%. An infant who has a strong side bias, is distracted by an internal state or an external stimulus, or who is blind might show the same pattern, and any of these circumstances warrants a different interpretation than an infant who has observed a series of trials and does not have the cognitive ability that is being assessed.

EDA for bogus data should look for randomness and systematic incorrectness, although randomness can be difficult to detect in behavioral responses. Surveys can include a lie scale based on some questions that are randomness detectors (e.g., Question 2: Please select the box labeled Never) or questions

raw data. The confirmatory phase is an effort to evaluate the degree to which conclusions are solidly supported by these patterns rather than reflecting a chance distribution of scores. One obvious metaphor is to view the exploratory process as detective work and the confirmatory process as the courtroom trial in which claims about the evidence are evaluated. To add another metaphor, the exploration process helps us notice that the data analysis process contains some opportunities that could be viewed as art. Performing traditional statistical analyses without exploring the data is comparable to painting a canvas with a roller and a can of paint rather than an array of brushes and a pallet with various colors.

Exploratory and confirmatory approaches are relevant for successful research, but when modern electronic analytic techniques emerged and became increasingly prominent, some statisticians noticed that our connection with our raw data was being undermined. Exploratory Data Analysis (EDA) was formalized by John Tukey in the 1970s (e.g., Tukey, 1977), with further promotion by Behrens (1997) and others to establish techniques to help researchers become intimately familiar with their raw data. Unfortunately, a quick scan of courses being offered by prominent Quantitative Psychology Programs suggests that formal training in EDA has abated. The recent tendency for researchers to delegate their data management, and sometimes their data analysis, to professional consultants makes data entry more reliable and data analysis more sophisticated. However, it also can cause researchers to be less familiar with their raw data, less likely to detect the obvious effects (and lack of effects) that emerge at a primitive but compelling level of EDA, and less likely to present data using informative graphs (e.g., see Lane & Sándor, 2009).

In my own experience, I distinctly remember using a Monroe calculator to perform the correlations, analyses of variance, and other statistics in my master's thesis four decades ago (Reznick & Richman, 1976). The analysis process was cumbersome, I probably made many arithmetic mistakes, additional analyses might have revealed some additional effects, and modern analytic techniques could have provided insight and unique perspectives. However, one of the main results in my master's thesis was my discovery that the performance of participants in my rule-learning task was affected by the perceptual characteristics of the stimuli that were used to define the rule. I noticed this effect when I examined each participant's response pattern in my effort to understand individual differences in performance. I doubt that I would have noticed the effect if I had not been looking at the raw data, and I doubt that our contemporary statistical tools would have detected this interesting and unexpected influence on rule learning, which I labeled "pre-experimental bias."

Some aspects of EDA can be accomplished using graph paper and a pencil. However, we can also include EDA as part of our electronic processing, and many electronic EDA tools are much more useful than our archaic graphs. For example, radar charts and spider plots can be viewed as initial steps toward modeling data. These multivariate graphs combine multiple variables as spokes starting from the same point with the length of the spoke reflecting the magnitude of the variable and with lines connecting comparable values among the spokes. This view of the data can reveal similarity and outliers among the observations. Another advantage of effective graphic EDA is that it provides visual tools that can be incorporated into publications and presentations to enhance the effectiveness of communication. Lane and Sándor (2009) demonstrated the effectiveness of bar charts containing distributional information, graphics that reveal trends, and figures that include graphics and inferential statistics.

Another activity that could be labeled EDA is beginning statistical analysis before a full data set is collected. Here is my favorite abstract metaphor on this: assuming that you are working on some sort of project that will ultimately lead to a structure constructed on the top of a mountain, one obvious strategy is to acquire all of the relevant tools and materials, and move the entire array to the top of the mountain and then begin construction. Some problematic aspects of this strategy are that additional tools might be needed, the materials that have been selected might not be appropriate, or the top of the mountain might not be as aesthetically pleasing as expected. The alternative strategy is to assemble a minimal collection of tools and materials, transport this small collection to the top of the mountain, and assemble a preliminary version of the ultimate structure. Additional effort will be needed to bring the full array of tools and material to the top of the mountain, but the exploratory phase can indicate changes in the tools and materials that will make the project notably better.

When I talk to a student about plans for an upcoming project, I recommend beginning data analysis before the study with data from some pilot participants and/or virtual data that has been created through mock coding, random completion of questionnaires, or other synthetic processes such as simulation techniques. When these ad hoc data are available, I recommend downloading data from online surveys and coding videos and then inputting the data into whatever statistical analysis tool will be used and setting up the analyses that will be used to test hypotheses. Conducting analyses based on data from a few pilot participants obviously does not lead to conclusions. However, these analyses do lead to insights about additional variables that might be needed (e.g., how long the procedure lasted, a qualitative note after each trial assessing the participant's engagement in the task, etc.), additional measures that might be relevant (e.g., noting the participant's gender, measuring the participant's

weight, an additional test of the same construct), and the statistical will be needed to explore relevant hypotheses. Engaging in this data activity before actually beginning the study is not inefficient becau activities will occur eventually, and engaging in them before formal d lection begins could lead to modifications that greatly improve the qua the research.

Carrying this idea of pre-study data analytic activity a step furthe remember attending a series of meetings in which colleagues and I met w a statistical consultant to discuss how to analyze the data we had accrued a large intervention project. Our original grant included data analytic plans but we had initially explored this topic from a relatively abstract perspective. In retrospect, we could have begun our project plans by creating a more or less random data set in which we altered the data from some virtual participants to reflect a range of scores that we would expect if the intervention was effective. In analyzing these potential data, we would have noticed that one possible outcome would be effective intervention for some participants but not all. Alternatively, all participants could have been affected somewhat by the intervention but with relatively subtle changes in their performance. Some participants could also have manifested some negative effects of the intervention. Looking at these and other potential outcome patterns, we could have examined statistical techniques that would identify and validate each possible outcome. From this perspective, we would have become more aware of outcome measures that should have been implemented before the intervention so that we could look at change rather than group differences per se. We could also have implemented additional measures of outcomes that we felt would be most affected by the intervention. From a broader perspective, we could have identified some aspects of participants and their family that could contribute variance to the effectiveness of the intervention, and thus could have been measured so that we could reduce some variance. Having a discussion of this topic in a context that included a statistical consultant and that focused on ad hoc data could have led to many changes that would have improved the quality of the research.

9.2 Identifying Bogus Data and Outliers

An extremely effective design and implementation of a research project that includes offering a salient incentive for participation or a salient punishment for not participating could prevent participants from discarding a mailed survey or avoiding a lab-based assessment, and thus lead to a data set that is 100%

that are an exact repetition of previous questions. Potential systematic incorrectness could be detected based on repeated response in a particular column or a systematic pattern across questions (1.a, 2.b, 3.c, 4.d, 5.a, 6.b, 7.c, etc.). I remember participating on a committee that was reviewing applicants for a fellowship, and I noticed that a reviewer (who was not attending the meeting) often rated applicants at the opposite extreme than the rating offered by other reviewers. I called her mobile phone and confirmed my hypothesis: she had used the correct range, but did not realize that excellence received a low score and lack of excellence received a high score.

9.3 Analyzing Missing Data

Given the virtual impossibility of attaining valid data across all measures for all participants, our analysis of every research project faces the challenge of handling some missing data. Some statistical techniques sail smoothly (and blindly) despite the missing data, but statistical techniques that focus on relationships among measures and/or change over time or across conditions encounter a need to estimate the most likely value of the missing data and include these simulated values in the analyses. Random missing data impose a loss of power, and systematic missing data can impose not only a loss of power, but also false generalizations. For example, the infants or toddlers who have missing data can also differ in cognitive, linguistic, temperament, motivation, or focal constructs. One strategy to explore this problem is to compare participants with missing and non-missing data on auxiliary measurements of other potentially relevant dimensions and use these data to define and defend appropriate generalizations.

One traditional technique for the statistical estimation of missing data was to replace the missing value with the mean of the values attained by comparable participants. This model has some intuitive appeal based on the definition of comparable participants, and it also has some problems (e.g., adding a new score that is the same as the mean will automatically reduce the variance of the distribution).

Recent statistical innovation uses a simulation-based approach in which missing data are replaced by multiple simulated values (see Enders, 2013 for an easily readable summary of relevant approaches). The resulting set of analyses is then combined in an effort to support inferential conclusions that incorporate uncertainty that is caused by simulated missing data. Some statisticians are confident that their estimated data are based on the higher powers that govern or predict behavior. Those of us who are more rational and less statistical will believe that all estimated data are built upon some aspect of estimation and are thus ultimately a form of clairvoyance: no statistical estimation technique gives us the power to see objects or events that do not exist and thus cannot be directly perceived by our senses. However, we also recognize that some forms of imputation are more impressive than others. Single-imputation methods treat imputed values no differently from observed ones. In contrast, multiple imputation uses a distribution of imputed data to evoke the most credible simulation.

Returning to a previous topic, it seems possible that multiple imputation tools can provide an innovative and statistically sophisticated strategy for detecting outliers. For example, it could be informative to reverse the process of multiple imputation and use it to perform selective amputation in which we identify an outlier, change it to missing, look at the distribution of replacement values that emerge via multiple imputation, evaluate the suspicious value's position within the distribution, and if it is extremely unlikely, we label it an outlier and remove it.

9.4 Assessing the Significance of Statistical Significance

English statistician, biologist, and geneticist Ronald Fisher gets mixed reviews. His productive career during the first half of the 20th century created many statistical techniques that are still widely used (e.g., analysis of variance, maximum likelihood estimation, and the z-distribution), and Queen Elizabeth II promoted him to Sir Ronald Fisher in 1952. In contrast, methodologic guru Paul Meehl (1978) claims that "Sir Ronald has befuddled us, mesmerized us, and led us down the primrose path. I believe that the almost universal reliance on merely refuting the null hypothesis as the standard method for corroborating substantive theories in the soft areas is a terrible mistake, is basically unsound, poor scientific strategy, and one of the worst things that ever happened in the history of psychology" (p. 817). The issue here is inference based on the idea that we can use statistical techniques to reject or disprove the null hypothesis (i.e., that there is no effect) and thus claim to have found what is labeled a statistically significant effect. In Fisher's classic "lady tasting tea" experiment (Fisher, 1935), a lady claimed the ability to discriminate cups in which tea was added first versus cups in which milk was added first. The protocol of the experiment was that the lady received 8 randomly ordered cups in which 4 were tea-then-milk and 4 were milk-then-tea, and she correctly identified milk-first versus tea-first for all 8 cups. Fisher estimated that the probability of her attaining this performance based on random selection would be approximately 1.4%. Thus, she could have been a lucky guesser, but he considered the level of probability for this interpretation to be low enough to interpret her claim as statistically significant and therefore reject the null hypothesis that she cannot discriminate the two conditions. The specific criterion for claiming statistical significance was eventually set at probability < 0.05.

For a more contemporary example of testing statistical significance, imagine the following scenario: You are teaching a lecture class to 25 students, and you occasionally lecture in a new format that you hope students will find helpful. To evaluate the efficacy of your new strategy, you distribute a card to each student and ask them to rate the class on a scale from 4.0 for a great class to 1.0 for a terrible class, and you collect these cards on a day in which you use the new format and a day in which you use the old format. When you examine the data, the mean score on the cards is 3.4 for the new format and 3.0 for the old format. This difference is relatively small and you wonder if your new format is having an effect. You then invent a method to evaluate the difference. You shuffle the index cards for each day, deal a set of 10 cards and calculate the mean, combine the cards and shuffle them again, deal another set of 10 cards and calculate another mean, repeat this process 20 times, and then calculate the standard deviation of the 20 means. If the standard deviation is 0.10, the difference between the mean scores for the two formats is impressive. If the average standard deviation is 1.2, the difference between the mean scores for the two formats is unimpressive and can be viewed as reflecting no effect. In a contrasting scenario, you are now teaching the lecture class to 250 students. You use a similar strategy, but this time you deal sets of 50 cards. You now get a relatively low standard deviation, and even a difference between 3.2 and 3.3 looks relatively impressive.

Critics see many problems associated with using null hypothesis statistical testing (NHST) to interpret data. Most saliently, rejecting the null hypothesis provides relatively little information about whether or not a theory is correct. For example, the null hypothesis that A = B could be rejected if A > B or if B > A, and the magnitude of the difference could be small or large. Failure to reject the null hypothesis could indicate that A = B, but could also indicate that the experiment was under-powered or flawed in some other way, and thus failure to reject the hypothesis would support no persuasive conclusions regarding the truth of the hypothesis. From this perspective, the probabilistic criterion for statistical significance does not necessarily align with practical or theoretical significance, and thus creates a context in which an extremely large number of statistical tests will almost always generate false rejection of some null hypotheses. Another perspective for criticizing NHST is that it can lead to two different categories of error. A Type I error is a false positive in which we claim that a hypothesis was correct (e.g., an analysis suggests that confidence has a positive effect on performance but confidence does not have a positive effect on performance). A Type II error is a false negative in which we claim that our hypothesis was not supported (e.g., an analysis suggests that confidence has no effect on performance but confidence does have a positive effect on performance).

I do not see NHST as inherently evil, but it can definitely be problematic. For example, NHST can claim that a correlation of 0.33 is statistically significant and thus supports the claim that A predicts B. Here is a metaphor I frequently use to put this into perspective: A correlation of 0.33 accounts for 10% of the variance. Imagine that a piano player is preparing to put 10 fingers on a keyboard, and we know that one of the fingers will be on B^b. Given that we know one note and we do not know the other nine notes, in what sense can we predict what the chord will sound like? All we can say is that one particular note will be among the notes and thus play a small role in the overall effect. That is a very weak definition of prediction, and it introduces a perspective called effect size. Effect size is an index of the relation between variables that is much more informative than statistical significance per se. Various measures of effect size are available, and Hedges (2008) provides a useful summary. Interpretations of effect size will evolve when this parameter is included in all publications, and contemporary journal editors are steering developmental science toward this important goal.

From the perspective of prediction, I am more comfortable with NHST when research is based on a specific set of point predictions that are being tested with the grave risk of refutation. For example, a study could test the hypothesis that people who are feeling more confident will have stronger working memory and thus be able to respond faster and more accurately in a task in which a response is based on their working memory. The zone of research where I often see this opportunity is longitudinal studies where a new proposal emerges to use already collected data to identify participants who would be expected to have some specific outcome eventually and then conduct research that tests this specific hypothesis. For example, if aspects of early vocabulary are expected to have some specific implications for success in classrooms, preliminary examination of early vocabulary scores could identify one group of participants who are at risk and another group who should have no problems. A dissertation could then be proposed in which members of the risk group and the control group are assessed using measurements such as grades in elementary school, language assessments conducted in a laboratory, or interviews with teachers and/or parents regarding ongoing academic success. If the risk complete. This accomplishment could evoke a standing ovation from some reviewers, particularly if the results are interesting, and it could also evoke some concern because it is extremely unusual to conduct research in which 100% of invitees participate diligently and administrators and data coders make no mistakes. As discussed in previous chapters, research can be implemented using strategies that increase the likelihood of acquiring accurate data. However, it is virtually impossible to implement a research project that accommodates the idiosyncrasies of all participants, and some participants will view their participation in research as an incursion on their privacy, an insult to their intelligence, or a waste of their time. They will accommodate to this challenge by using a strategy such as answering randomly or checking all the boxes under the "sometimes" column to complete their participation. All measurements are data, but not all data are measurements. Identifying bogus data is an important step toward successful developmental science because even a well-intentioned participant might adopt a strategy that creates data that are misleading.

One strategy for identifying bogus data is to look for outliers. A traditional statistical approach defines outliers based on data points that are too far above or below the mean defined by the standard deviation of the unit of measurement. This approach has some appeal in the confirmatory phase and would have enhanced credibility if it was consistent with the exploratory phase. Inspection of a distribution of scores will confirm the extent to which a standard deviation (in a sample that includes outliers) is an appropriate metric for outliers. Additionally, from a broader perspective, the distribution could be skewed or bipolar, which would completely change the identification of outliers. Using this perspective, I have often defined outliers based on their distance from their nearest neighbor in units of standard deviation. If the outlier is one of many scores in a neighborhood that is notably separate from the other scores, this could lead to the identification of a small but homogeneous outlying group.

EDA also allows us to detect bogus data based on individual patterns. For example, an infant who is coded as looking continually at one of two screens in a randomly distributed set of trials in which one screen is designated as correct will receive a percentage correct score of 50%. An infant who has a strong side bias, is distracted by an internal state or an external stimulus, or who is blind might show the same pattern, and any of these circumstances warrants a different interpretation than an infant who has observed a series of trials and does not have the cognitive ability that is being assessed.

EDA for bogus data should look for randomness and systematic incorrectness, although randomness can be difficult to detect in behavioral responses. Surveys can include a lie scale based on some questions that are randomness detectors (e.g., Question 2: Please select the box labeled Never) or questions weight, an additional test of the same construct), and the statistical tools that will be needed to explore relevant hypotheses. Engaging in this data analytic activity before actually beginning the study is not inefficient because these activities will occur eventually, and engaging in them before formal data collection begins could lead to modifications that greatly improve the quality of the research.

Carrying this idea of pre-study data analytic activity a step further, I remember attending a series of meetings in which colleagues and I met with a statistical consultant to discuss how to analyze the data we had accrued in a large intervention project. Our original grant included data analytic plans, but we had initially explored this topic from a relatively abstract perspective. In retrospect, we could have begun our project plans by creating a more or less random data set in which we altered the data from some virtual participants to reflect a range of scores that we would expect if the intervention was effective. In analyzing these potential data, we would have noticed that one possible outcome would be effective intervention for some participants but not all. Alternatively, all participants could have been affected somewhat by the intervention but with relatively subtle changes in their performance. Some participants could also have manifested some negative effects of the intervention. Looking at these and other potential outcome patterns, we could have examined statistical techniques that would identify and validate each possible outcome. From this perspective, we would have become more aware of outcome measures that should have been implemented before the intervention so that we could look at change rather than group differences per se. We could also have implemented additional measures of outcomes that we felt would be most affected by the intervention. From a broader perspective, we could have identified some aspects of participants and their family that could contribute variance to the effectiveness of the intervention, and thus could have been measured so that we could reduce some variance. Having a discussion of this topic in a context that included a statistical consultant and that focused on ad hoc data could have led to many changes that would have improved the quality of the research.

9.2 Identifying Bogus Data and Outliers

An extremely effective design and implementation of a research project that includes offering a salient incentive for participation or a salient punishment for not participating could prevent participants from discarding a mailed survey or avoiding a lab-based assessment, and thus lead to a data set that is 100%

many electronic EDA tools are much more useful than our archaic graphs. For example, radar charts and spider plots can be viewed as initial steps toward modeling data. These multivariate graphs combine multiple variables as spokes starting from the same point with the length of the spoke reflecting the magnitude of the variable and with lines connecting comparable values among the spokes. This view of the data can reveal similarity and outliers among the observations. Another advantage of effective graphic EDA is that it provides visual tools that can be incorporated into publications and presentations to enhance the effectiveness of communication. Lane and Sándor (2009) demonstrated the effectiveness of bar charts containing distributional information, graphics that reveal trends, and figures that include graphics and inferential statistics.

Another activity that could be labeled EDA is beginning statistical analysis before a full data set is collected. Here is my favorite abstract metaphor on this: assuming that you are working on some sort of project that will ultimately lead to a structure constructed on the top of a mountain, one obvious strategy is to acquire all of the relevant tools and materials, and move the entire array to the top of the mountain and then begin construction. Some problematic aspects of this strategy are that additional tools might be needed, the materials that have been selected might not be appropriate, or the top of the mountain might not be as aesthetically pleasing as expected. The alternative strategy is to assemble a minimal collection of tools and materials, transport this small collection to the top of the mountain, and assemble a preliminary version of the ultimate structure. Additional effort will be needed to bring the full array of tools and material to the top of the mountain, but the exploratory phase can indicate changes in the tools and materials that will make the project notably better.

When I talk to a student about plans for an upcoming project, I recommend beginning data analysis before the study with data from some pilot participants and/or virtual data that has been created through mock coding, random completion of questionnaires, or other synthetic processes such as simulation techniques. When these ad hoc data are available, I recommend downloading data from online surveys and coding videos and then inputting the data into whatever statistical analysis tool will be used and setting up the analyses that will be used to test hypotheses. Conducting analyses based on data from a few pilot participants obviously does not lead to conclusions. However, these analyses do lead to insights about additional variables that might be needed (e.g., how long the procedure lasted, a qualitative note after each trial assessing the participant's engagement in the task, etc.), additional measures that might be relevant (e.g., noting the participant's gender, measuring the participant's raw data. The confirmatory phase is an effort to evaluate the degree to which conclusions are solidly supported by these patterns rather than reflecting a chance distribution of scores. One obvious metaphor is to view the exploratory process as detective work and the confirmatory process as the courtroom trial in which claims about the evidence are evaluated. To add another metaphor, the exploration process helps us notice that the data analysis process contains some opportunities that could be viewed as art. Performing traditional statistical analyses without exploring the data is comparable to painting a canvas with a roller and a can of paint rather than an array of brushes and a pallet with various colors.

Exploratory and confirmatory approaches are relevant for successful research, but when modern electronic analytic techniques emerged and became increasingly prominent, some statisticians noticed that our connection with our raw data was being undermined. Exploratory Data Analysis (EDA) was formalized by John Tukey in the 1970s (e.g., Tukey, 1977), with further promotion by Behrens (1997) and others to establish techniques to help researchers become intimately familiar with their raw data. Unfortunately, a quick scan of courses being offered by prominent Quantitative Psychology Programs suggests that formal training in EDA has abated. The recent tendency for researchers to delegate their data management, and sometimes their data analysis, to professional consultants makes data entry more reliable and data analysis more sophisticated. However, it also can cause researchers to be less familiar with their raw data, less likely to detect the obvious effects (and lack of effects) that emerge at a primitive but compelling level of EDA, and less likely to present data using informative graphs (e.g., see Lane & Sándor, 2009).

In my own experience, I distinctly remember using a Monroe calculator to perform the correlations, analyses of variance, and other statistics in my master's thesis four decades ago (Reznick & Richman, 1976). The analysis process was cumbersome, I probably made many arithmetic mistakes, additional analyses might have revealed some additional effects, and modern analytic techniques could have provided insight and unique perspectives. However, one of the main results in my master's thesis was my discovery that the performance of participants in my rule-learning task was affected by the perceptual characteristics of the stimuli that were used to define the rule. I noticed this effect when I examined each participant's response pattern in my effort to understand individual differences in performance. I doubt that I would have noticed the effect if I had not been looking at the raw data, and I doubt that our contemporary statistical tools would have detected this interesting and unexpected influence on rule learning, which I labeled "pre-experimental bias."

Some aspects of EDA can be accomplished using graph paper and a pencil. However, we can also include EDA as part of our electronic processing, and that are an exact repetition of previous questions. Potential systematic incorrectness could be detected based on repeated response in a particular column or a systematic pattern across questions (1.a, 2.b, 3.c, 4.d, 5.a, 6.b, 7.c, etc.). I remember participating on a committee that was reviewing applicants for a fellowship, and I noticed that a reviewer (who was not attending the meeting) often rated applicants at the opposite extreme than the rating offered by other reviewers. I called her mobile phone and confirmed my hypothesis: she had used the correct range, but did not realize that excellence received a low score and lack of excellence received a high score.

9.3 Analyzing Missing Data

Given the virtual impossibility of attaining valid data across all measures for all participants, our analysis of every research project faces the challenge of handling some missing data. Some statistical techniques sail smoothly (and blindly) despite the missing data, but statistical techniques that focus on relationships among measures and/or change over time or across conditions encounter a need to estimate the most likely value of the missing data and include these simulated values in the analyses. Random missing data impose a loss of power, and systematic missing data can impose not only a loss of power, but also false generalizations. For example, the infants or toddlers who have missing data can also differ in cognitive, linguistic, temperament, motivation, or focal constructs. One strategy to explore this problem is to compare participants with missing and non-missing data on auxiliary measurements of other potentially relevant dimensions and use these data to define and defend appropriate generalizations.

One traditional technique for the statistical estimation of missing data was to replace the missing value with the mean of the values attained by comparable participants. This model has some intuitive appeal based on the definition of comparable participants, and it also has some problems (e.g., adding a new score that is the same as the mean will automatically reduce the variance of the distribution).

Recent statistical innovation uses a simulation-based approach in which missing data are replaced by multiple simulated values (see Enders, 2013 for an easily readable summary of relevant approaches). The resulting set of analyses is then combined in an effort to support inferential conclusions that incorporate uncertainty that is caused by simulated missing data. Some statisticians are confident that their estimated data are based on the higher powers that govern or predict behavior. Those of us who are more rational and less statistical will believe that all estimated data are built upon some aspect of estimation and are thus ultimately a form of clairvoyance: no statistical estimation technique gives us the power to see objects or events that do not exist and thus cannot be directly perceived by our senses. However, we also recognize that some forms of imputation are more impressive than others. Single-imputation methods treat imputed values no differently from observed ones. In contrast, multiple imputation uses a distribution of imputed data to evoke the most credible simulation.

Returning to a previous topic, it seems possible that multiple imputation tools can provide an innovative and statistically sophisticated strategy for detecting outliers. For example, it could be informative to reverse the process of multiple imputation and use it to perform selective amputation in which we identify an outlier, change it to missing, look at the distribution of replacement values that emerge via multiple imputation, evaluate the suspicious value's position within the distribution, and if it is extremely unlikely, we label it an outlier and remove it.

9.4 Assessing the Significance of Statistical Significance

English statistician, biologist, and geneticist Ronald Fisher gets mixed reviews. His productive career during the first half of the 20th century created many statistical techniques that are still widely used (e.g., analysis of variance, maximum likelihood estimation, and the z-distribution), and Queen Elizabeth II promoted him to Sir Ronald Fisher in 1952. In contrast, methodologic guru Paul Meehl (1978) claims that "Sir Ronald has befuddled us, mesmerized us, and led us down the primrose path. I believe that the almost universal reliance on merely refuting the null hypothesis as the standard method for corroborating substantive theories in the soft areas is a terrible mistake, is basically unsound, poor scientific strategy, and one of the worst things that ever happened in the history of psychology" (p. 817). The issue here is inference based on the idea that we can use statistical techniques to reject or disprove the null hypothesis (i.e., that there is no effect) and thus claim to have found what is labeled a statistically significant effect. In Fisher's classic "lady tasting tea" experiment (Fisher, 1935), a lady claimed the ability to discriminate cups in which tea was added first versus cups in which milk was added first. The protocol of the experiment was that the lady received 8 randomly ordered cups in which 4 were tea-then-milk and 4 were milk-then-tea, and she correctly identified milk-first versus tea-first for all 8 cups. Fisher estimated that the probability of her attaining this performance based on random selection would be approximately 1.4%. Thus, she could have been a lucky guesser, but he considered the level of probability for this interpretation to be low enough to interpret her claim as statistically significant and therefore reject the null hypothesis that she cannot discriminate the two conditions. The specific criterion for claiming statistical significance was eventually set at probability < 0.05.

For a more contemporary example of testing statistical significance, imagine the following scenario: You are teaching a lecture class to 25 students, and you occasionally lecture in a new format that you hope students will find helpful. To evaluate the efficacy of your new strategy, you distribute a card to each student and ask them to rate the class on a scale from 4.0 for a great class to 1.0 for a terrible class, and you collect these cards on a day in which you use the new format and a day in which you use the old format. When you examine the data, the mean score on the cards is 3.4 for the new format and 3.0 for the old format. This difference is relatively small and you wonder if your new format is having an effect. You then invent a method to evaluate the difference. You shuffle the index cards for each day, deal a set of 10 cards and calculate the mean, combine the cards and shuffle them again, deal another set of 10 cards and calculate another mean, repeat this process 20 times, and then calculate the standard deviation of the 20 means. If the standard deviation is 0.10, the difference between the mean scores for the two formats is impressive. If the average standard deviation is 1.2, the difference between the mean scores for the two formats is unimpressive and can be viewed as reflecting no effect. In a contrasting scenario, you are now teaching the lecture class to 250 students. You use a similar strategy, but this time you deal sets of 50 cards. You now get a relatively low standard deviation, and even a difference between 3.2 and 3.3 looks relatively impressive.

Critics see many problems associated with using null hypothesis statistical testing (NHST) to interpret data. Most saliently, rejecting the null hypothesis provides relatively little information about whether or not a theory is correct. For example, the null hypothesis that A = B could be rejected if A > B or if B > A, and the magnitude of the difference could be small or large. Failure to reject the null hypothesis could indicate that A = B, but could also indicate that the experiment was under-powered or flawed in some other way, and thus failure to reject the hypothesis would support no persuasive conclusions regarding the truth of the hypothesis. From this perspective, the probabilistic criterion for statistical significance does not necessarily align with practical or theoretical significance, and thus creates a context in which an extremely large number of statistical tests will almost always generate false rejection of some null hypotheses. Another perspective for criticizing NHST is that it can lead to two different categories of error. A Type I error is a false positive in which we claim that a hypothesis was correct (e.g., an analysis suggests that confidence has a positive effect on performance but confidence does not have a positive effect on performance). A Type II error is a false negative in which we claim that our hypothesis was not supported (e.g., an analysis suggests that confidence has no effect on performance but confidence does have a positive effect on performance).

I do not see NHST as inherently evil, but it can definitely be problematic. For example, NHST can claim that a correlation of 0.33 is statistically significant and thus supports the claim that A predicts B. Here is a metaphor I frequently use to put this into perspective: A correlation of 0.33 accounts for 10% of the variance. Imagine that a piano player is preparing to put 10 fingers on a keyboard, and we know that one of the fingers will be on B^b. Given that we know one note and we do not know the other nine notes, in what sense can we predict what the chord will sound like? All we can say is that one particular note will be among the notes and thus play a small role in the overall effect. That is a very weak definition of prediction, and it introduces a perspective called effect size. Effect size is an index of the relation between variables that is much more informative than statistical significance per se. Various measures of effect size are available, and Hedges (2008) provides a useful summary. Interpretations of effect size will evolve when this parameter is included in all publications, and contemporary journal editors are steering developmental science toward this important goal.

From the perspective of prediction, I am more comfortable with NHST when research is based on a specific set of point predictions that are being tested with the grave risk of refutation. For example, a study could test the hypothesis that people who are feeling more confident will have stronger working memory and thus be able to respond faster and more accurately in a task in which a response is based on their working memory. The zone of research where I often see this opportunity is longitudinal studies where a new proposal emerges to use already collected data to identify participants who would be expected to have some specific outcome eventually and then conduct research that tests this specific hypothesis. For example, if aspects of early vocabulary are expected to have some specific implications for success in classrooms, preliminary examination of early vocabulary scores could identify one group of participants who are at risk and another group who should have no problems. A dissertation could then be proposed in which members of the risk group and the control group are assessed using measurements such as grades in elementary school, language assessments conducted in a laboratory, or interviews with teachers and/or parents regarding ongoing academic success. If the risk group is performing notably worse than the control group on these outcome measures, the initial hypothesis has survived grave risk of refutation and thus has attained additional credibility. If the scores on the outcome measures overlap, either the initial hypothesis has been undermined or the measurement techniques are questionable. The bottom line here is that the cumulative knowledge about group differences that we accrue from this type of research seems much more valuable than the cumulative knowledge we would accrue from a generic longitudinal follow-up in which multiple analyses were used to find any variables that have statistically significant group differences linked to previous assessments.

Another important tool for moving forward in statistical analysis is Bayesian analysis, which is a traditional idea that has emerged recently as a potential statistical tool that would be more effective than null hypothesis statistical testing. This topic is too complicated to summarize in the present context, particularly for a relatively unsophisticated user of statistics like me. For an introduction to this topic, I highly recommend a series of articles introduced by John K. Kruschke (2011) that explain how Bayesian inference is intuitively more coherent than NHST because it provides factors that correlate with traditional probability calculations and also offers a notably different perspective on statistical significance. The articles explore "the intuitiveness of Bayesian inference, the consistency of Bayesian conclusions with conclusions from NHST, and the richness of Bayesian inference when used in its full-fledged form of parameter estimation and hierarchical modeling." Johnson (2013) carries this conclusion a step further by connecting Bayesian hypothesis tests and traditional NHST in a way that leads to altering the probability values associated with significant findings. Another useful perspective on Bayesian analysis is an article by Gopnik and Wellman (2012) in which they offer an updated "theory theory" using a computational framework based on probabilistic causal models and Bayesian learning. The bottom line here is that a developmental scientist who finds these articles too difficult to read (e.g., me) should realize that this lack of statistical sophistication indicates the need for further education in statistical analysis.

9.5 Modeling

The term modeling has a broad range of definitions and generally refers to the strategy of using a particular entity as a tool for helping us envision, understand, or predict a phenomenon. For example, retailers show photographs of people wearing fancy, expensive clothing with the goal of having us envision how attractive we would be if we wore these clothes. Basketball analysts show us an array of X's, O's, and arrows to help us understand how so many basketball teams shoot 3-point shots with little defensive pressure when they are playing against the Carolina Tar Heels coached by Roy Williams. From a more scientific perspective, meteorologists have developed a wide array of models that use atmospheric parameters to predict potential changes in those parameters at particular locations. The weather reports that we see in the media are based on these models, but if we use a weather website to monitor the discussion among forecasters, we realize that they are viewing multiple models that are not necessarily offering the same predictions. Their challenge is to select the model that is most likely to be correct at a specific location under specific circumstances. For an even better introduction to this topic, read Simmering, Triesch, Deák, and Spencer (2010), an article that "explores the concerns, attitudes, and historical trends that underlie the tension between two cultures: one in which computational simulations of behavior are an important complement to observation and experimentation and another that emphasizes evidence from behavioral experiments and linear models enhanced by verbal descriptions."

Advances in the world of computing and statistics have led to a strong tendency for developmental scientists who conduct research that has relatively large numbers of participants to model their data and to report a model as their conclusion. From this perspective, a model is a structural description of the data in a format that could allow description, prediction, or explanation of how various constructs are interrelated. When data are modeled, the statistics that are applied to the model give us a metric of the degree to which the model fits the data and the chances that this alignment could occur by chance. When a model is statistically significant, we conclude that this fit would not have occurred by chance, although this does not necessarily mean that the model is an excellent fit for the data, or even the best fit, or that it provides us a useful tool for making predictions. Looking back at the history of models, this approach was very compelling when we used a mean to describe the expected value for a group or a scatterplot to describe the most likely combination of two parameters. The more complicated models in recent time are less compelling, and in my opinion as a naïve data analyst, they are notably vulnerable to misleading us in various ways if we simply focus on numbers and equations without considering variables and definitions of fit.

Consider this perspective on the complexity of modeling: A very supportive friend decides to update your wardrobe by giving you a new outfit composed of a sweater, a button-down shirt, pants, gloves, socks, and shoes. You put on these clothes, and your friend asks you to evaluate how well they fit. From a statistical modeling perspective, a number could be calculated that describes how well each item fits and the overall fit of the wardrobe. However, the fact that the fit of the clothes can be modeled does not mean that these are the best clothes for you. A different set of clothes might fit much better and be more comfortable. Individual items might require different definitions of fit. A button-down shirt is relatively inflexible, so its metric of fit would be different than the fit of a sweatshirt, which is much more flexible. Similarly, gloves would need a much more specific fit in comparison to socks. And, some items are more affected by a particular aspect of poor fit: pants and gloves that are a bit too large are much better than pants and gloves that are too small. For socks and sweatshirts, being too small or too large is less problematic. Finally, some items could be more important than others: The fit of shoes is very important, and much more important than the fit of a sweater. From the perspective of these various complications, it seems notably unrealistic to evaluate a model that uses a simplistic, undifferentiated, generic metric of fit.

Another perspective is to consider an alternative interpretation of your friend's question about how well the clothes fit. Size is relevant, but fit could also be defined as how well the clothes align with your personality, goals, closet, or suitcase. The challenge here is to recognize that statistical fit can support various theoretical interpretations. At one extreme, we could construct a model based on a priori hypotheses about the direction and strength of the relation among all variables in the model. In this situation, statistically significant fit supports the a priori theory. At the other extreme, and more commonly occurring in the research that we see, the model is adjusted to maximize fit with the data and is then given a theoretical façade. The difficulty that emerges for cumulative developmental science is to interpret this configuration as the test of a hypothesis rather than the more appropriate interpretation of it being the generation of a hypothesis that now needs to be tested.

Bauer and Reyes (2010) describe a strategy for modeling data that seems particularly compatible with the challenges faced by developmental scientists. Longitudinal data can be analyzed using latent curve models, hierarchical linear growth models, group-based trajectory models, or growth mixture models. It would be far beyond my competence to present the pros and cons of each of these models. However, Bauer and Reyes provide a demonstration that helps us understand the differences among models and the need to select the appropriate model. At the lowest level of understanding of the different types of models, one perspective is that individual differences constitute a continuum. Our focus in developmental science is usually on how individuals change over time, and from this perspective, we know that some individuals change rapidly, and others change slowly. Bauer and Reyes then note a second approach that acknowledges that some individuals differ from other individuals qualitatively. That is, one group changes over time in a different way than another group. Carrying this one step further, a third approach to modeling is the realization that there can be qualitatively different patterns of change and quantitative differences within each particular pattern. Another sophisticated approach to modeling is described by Bauer, Gottfredson, Dean, and Zucker (2013) as a strategy for looking at individuals nested within groups. Specifically, they describe a multilevel model that uses repeated measures data on individuals clustered within groups to notice the effects of groups.

From a broader perspective, Bauer and Reyes (2010) demonstrate that different approaches to modeling can be applied to the same set of data. As each model is applied and explored, we see that different tools can be used and that the explanation that emerges is different, although not obviously right or wrong. The bottom line is the challenge we face regarding how to choose the appropriate model. The Bauer and Reyes explanation is somewhat bewildering: Theory can suggest a model being better, but theory is often ambiguous regarding details like the nature of individual differences. The bottom line is that modeling is an art and a science. There is no automatic rule that says exactly which model should be used, how many variables the model should include, or how models can be compared, but by being aware of the different types of models and by accruing skills in how models function, we will be advancing toward an improved developmental science. It is also important to have independent validation to prove that each of the influences have been measured correctly. Without this, the lack of influence could be a lack of measurement, and a model could reflect degree of measurement per se rather than relative influence.

10 Interpreting Research Results

Whatever perspective we use to describe the endeavor that we call science, the obvious definition of success in science is the accrual of new knowledge that includes the description of a phenomenon and some degree of generalized interpolation or extrapolation on the basis of that description. When constructs and variables have been defined appropriately, measured in an appropriate sample and context, and analyzed using appropriate statistics, the next step is to interpret the statistical analyses appropriately. If the interpretation does not yield an accurate and replicable description of a phenomenon, the research process would be more appropriately labeled creative writing, philosophy, or spiritualism. And, if the interpretation does not yield generalized interpolation or extrapolation, the research process would be labeled archival storage, inventory, or census-taking.

10.1 General Concerns

It is hard to imagine that any experienced developmental scientist has not encountered various moments in which imperfect aspects of data have become apparent. Using a comparison of data across multiple studies addressing the same phenomenon, Schmidt (2010) accrued an array of inconsistencies that led him to conclude that "data often look you in the eye and lie to you – without even blinking – and this is especially true when interpretation of data is based on significance testing" (p. 239). Some developmental scientists would consider this conclusion to be exaggerated, but Schmidt's analysis does yield an important list of topics to keep in mind when interpreting results. These topics include a lack of awareness of variability due to incorrect measurement; a failure to recognize that some new constructs are completely redundant with existing constructs; the presence of unrecognized errors in data coding and transcription; measurement that has caused artificial restriction of range; data that have been dichotomized into two groups rather than being viewed as a continuous distribution, etc.

Fiedler, Kutzner, and Krueger (2012) provided an important perspective to consider when interpreting data: there are some problems that emerge in the context of conclusions that are false positives (i.e., that falsely claim the success of a hypothesis) and these problems can be contrasted with problems that emerge in the context of false negatives (i.e., that falsely claim the failure of a hypothesis). Scrutiny on incorrect conclusions can be shifted to pay more attention to either type of error. Traditionally, false positives seem particularly problematic because we are asserting a truth that is actually false. Fiedler et al. persuasively assert that the opposite is true. Specifically, a false positive is initially problematic, but as discussed in previous chapters, evolutionary epistemology will impose additional scrutiny on all hypotheses and eventually will reveal hypotheses that should be rejected. The problem with a false negative is that the hypothesis has now been declared unconscious (if not dead) and may experience an extremely long coma. The general message here is that we should always consider alternative hypotheses and more general explanations when interpreting our data, which include appropriately constrained interpretations of our hypotheses that were supported by statistically significant results and appropriately optimistic sympathy for our hypotheses that were not supported.

Wagenmakers, Wetzels, Borsboom, van der Maas, and Kievit (2012) provide another perspective on why we should diligently constrain our support for our own hypotheses. Given that developmental scientists are human beings, we are vulnerable to a confirmation bias that can have various manifestations: interpreting ambiguous information as consistent with our inherent beliefs; searching for information that confirms our favorite hypotheses; disproportionately remembering evidence that supports our hypotheses; and covertly or overtly dismissing evidence that is inconsistent with our hypotheses. One interesting strategy that could address this problem would be to have all research proposals registered in a format that will dictate eventual reporting of the results from predetermined analyses whether or not the scientists like them. This constraint is currently in place for clinical trials and could be extended to include a much wider array of research. Wagenmakers et al. also propose a more localized strategy that could help us avoid confirmation bias: divide a new data set into two halves and analyze each half separately. The first half could be used for an exploratory analysis in which various tools are used to identify possible effects. The second half of the data could then be used for a confirmatory analysis in which specific statistical techniques are used to test the effects that emerged in the exploratory analysis. The obvious constraint of this strategy is having enough data to implement it.

10.2 Interpreting Correlations

If x is correlated with y, it is possible that x causes y, and if x is not correlated with y, it is unlikely that x causes y. The logic here seems relatively simple, but with deeper scrutiny, a complex issue is being assessed with inappropriate simplicity. For example, a correlation between maternal talkativeness and infant vocabulary could possibly support the claim that maternal talkativeness causes increased infant vocabulary (Hart & Risley, 1995; Pan, Rowe, Singer, & Snow, 2005). It is also possible that infants with increased vocabulary evoke more talk from their mothers, or that talkative mothers are also likely to engage in more book reading and family discussion, have higher IQ scores, pay attention to the intellectual aspects of the child's environment, or be married to a talkative father, all of which could have an effect on infant vocabulary. And if an epigenetic influence can make a person more talkative, the genetic influence that creates the talkative mother and the talkative environment might be passed directly to the child. If a randomly assigned treatment is available that makes mothers more talkative and their infants subsequently have increased vocabulary, this adds credibility to the claim that maternal talkativeness causes increased infant vocabulary. However, here too there are alternative interpretations to consider. For example, the talkativeness manipulation might cause a mother to be more attentive to her infant in many contexts, which may lead to an infant's increased curiosity about learning the names of things. Or, the manipulation might lead a mother to do other things such as read more or spend more time playing verbal games, with either of these peripheral activities causing an increase in the infant's vocabulary. The bottom line is that when we attempt to interpret a correlation we must always use explicit and open-minded considerations of the possibilities that x causes y, y causes x, or z causes both x and y.

Another problematic zone of correlation interpretation emerges in research that attempts to identify a risk factor that has a causal influence on a later emerging problem. For example, consider the claim that excessive exposure to media violence causes children to become inappropriately aggressive, which could be based on a correlation between exposure to media violence and inappropriate aggressiveness. An alternative explanation of this correlation is that children who are inappropriately aggressive enjoy media violence and thus willingly obtain excessive exposure. Or, the effect could be due to a particular risk factor or something that caused the risk factor (e.g., having a younger mother, a less educated mother, or a lower SES). General clinical risk factors such as exposure to alcohol, smoking cigarettes, poor nutrition, excessive stress, etc. are likely to be components of a broader spectrum of influences, and thus while they are correlated with risk, the model for explaining the mechanism that leads to clinical problems does not view the risk factor itself as being causal. A further complication here is the recently emerging science of epigenetics in which aspects of the environment, which include not only air, water, food, etc., but also parent behavior, stress, mood, etc., can alter the configuration of the genomic processes that underlie all aspects of behavior (Moore, 2015).

A similar problem emerges when a treatment is interpreted as causing a beneficial effect. Even if individuals are randomly assigned to receive a treatment or a control, variations in uptake of treatment can reflect underlying self-selection of treatment. For example, a child who is being tutored to become a better reader may engage in more treatment because the child finds reading more interesting. Or, the child may engage in more treatment because a parent is advocating for, implementing, and enforcing the use of an obvious intervention. Random assignment to treatment or control should reduce this problem, but it is also relevant to consider various possible explanations for why the treatment is working.

Correlations are an obvious way to explore individual differences, but it is important to note and remember that they are not the only way. Bauer (2011) points to the value of correlations, and then describes moderation models, finite mixture models, and random effects models, and each model shows how it provides a better understanding of phenomena, like the relationship between depression and drug consumption. Another important perspective is the distinction between measuring individual differences on a particular pair of variables across many people concurrently versus monitoring people longitudinally and looking at possible changes over time and different patterns in that aspect of individual difference. The bottom line is that inferring "causes" from correlations often has negative/adverse ramifications and is never logically justified.

10.3 Interpreting Change Over Time

Longitudinal studies are crafted as a mechanism for exploring the functionality of developmental processes. For example, how does an infant develop an attachment to her parent? To explore this question, we could note the infant's relationship with her parent at a particular age, then observe aspects of the parent–child interaction that could be affecting the infant's relationship with her parent, and then monitor this dyad longitudinally to see how the relationship emerges into the phenomenon that we have labeled attachment. Or, how does a child develop a strategy to use when solving a problem? This could be explored in a short-term longitudinal study, but the general design again is to present the problem, monitor the child's behavior, monitor how that behavior changes over time, and identify the approach that the child uses that could be labeled a strategy.

Researchers who measure attachment using the Ainsworth Strange Situation (Ainsworth & Bell, 1970) usually administer this tool at 12–14 months because this is the time frame in which the Strange Situation is effective. The fact that attachment is measured at 12–14 months does not imply that attachment emerges at this point in time. Rather, attachment reflects a complex interactive process that begins early in life and is reflected in many aspects of infant behavior. Researchers tend to measure aspects of the process such as parent–child interaction earlier than they measure the attachment classification that emerges in the Strange Situation, so we often see empirical reports that suggest that attachment is a causal outcome of earlier influences such as parent–child interaction. Given that attachment has emerged during the same time frame, it could have caused the earlier predictors rather than have been a result of aspects of the infant that were measured earlier. Also, assessing attachment using a measurement tool that is only effective at a particular age ignores the important question of how attachment develops. Age-specific measurement tools raise comparable concerns for many other constructs in addition to attachment.

Longitudinal studies also have some inherent design characteristics that could influence the viability of a causal interpretation. One characteristic is repeated testing. Researchers often repeat a test many times because the test is being used to monitor the child's level of competence. However, administering the procedure multiple times could be altering how the child is responding to the procedure. Thus, the testing per se in a longitudinal study can be causing a change. Another problematic aspect of a longitudinal study is that although it is occurring within the temporal framework of the experimental design, the participant is also living in a real world in which other changes might be occurring across time. From a simple perspective, at some points in a longitudinal study a child will be on summer vacation, in school, and affected by other seasonal variations. Furthermore, the efficacy of an educational intervention could be altered if participants are attending a school attacked by a person with a gun, a tropical storm, or a tornado. These are extremely dramatic examples, but the general point is that from a historical perspective, any range of time can contain various influences that affect the outcomes of ongoing longitudinal studies.

A cumulative developmental science requires realistic longitudinal models that recognize the complexity of development. For example, causal relations over time can reflect equifinality and/or multifinality. In equifinality (also called convergent causality), significant differences that are detected at the beginning can all lead to the same outcome. In multifinality (also called divergent causality), individuals who are identical at the beginning can eventually attain significant differences. One obvious example of this is the various differences eventually present in identical twins. Another realistic longitudinal model that incorporates complexity is the situation described by Meehl (1978) as a "random walk" in which a person's atypical carbohydrate breakfast leads to mid-morning hypoglycemia, which leads to a temper outburst at the boss, which leads to a failure to get an expected promotion, which leads to notable disappointment for an ambitious wife, which leads to a divorce scandal, followed by emergence of alcoholism, and eventual suicide. Finally, an autocatalytic model includes the complication of a change becoming self-sustaining. For example, when depression emerges, the depressed person then spends too much time in bed, loses his/her job, and the person's life deteriorates further, thus promoting deeper depression.

10.4 Interpreting Clinically Relevant Data

Developmental science can address various clinically relevant themes such as diagnosing clinical disorders, exploring their causes, or mapping the array of challenges they evoke. However, one of the most prominent of these themes is to identify and evaluate possible interventions. The assessment of interventions is often conducted using a randomized clinical trial (RCT) in which participants receive a treatment or a placebo and are evaluated subsequently for potential change. Outcomes in RCTs are often based on standardized developmental assessments, and one obvious strategy is to compare the effects of the treatment with the effects of a placebo. Two areas of potential improvement in developmental science are to incorporate a broader perspective on outcomes and whether or not the intervention has been effective.

Standardized developmental assessments and other behavioral procedures can be affected by clinically relevant themes and also by peripheral aspects of a clinical problem. For example, a child who has suffered from a difficulty with attention can be experiencing improved attention evoked by an intervention but will still be affected by the lack of knowledge, confidence, motivation, etc. that has evolved during the clinical problem. Some developmental assessments and behavioral procedures could be better than others as direct assessments of the change that has potentially occurred due to the intervention. Another zone of assessment with potential advantages is biomarkers. For almost all clinical problems, access to an internal biomarker could provide evidence indicating the timing of the intervention's effect, the amplitude of the effect, and the stability over time. Each of these aspects can be, and are typically, measured less directly using behavioral data.

Another zone of productive assessment of outcomes is to include the clinically challenged individuals' perspectives on how they are functioning and their feelings regarding their clinical problems. These measures can detect various aspects of the treatment that are not tapped by the assessment procedures, and they can also evaluate the efficacy of a placebo effect. When research demonstrates a placebo effect, this is typically seen as less successful from a scientific perspective. However, it can also be seen as vitally important from a broad therapeutic perspective.

A simple statistical assessment of a treatment effect has value but is not the only perspective that is relevant. Interventions in developmental science may or may not be effective for various reasons, such as not changing the parent, changing the parent but not changing the child, or changing the parents' behaviors or beliefs but not both. These factors lead to a perspective in which we should not only conduct group comparisons of treatment and placebo, but also identify the individuals who were positively affected by the treatment, those who were not affected by the treatment, and those who were negatively affected by it. This perspective allows identification of variables such as the child's cognitive style, temperament, motivation, family support, etc. that can be used to determine who will be positively affected by a particular intervention. Some interventions will be appropriate for a relatively wide range of children, but it seems highly unlikely that a single intervention would work equally well for everyone suffering from a particular clinical problem.

Finally, we should consider deficit versus surplus effects of clinical treatment. A frequently occurring theme in research on behavioral development is to identify a deficit and find ways to remediate it. For example, research might indicate that a child who is a poor reader in comparison to his or her peers benefits from supplemental exercises that facilitate an appropriate eye movement pattern or a more extensive comprehension of terms. It is important to note that an intervention that remediates a deficit does not necessarily help children who do not have a deficit. For example, children who suffer from anemia show significant increases in various aspects of cognitive development when they receive supplemental iron, but this does not imply that iron would provide a general enhancement of cognitive ability in children with normal levels of iron.

10.5 Harvesting Conclusions in the Context of Discovery

Many developmental scientists view the statistical analysis of quantitative data as the only mechanism for harvesting results from their research. From a broader perspective, many aspects of the research process provide insights into the questions we are trying to answer through our research. Thomas Kuhn (1962/1970) used the phrase "context of discovery" as a way to describe the process of generating hypotheses and contrasted it with the "context of justification," which is the process of determining whether a hypothesis should be accepted or rejected. Popper (1934) viewed the contexts of discovery versus justification as a distinction between how an idea is generated and whether or not the idea survives. Hans Reichenbach (1951) saw the distinction between the contexts of discovery and justification as theory creation versus criticism. Consolidating these definitions, the context of justification allows us to move forward by testing hypotheses; the context of discovery allows us to clarify questions, generate hypotheses, and become familiar with the constructs that will allow us to measure, predict, and explain phenomena, but neither context provides definitive answers.

Developmental science can be improved if we are always looking for ways to use the qualitative understanding that emerges in the context of discovery to improve our research by helping us encounter the actual phenomenon that we are trying to understand. My students quickly learn that their implementation of a new procedure for assessing infants will almost always include a pilot phase in which they administer the infant assessment procedure to me. A particularly salient memory of this context is what I learned as a participant observer in a study decades ago in which a student was presenting stimuli to infants via rear-projection slides. Viewing the stimuli myself, I noticed that stimuli that had a circular shape projected a very bright core that would probably cause infants to divert their gaze. Without knowing the actual cause, this diversion could be incorrectly interpreted as reflecting disinterest in the stimuli rather than avoidance of an uncomfortable light. In another study, I noticed that the examiner kept appearing and disappearing on the left side of the screen, which might induce a bias toward the stimuli on that side.

Early in my career, I had the opportunity to work with a prominent developmental psychologist who was sometimes described as "shooting from the hip" (i.e., making assertions on the basis of relatively limited empirical support) but who also had a remarkable tendency to "hit the target." From my perspective, the mechanism that supported this apparent contradiction was the fact that his perspective on empirical research included observing almost every testing session in which empirical data were accrued. The notes that he recorded in this context of discovery influenced his subsequent analysis in the context of justification. He may have tended to focus on findings that objectively confirmed his hypotheses (i.e., shoot from the hip), but his familiarity with his target had a positive influence on his marksmanship.

Research conducted in the context of discovery does not replace the need for an eventual quantitative test of a specific hypothesis in the context of justification. However, a thorough harvest of the rich and varied information that is available in the context of discovery can confer a major improvement in the efficacy of the subsequent quantitative research. I often recommend that students who are writing an honors project, master's thesis, or dissertation optimize the discussion section by extending the conclusions based on statistical analyses with whatever else they learned from the context of discovery. This can include interpretation of the data, but also explanations of why the results did not align with expectations. Another example is to identify participants in a longitudinal study who have experienced an outcome of interest and then conduct a retrospective examination of early data to identify possible predictors of that outcome. And broadly, insights in the context of discovery can also generate a collection of creative new hypotheses and measurement strategies that will improve subsequent research. Incorporating a macroscopic perspective in addition to a microscopic focus is a valuable strategy for noticing, examining, and engaging in phenomena of possible relevance in developmental science and many other sciences.

10.6 Meta-Analyses

Meta-analysis is a statistical strategy for combining results across a large number of studies. This is obviously a very important technique for attaining the goal of a cumulative array of knowledge. From a broad pre-statistical perspective, Cooper and Koenka (2012) described their exploration of published articles that are reviews of research. Their analysis moves beyond meta-analysis, and looks more generally at how we can combine studies. They see the advantages and purposes of reviews and offer guidance through the steps that lead to reducing them effectively. Specifically, these steps include formulating the problem, searching the literature, gathering information from syntheses, evaluating the quality of evidence, analyzing and integrating the outcomes of the syntheses, interpreting the evidence, and presenting the results. Focusing on each of these steps could help us craft better reviews ourselves and seek better reviews from our colleagues.

Reviews can definitely be helpful when we have attained "multiple measurement" by combining the measurements of a construct that have been conducted by multiple researchers. For example, Wellman, Cross, and Watson (2001) compared 178 separate conditions in which a false belief task was used to assess theory of mind in children aged 30–100 months. A developmental curve mapping the average proportion of correct scores in this meta-analysis suggested a systematic increase in theory of mind ability. However, the more sobering aspect of these data was the large number of conditions that dramatically overstated or understated theory of mind development at each age. For example, in the 40–50 month age range, proportion correct scores across conditions included dozens of conditions with scores of less than 20% correct on the focal test of theory of mind, and dozens of conditions with scores of more than 80% correct on a comparable test.

From a positive perspective, we can see many obvious advantages in statistical meta-analyses. For example, Chan and Arvey (2012) examined the role of meta-analyses and noted many advantages in comparison to single studies: meta-analyses provide a larger sample, allow a general correction for methodologic artifacts within individual studies, and open the possibility for broader explanations or interpretations of results. From an alternative perspective, meta-analyses have weaknesses such as subjectivity in judgments regarding what studies to include and the classic "file drawer problem" noted by Rosenthal (1979) decades ago that refers to studies that are systematically excluded from the review.

Studies that have been published are public information that is usually the primary material in the meta-analysis. However, anyone who has had experience in the world of developmental science knows that not all studies get published. Indeed, the term "publication bias" is based on the recognition that we tend to publish studies that have statistically significant results suggesting a prominent effect. When research shows that there is no effect, or a hypothesis is not correct, the results are usually viewed as negative by journal editors and reviewers, and thus they are likely to not be published. These are file drawer studies in the sense that the data are only accessible to the researcher, and are not made public. Therefore, when a meta-analysis summarizes the effect size across published studies, there is a possibility that it is generalizing based on a subset of studies and thus has a very incorrect conclusion.

Ferguson and Brannick (2012) explored publication bias by examining published meta-analyses. A large percentage of the studies indicated some effort to analyze publication bias, with many finding evidence of the bias. Authors used different techniques to access unpublished studies and to incorporate this phenomenon into their overall synthesis. Searching for unpublished studies obviously seems important, but a systematic analysis suggests that this effort for improvement can actually cause problems. Ferguson and Brannick found that the authors of the meta-analyses themselves were the main contributors of unpublished studies, and authors also tended to acquire more unpublished results from friends and well-known authors than from others. This leads to the disappointing conclusion that meta-analyses that include unpublished studies can be more likely to show bias (albeit of a different type) than meta-analyses that do not include unpublished studies.

In recent years, statisticians have developed techniques for evaluating meta-analyses. One visual tool is a funnel plot in which the treatment effect is paired with the size of the study. If the distribution is a symmetric triangle, a summary of the included studies seems representational. If the distribution is asymmetric, this can indicate a publication bias or a systematic difference based on the size of the study or the measure of effect size. The possible causes of asymmetry in the final plot are complicated, but it is important to explore this warning flag before offering a simple interpretation.

11 Building Better Developmental Science

Previous chapters have examined each component of developmental science research with the goal of providing a perspective that will allow us to scrutinize our research (and the research of our colleagues and students), detect aspects of the research that can be improved, and implement changes that will move us toward that improvement. From a broader perspective, developmental science is occurring in the context of our academic or research institutions, our professional organizations, our community of developmental scientists, our sources of funding for research, and how we are perceived by our academic peers and the public. This chapter will offer some suggestions for improving our profession.

11.1 Better Research Support

From an optimistic perspective, it is obvious that we could create better developmental science if we had easier access to ample funding to support our research. From a more realistic perspective, we should try to improve the policies that guide current research funding from governments and institutions. Developmental scientists who are currently receiving adequate funding to support their ongoing research will probably be less supportive of changes than those of us who are currently unfunded. But, from a broad perspective that includes the ongoing diminishing of research funding, the majority of us would probably see advantages in reducing the support for large ongoing studies and redeploying funding to support the pilot work and measurement development that would allow new studies to emerge. For example, De Los Reyes and Wang (2012) provide a sobering description of the grant review process and recommend that we shift from our current "fund or not fund" model and move toward a more broad distribution of funds that provides some research funding to a very large proportion of scientists who have submitted grants. One obvious constraint is that some research cannot be done with less money, but some institutions and some countries have adopted a productive broad-distribution funding model in which all academic researchers receive minimal but constant annual research funding.

The criteria used to evaluate grants are in a domain in which the decisions sometimes seem to be guided by the arbitrary perspectives of politicians or wealthy controllers of foundations. Funding sources have begun preferring research in developmental science that incorporates underlying biomarkers and neurological measurement. As discussed previously, these tools offer opportunities to improve developmental science and they also offer constraints that will limit developmental science and shift it toward some topics that have questionable relevance. Other funding sources have begun focusing more on translational research that has specific relevance for developmental disorders and other problems such as poor academic performance. All developmental scientists should maintain some focus on the translational implications of their research, but innovative interventions are as likely to emerge from fundamental science as they are from focus on the targeted problem. And, despite the obvious importance of improving measurement, it has always been difficult to obtain funding for this zone of research. From a broader perspective, Nobel science awards are much more likely for contributions to method than for contributions to theory (Greenwald, 2012). Funding in developmental science should be redistributed based on this fact.

The methodological criteria that are used to evaluate grants are another domain in which improvement would be possible. Stronger criteria for effective measurement would improve developmental science and place researchers in a context in which their goal is to implement strong measurement of a limited number of constructs and thus provide cumulative knowledge regarding those constructs. Reviewers with a strong methodologic focus could steer grants toward this goal rather than the goal of measuring enough different constructs to increase the probability of finding at least one statistically significant result. Reviewers should advocate appropriate and effective data analysis, require going beyond single measurements, and encourage the inclusion of explicit replication.

When research is funded at any level, funding sources should require a contract that will lead to having a more formal harvest. For example, all data can be analyzed according to a pre-approved plan and archived in a repository that will be open to other researchers (e.g., meta-analysts). Information in this data archive should include details about recruitment, treatment of missing data, and all analyses including those that are incorporated in publications and those that are not. The data archive could also include some metric of quality. For example, Jarde, Losilla, Vives, and Rodrigo (2013) describe the Q – COH, which is a tool to measure the methodologic quality of specific types of studies. Or, reviewers could be asked to grade each study on a predefined set of dimensions. Archiving all data and including an appropriate formal evaluation will not only help us conduct meta-analyses and literature reviews, but also help us adjust our consciousness toward finding better ways to implement our research. Here is an example of the dimensions that could be evaluated to assess each study's potential for cumulative contribution: appropriateness of study design, breadth and depth of measurement strategy for relevant constructs, inclusiveness of appropriate array of stimulus materials, diversity of participants, degree of anchoring to previous studies, assessment of reliability, appropriateness of statistical analyses, recognition of weaknesses in discussion, harvest of information in the context of discovery, etc. Educational institutions currently provide start-up funds to allow incoming academic scientists to configure their laboratory and launch their research. This policy fails to recognize that equipment can deteriorate, technology can advance, and academic scientists can shift their interests to other topics. Educational institutions and professional organizations should establish a collaborative relationship that will facilitate the transfer of used research equipment among scientists who recognize that "something is better than nothing" and provide support for new equipment that can be in individual laboratories or in institutional laboratories that are available for use by a wide array of academic scientists.

Another zone of research support is the control imposed by the local Institutional Review Board (IRB). Many decades ago some researchers failed to recognize – and attempt to avoid – the possibility that they could harm their research participants. Some examples of this failure are notably salient, but many of us who were engaged in research at this time would not see this as a disastrous context. The implementation of research supervision conducted by the IRB definitely reduced the probability of problems. However, some of us would describe the ongoing evolution of the IRB as promoting a somewhat self-serving survival of this institution. That is, rather than attempting to reduce its role via efficiency and appropriate, more specialized training of researchers, the IRB has attempted to expand and concretize its role. One obvious improvement would be to centralize the review process and provide a mechanism whereby a research project that will be conducted at multiple sites can undergo a single evaluation that not only allows comparable implementation at each site but also offers suggestions to help improve the consistency of implementation across different sites. Another improvement would be to centralize the description of well-established approved measurement tools and their age-specific administration in a formal registry and allow researchers to simply refer to this well-established information rather than provide extensive description and then receive unneeded feedback. One strategy for implementing these improvements would be to shift control of the IRB to researchers and participants rather than the professional administrators whose livelihood is linked to the IRB.

When a study has been completed and further steps are being considered, one important step is replication. This suggestion has been offered by many authors in recent articles, and it reminds me of a creative idea I suggested many decades ago: developmental science students who are pursuing a master's thesis on their path to a Ph.D. should conduct a replication of some published study. This would allow them to understand how important it is to give a functional description of a study and show them how aspects of the implementation of a study can have a dramatic effect on its outcome. And, of course, it would lead them to a creative perspective in which they might see a better way to conduct the experiment that had been designed to answer a specific question in the past and from a possibly unique perspective.

11.2 Promoting Diversity of Culture and Ethnicity

Diversity is a topic that has emerged repeatedly when we ponder research participants, effective measurement tools, problems with missing data, etc. As mentioned previously, conducting cross-cultural research from a single cultural perspective can evoke what Medin et al. (2010) describe as the "home-field disadvantage" in which validity is reduced because the initial culture defines the normative level, the measurement techniques, and the data gathering context. Cultural differences would be rampant in the relative availability of research participants, the comfort participants have with laboratory visits or home visits, and the familiarity participants have with the topics and procedures used to assess constructs.

Hartmann and colleagues (2013) report a literature scan in which they searched for research that is cross-cultural and/or includes ethnic minorities, and they compared a previous scan for 1993–1999 with their new scan for 2003–2009. Their research indicates a relative lack of attention to this topic and they noticed potential causal problems such as the lack of relevant personnel in universities where the research was being conducted and the lack of diversity on journal editorial boards.

Jones (2010) offers a very articulate review of the history of biased or ethnocentric science, particularly regarding the putative inferiority of African Americans. He describes the racist assumptions and stigmatizing beliefs that he has encountered and then recommends various strategies for diversifying psychological science. The first strategy is to diversify those who do the research. The second is to broaden our perspective and diversify theory and research ideas. Finally, he describes the need to develop what he calls a formal diversity science that focuses on diversity per se.

An inspection of photographs of the current faculty in departments and programs in the United States who are pursuing developmental science authenticates the obvious realization that Caucasian men and women continue to dominate this field. Many of us have conducted research focused on other cultures and ethnicities, but as noted in previous chapters, researchers can be strongly affected by their personal perspective. Equal opportunity positions have helped us increase the diversity of professional developmental scientists. However, this is a relatively shallow solution to the problem. Activities such as engaging a diverse array of students in developmental science research when they are in high school or college will greatly increase the probability that they will eventually be developmental scientists who are candidates for academic positions. I remember giving a series of talks to students attending Historically Black Colleges and Universities (HBCUs) regarding graduate school, and being surprised and encouraged by the large number of students who had not realized that most graduate programs in Developmental Psychology and other zones of developmental science offer a stipend and tuition remission to graduate students pursuing a Ph.D.: this new insight could affect their future plans.

11.3 Supporting and Improving Professional Organizations

Our professional organizations face challenges in the current economy and have become less "necessary" now that most professionals have electronic access to all of our contemporary journals. Despite these challenges, the organizations remain present and salient, and continued membership in the relevant professional organizations is helpful for individuals and also can leverage broader changes in our profession. Large professional organizations tend to have maximal potency and can also have an agenda that is strongly influenced by their staff. I have worked with several professional organizations in which I felt that I was advocating for my fellow developmental scientists in a negotiation with staff who were more focused on the fiscal health of the organization that would affect their own job security. In contrast, smaller organizations have less potency but are administrated primarily by developmental scientists who have no fiscal connection to the organization. This leads these organizations to activities that are much more focused on the needs of developmental scientists. For example, the Cognitive Developmental Society holds its biennial meeting in a format in which the meeting begins with a plenary session in which all attendees will hear the same talks, learn from them, and have topics to discuss with colleagues throughout the meeting. Subsequent sessions are a few seminars held simultaneously, which divides the attendees but into relatively large groups so that they learn together about topics of interest. Other professional meetings have extensive simultaneous presentations because their goal is to have all attendees "on the program." This strategy obviously enhances the fiscal benefits of the meeting but it does not seem focused on enhancing the quality of developmental science and developmental scientists.

Any perspective about optimal developmental science should include familiarity with the Center for Developmental Science in Chapel Hill, North Carolina. The initial developmental science initiative that led to the Center for Developmental Science began in the late 1980s when Bob Cairns, Glen Elder, Gilbert Gottlieb, Peter Ornstein, Martha Cox, Jane Costello, and others began a series of weekly meetings that continue today, known as the Carolina Consortium. On the basis of these meetings, a group a faculty at UNC-Chapel Hill, Duke, N.C. State, UNC Greensboro, N.C. Central, and Meredith College banded together to form the Center for Developmental Science, which has continued to be housed on the campus of UNC-Chapel Hill. Developmental science as promoted and supported by the Center for Developmental Science encompasses all aspects of developmental psychology, and expands its perspective to also include relevant fields such as clinical psychology, psychiatry, biological psychology, nutrition, sociology, social work, nursing, education, pediatrics, anthropology, and any other perspective that can contribute relevant expertise to efforts to understand human development.

To improve developmental science, we should seek more efficacy from our professional organizations. For example, some professions stipulate regular updates of relevant knowledge and skills, and to accomplish this goal they offer the relevant training through professional organizations. Developmental science should do this. I can applaud SRCD for their recent institution of some relatively small thematic meetings in addition to their large generic biennial meeting, a change that is more consistent with the educational goal prominent in other organizations such as the Cognitive Developmental Society. I can also note suggestions for improving SRCD that were generated by the task force that I led in 2004 with the charge that we develop strategies to help SRCD "be a central professional organization for researchers and students in all aspects of infant, child, and adolescent development, and its life-long implications." Our suggestions included a wide array of topics:

- providing members with useful information such as job openings and training opportunities;
- forming online connections among communities that shared common interests;
- organizing and/or funding opportunities for members to receive advanced training in new skills and techniques such as statistics and data analysis, physiologic measurement, dissemination and media skills, successful graduate training, the funding process, and writing and oral presentation;
- promoting the development of academic faculty and preparing graduate students and post-docs for success in academic positions in institutions with a wide range of missions or for careers outside academia;
- providing resources to facilitate research such as helping monitor and influence changes in IRB and HIPPA requirements;
- developing resources to help members with IRB issues such as providing a clearinghouse for "adverse effects," providing IRB-relevant materials such as consent forms, and maintaining an archive of descriptions of standard procedures and measures;
- helping members obtain grants through effective lobbying of government organizations and foundations, and education or training of members;
- providing resources to facilitate teaching such as model syllabi and handouts, reviews of textbooks, notes or graphics to accompany specific lectures, photographs or videos relevant to themes in child development, ideas for innovative projects, class assignments, and discussion themes, and listings of useful articles and readings;
- providing resources to facilitate dissemination to audiences outside the research community;
- exploring ways to improve the biennial meeting to bring the membership together to share current research and ideas across a wide range of topics, exploring different presentation formats and alignment of timeslots, ensuring strong program presence for translation and policy, interdisciplinary work, and international perspectives in addition to traditional research, doing more to help first-time attendees feel welcome and to help them navigate the plethora of activities, exploring ways to facilitate the continuing participation of retired members;
- creating new publications when warranted.

The implementation of some of these suggestions occurred and the organization may have been improved. I include this long list of suggestions here because I see them as a broad array of ideas that can direct us toward improvement in many professional organizations relevant for developmental scientists.

11.4 Sharing Our Harvest

Developmental scientists are engaged in developmental science in various ways that should advance our accrual of relevant knowledge. The mechanism for this accrual can include teaching classes or writing books or monographs. The most prominent form of knowledge accrual in recent decades is the publication of peer-reviewed articles in journals and chapters in edited volumes. We share our findings more socially via invited addresses at institutions or speeches, symposia, and posters at professional conferences. Another form of publication, which we have less control over, is articles written by journalists in newspapers, magazines, or websites. Our least prominent form of potential knowledge accrual is our personal collection of grants not accepted for funding, manuscripts that were not accepted for publication, and data from research projects that were unsuccessful.

The physical sciences have a long history and have accrued a theoretical and technological infrastructure that has led to increasingly sophisticated science over many centuries. Given that developmental science has emerged more recently, there is often a more or less implicit assumption that developmental science should be held to the standards that one can derive from other sciences, and developmental scientists are encouraged to borrow from physical science expertise whenever possible. It is important to identify the unique challenges evoked by developmental science, and we must be careful to not presume that all tools of physical science can enable our effort to understand open systems. Awareness of our potential weaknesses should help us strengthen these areas and avoid problems that the weaknesses can cause. As noted frequently in this book, folk psychology is the long-term context that generated many of the theories and constructs that have been incorporated into developmental science. Our progress has helped us confirm or deny many of these theories and evolve increasingly valid measurement techniques. We cannot deny this folk psychological background, but we should realize that it can cause our research to be viewed as gossip or common sense. The obvious remediation here is to clarify our testing of these hypotheses and our assessment of the validity of these constructs. As mentioned previously, we work in an open system rather than a closed system and conduct much of our research with complicated human participants. We cannot use the concrete scientific methods common in the physical sciences and we must scrutinize our methods to keep them as scientific as possible. Physical scientists across the world have access to materials and contexts that are identical. Developmental scientists are all examining limited samples in potentially unique contexts, and must be careful when making generalizations. Despite the reality that human development is too complicated to ever generate specific predictions and universally successful interventions, developmental science is making progress that is impressive and deserves praise rather than dismissal.

Shonkoff and Bales (2011) offer a very interesting strategy for improving our communication. They note the efficacy of developing a relevant and coherent story based on research and then translating it into a format that will provide information effectively for the target audience. The specific goal they describe is to translate research on developmental science into a format that will influence the public and particularly policy makers. The goal of identifying and focusing on a target audience became very salient for me when I attempted to develop a new course called "Practical Perspectives on Early Psychological Development: Parents, Practitioners, & Politicians" that focuses on the description and discussion of research on various aspects of early psychological development that are relevant for the decisions faced by parents, practitioners, and politicians. My target audience in this course was undergraduates majoring in psychology, and my goal in the course was to help these students understand how developmental science is perceived by the obviously important target audiences: parents, practitioners, and politicians. From a broader perspective, to attain the goal of creating developmental science that has important translational implications, we must monitor our publications to ensure that they can be and will be read by individuals who will understand, recommend, and/or implement our translational research.

An additional challenge comes with our efforts to balance research with practical and professional constraints. Most scientists who work in academic settings feel that they face a "publish or perish" admonition that links the quality and quantity of their publications to hiring, promotion, tenure, and the rewards that are linked to productivity. From this perspective, we tend to make the unfortunate decision that every study is publishable whether or not publishing it contributes to the accrual of cumulative knowledge. And, this perspective can bias scientists toward distorted analyses, inappropriate linking of results and hypotheses, and lack of interest in replication (Giner-Sorolla, 2012). Every study could be seen as contributing to our cumulative developmental science in some ways, and the statistically significant rejection of a null hypothesis is not the only definition of contribution. One strategy that will help us attain this goal is to hold ourselves to higher standards for our publications in journals. As mentioned frequently in previous chapters, developmental science can improve if we expect published manuscripts to have better analyses, and the improvement will be more effective if authors understand what is changing and explain their new analyses effectively. If journals add statisticians to their review teams, these statistical experts will be holding us to higher standards and evaluating our ability to understand and describe our data analysis. LeBel et al. (2013) conducted an interesting experiment to see how authors felt about providing four specific details in their manuscripts: excluded subjects, non-reported conditions and measures, and sample size determination. Their conclusion is that researchers like this idea, and that journals should include this information.

I worked with SRCD to launch a new journal that would be a source of brief, accessible, synthetic reports that summarize emerging trends and conclusions within various domains of developmental research that is intended primarily for people trying to stay abreast of progress in areas outside their specialties. The plan was to have articles that are brief and nontechnical but high-quality science. Most of the papers would be research-oriented, providing integrative reviews of a research program or area, but some would address theoretical advances or innovative designs and methods. Topics related to policy and translation would be included as well. Most articles would summarize existing research, but some would focus on promising new directions, research that is needed, or broader issues that relate developmental science to topics in neighboring disciplines such as medicine, health, history, philosophy, sociology, economics, anthropology, law, political science, biology, and neuroscience. We planned for this journal to be a good source of reading and teaching materials for child development courses at the undergraduate and graduate levels and useful for instructors teaching a range of topics, at least some of which are well outside their areas of specialized knowledge. The title of the journal is *Child Development Perspectives* and it continues to prosper.

11.5 Promoting Construct Unity

As we cycle between the context of discovery and the context of justification, we will focus on topics that deserve pursuit, and we will accrue insights into how they work and how to measure them. The ambient consciousness that will promote success is to improve constructs and measurement, with the criteria of validity, reliability, and unity. This allows us to make good use of the context of discovery and avoid being inundated with excessive content. Unity refers to the consolidation of similar constructs when possible, and the formal differentiation among similar constructs when consolidation is not appropriate.

Arthur Staats (1999) describes this problem within the context of the history of science. The initial phase of every science is a random fact-gathering about an interesting phenomenon. The next phase is to search for underlying principles and relationships among the phenomena. Unity can be viewed as a goal that is never complete, but it is a goal that science will always move toward more or less explicitly. E. O. Wilson (1998) labels unity "consilience," and asks why psychology has made so little progress toward unification. Obvious reasons are that this area of research is relatively young in comparison to other sciences, it addresses phenomena that are extremely complex, and it is currently being conducted by thousands of scientists. Sternberg and Grigorenko (2001) offer a broad perspective on unifying psychology and identify some problematic zones. First, as has been mentioned many times in this book, focusing on a single methodology or paradigm is less effective than identifying multiple converging measurement strategies that address the same phenomena. From a professional perspective, a second problem is that scientists in developmental science tend to segregate based on their subdisciplines rather than integrate based on a topic of interest.

From a professional perspective, we need to avoid ongoing tendencies to create and accept unnecessary diversity and redundancy, and we need to devote resources toward attaining unity. One strategy is to make a systematic effort to unify theories. I remember organizing a Consortium on Developmental Theory as an effort to pursue this strategy, and it did not work well. One problem is that our graduate training curriculum has shifted away from broad topics like history and theory, and is focusing more on narrow topics like neuroscience and statistics. Almost every book by Jean Piaget is out of print and many current students in developmental science learn almost nothing about theories. If attaining unity is important, altering curriculum in graduate training and presentations at professional meetings could remediate the problem.

A more practical strategy is to ask reviewers of grants and manuscripts to attempt to avoid redundancy in terminology and establish appropriate techniques for attaining unity. For example, any newly discovered phenomenon or measurement technique should be linked to existing phenomena and measurement techniques. And, we should encourage the creation and publication of reviews and meta-analyses that create linkages within the existing neighborhood of constructs. I can imagine an article that combines self-concept, self-image, self-perception, self-esteem, self-confidence, and self-efficacy, although it would be difficult to combine the 135,941 citations that emerge when we designate "Self" as a word in the Major Subject Heading in PsycINFO [as of August 2015]. Other terms that evoke numerous citations include "Memory" – 84,393, "attention" – 50,951, "Emotion" – 45,190, and "Attachment" – 15,427.

Our professional organizations can also help us attain unity. When I served as co-chair of the SRCD Biennial Meeting in 2011, I was concerned that the keywords that we used to index presentations had evolved as a grab bag of 356 terms that reflected a mixture of categories including broad topics, specific topics, disciplines, research participants, and some ambiguous words rather than an organized list. My colleagues and I devoted considerable effort to organize the keywords, and we attempted to segregate them into meaningful categories and levels. Feedback from over 100 colleagues led to a two-level keyword selection system with a high tier of 12 "Focal Areas" and up to two dozen specific "Aspects" within each Focal Area. For example, a submission under the Focal Area cognitive processes might tap the Aspects memory, attention, and/or categorization. And the same submission might also be associated with the Focal Area language/communication and tap the Aspects comprehension and bilingual.

A second section of the new keyword system was designed to collect what we labeled "Considerations." Specifically, one set of choices would allow submitters to indicate the participant ages that characterize their submission. A second set of choices would allow submitters to indicate the nationality, demographic, and cultural aspects of their sample, and whether or not their sample was selected to randomly represent a population of interest. Finally, submitters would be asked to select the disciplinary approaches that characterize their submission. The keywords selected for each submission were expected to provide information that could be used in various ways. For example, Review Panel Chairs could use the keyword information to help identify an appropriate reviewer for each submission. The Program Office could use the keyword information to facilitate optimal scheduling at the meeting. And, keywords could be used in search engines to help attendees organize their personal schedule. I am confident that moving in this direction was a helpful initial effort, and I hope that subsequent co-chairs and staff will recognize the importance of devoting time and resources toward this important goal and continue to expand or contract the keyword system as needed to improve it.

Another group that could promote our progress toward unity is the editors of our journals. Some journals are currently focused on general topics such as unity, but journals that are focused on more specific zones of research could adjust their policy to accept simple empirical studies and to also accept or invite theoretical manuscripts. Another strategy is to periodically devote issues of each journal to the topic unity/unification/consolidation.

A further step toward unity is for us to avoid the "measurement bandwagon." I add this step because a researcher could use unity as an excuse for conducting all research using a single measure. Publishing multiple studies using a measure like the Ainsworth Strange Situation (Ainsworth & Bell, 1970) does allow consolidation of these studies and relatively straightforward combination of these studies with other research using the same measurement tool. However, attachment is a broad construct that can refer to how a child feels about all parents, how parents feel about their child, and changes in these connections that occur at different ages. From this perspective, we may need to differentiate the term attachment into relevant components, and we definitely need to find an array of relevant measurement techniques.

12 Becoming Better Developmental Scientists

Strategies for improving the quality of developmental science should focus on all aspects of how developmental science is conducted. However, as a final perspective on attaining this goal, it is also important to focus on the individuals who are creating developmental science. Our culture has accrued a virtual library of books offering advice for self-improvement in all aspects of our personal and professional behavior. It would be impossible to summarize that library and present it here, but I do see some potential value in sharing my own perspective on personal and professional development, some based on my creative insights and some based on lessons learned from my mistakes and failures. I also recommend reading the original version of Dale Carnegie's *How to win friends and influence people* (1936). I read it in high school, and I reread it periodically.

12.1 Identifying and Navigating a Successful Career Path

I have a distinct memory of the decision I faced at the end of the second semester of my junior year in college: my father had strongly suggested that I not take over the management of Reznick's Music and Jewelry, and I began pondering "What will I be when I grow up?" My work-study job in Dr. Vincent LoLordo's laboratory in the Psychology Department at UNC-Chapel Hill had been very interesting. I knew many of his graduate students, and when I began pondering my future, I thought about him, and I realized that he had a great job. Specifically, college professors can pursue research on a topic they find interesting, they have much control over their schedule, they can be on vacation all summer, they spend their time on a college campus, and decades later when our economy faced strong challenges, I realized that many of them have notable job security. From this perspective, it became clear to me that I should pursue a career as a college professor, and that is what I did. Working as a college professor has been a great opportunity for me, and it is hard to imagine any career that would have been better.

We enter the world of developmental science in search of a career, and most of us are also motivated by our curiosity about some aspect of development, our enjoyment of conducting research on developmental science, or our broad goal of helping fellow humans who have clinical disorders, developmental disabilities, or problems associated with their demographics. These are goals that our profession allows us to attain. Our profession also allows us to work independently and focus on our own idiosyncratic perspective. Or, we can collaborate with colleagues in our domain or in related domains, and our choices among these options will change as our career progresses. For example, early in one's career, pursuing the same topic as a prominent mentor can create a situation in which our small tree is dwarfed beside our mentor's much larger tree. During mid-career pursuit of tenure and full professorship, first authorship and single authorship have distinct advantages for establishing the credibility of one's voice. During later career, collaboration becomes a strategy for participating in research with ample intellectual opportunities and fewer fundamental duties and responsibilities.

When I am advising/coaching graduate students, my general suggestion has become very predictable. I always recommend that students immediately start editing a slide presentation that is an ongoing draft of their first job talk and keep it in a salient location on the desktop so that the document will be noticed and possibly reviewed and modified every day. The title of the job talk succinctly identifies the question the student is attempting to answer in his/her research. The first slides explain why this question is interesting and important. Subsequent slides describe the progress the student has made toward answering the question of interest. The student's dissertation will eventually be the "heart" of this section, and there will also be some peripheral slides that identify relevant collaborations and research experiences that have helped the student develop skills and knowledge about this topic. These peripheral slides can be most notably valuable if they have a citation to a publication, a manuscript under review, or a conference presentation that includes the student's name. The penultimate slides in the job talk should summarize the progress the student has made toward answering the original question and verifying the claim that this question is interesting and important. The final slides should describe the next steps the student plans to use to pursue the original question and also possible shifts in direction based on what the student has learned thus far.

One advantage of implementing this strategy early in one's career is to attain a useful perspective on the tempting "candy shop" experience at the beginning of graduate school. Sampling a wide array of opportunities is an efficacious strategy for identifying the question we want to answer. However, monitoring this sampling from the job talk perspective can help us notice that our time in the candy shop and our consumption of candy will probably need some limits. Another advantage is that as research opportunities and potential collaborations emerge in our early career, it is important to say "yes" or "no" based on the extent to which these opportunities will fit within the context of our job talk. This perspective can also lead to efforts to enhance the value of these opportunities by attempting to have all of our collaborations include topics, duties, or goals that are more directly relevant to our job talk.

When students seek my advice regarding a postdoctoral experience, the job talk metaphor becomes more relevant and obvious. The decision of whether or not to pursue a postdoctoral experience can be evaluated based on the extent to which the postdoctoral experience will embellish the student's skill set and/or knowledge in ways that will expand and improve parts of the job talk. Another strategy is to use the postdoctoral experience as an opportunity to harvest more publications based on data that have been collected and include them in the job talk. And, while it is possible that the postdoctoral experience will lead to a new or notably modified job talk, this should be a conscious decision rather than a failure to retain focus on the original job talk and use this focus to maximize the value of the postdoctoral experience. Noticing the job talk on the desktop every day in graduate school can help us keep our early professional development salient and well guided.

The early draft of the job talk will eventually become an actual job talk and lead to a job for many developmental scientists. When I am advising/coaching assistant or associate professors, I recommend the same strategy: keep a draft of the job talk on the desktop, continue to revise it, and use it as a perspective to guide decisions regarding personal research endeavors, collaboration with colleagues and students, and prioritization in grants and publications. Early promotion and tenure for most developmental scientists includes some evaluation of teaching and administration, but focuses primarily on research productivity. The list of grants and publications in the CV is an important metric of success, and maintaining a focus on an interesting and important question and making progress toward answering it is the primary resource that young scholars need. The next steps are full professor and distinguished professor, which are steps that require the same progress with the additional criterion of attaining national credibility based on impressive progress being made toward answering an interesting and important question.

The validity of my job talk strategy is based on feedback I have received from people who have used it, and it is also based on information that I learned from my own salient mistakes. My job talk at Yale University in 1987 focused on my interest in infant cognitive development and particularly categorization and language as explored in my dissertation. I had also been working for many years in a laboratory that was focused on behavioral inhibition, so this productive zone added to the strength of my CV and was another topic that was discussed during my interview. Infant cognitive development was the centerpiece of my research at Yale, but my broad array of interests and my collegial collaborative tendency led to a wide array of research projects. When my non-tenure-track folding chair at Yale folded, I began searching for a job again and realized that my ongoing research would need to be distributed among three or more job talks. Fortunately, my interview at UNC-Chapel Hill in 1998 allowed me to include two presentations and my job talk itself was strong enough to attain my job. However, the challenge that I faced when I assembled my array of job talks led to the salient realization that engaging in a wide array of research on interesting topics was not an optimal strategy and that a primary job talk should have been a salient perspective for guiding many decisions throughout my early career.

Having become a full professor with tenure, I once again slipped into my mode of cordial collaboration on a wide array of topics, and I also engaged in teaching and in many administrative opportunities. I am comfortable with having done this, but it has also had some disadvantages. For example, I do not have the thematic research productivity that would warrant a Distinguished Chair or a Nobel Prize. Even within my research on cognitive development, I continued to pursue a wide array of initial studies on interesting topics followed by very little subsequent focused pursuit of those topics in search of significant advance and possible closure. I recently reviewed my history of publications, divided them into topic-oriented subsets, and scanned recent publications in search of advances on these topics. One pattern was very obvious: Research on most of these topics is still ongoing, and most of the questions I pursued have not yet been answered. In fact, my decades-old publications in infant cognitive development that seemed important at the time are now receiving very few citations. This observation made me realize that publications will always be available as evidence from a historical perspective, but the impact of previous publications will abate if the voice of those publications is no longer heard in the public forum. I remember organizing thematic sessions at conferences in which I integrated my findings on particular topics with those of my colleagues who were interested in those topics. When my voice left that chorus, my perspective was not maintained simply based on archival data. This leads to a choice that we should make explicitly: We can move forward on a topic of interest by staying involved in that topic, but if we shift repeatedly to new topics, the value of our previous contributions may abate.

Another decision is how to balance one's interest in measurement and methodology with one's interest in theory and translation. Measurement and methodology in developmental science is an important zone for creativity, technological sophistication, and direct experience. However, measurement and methodology can be viewed from some perspectives as less important than theory, and it can be more difficult to obtain funding for it. My own preference for measurement versus theory probably lowered the trajectory of my career path. However, I am proud of the collection of measurement tools I developed, and I am pleased to see that many of them are still being used.

My final suggestion for identifying and navigating a successful career path is to be aware that research in developmental science can create some difficulties. Recent articles by "Neuroskeptic" (2012) and Gullo and O'Gorman (2012) offer subjective evaluations of a range of phenomena that are inherent in our difficult world of developmental science and that can lead to problems that we will experience. For example, we are attempting to answer interesting and important questions, but the answers to our questions are almost never as straightforward as the answers accrued by our fellow scientists who work in closed systems with more easily measured variables. This difference can undermine our credibility and our access to research support. Another problem from some perspectives is that successful developmental science could be viewed as dehumanizing in the sense that it could allow devious entities to predict and control our fellow humans. This vulnerability is particularly salient in cases where such individuals have the political power to implement this sort of control. When we attain answers to our research questions, the formats some of us use to present our results can be described as overselling, plagiarism, or post hoc storytelling. And, the statistical analyses some of us report can include questionable techniques for dealing with outliers, missing values, probability values, selection of models, etc. Moving into publication mode, we face the challenge of deploying the data from studies that did not yield results that are considered "statistically significant." And, perhaps most disconcerting is the fact that some of our colleagues have been accused of fraudulently crafting data and have not denied this accusation. For example, the Retraction Watch website http://retractionwatch.com/ describes a wide array of published research in all sciences that have been retracted.

12.2 Publishing Our Research

As mentioned previously, most of us face the "publish or perish" admonition during many phases of our career. I will not offer strategies for attaining publications from everything we do in our laboratories, but I do have some suggestions that could help us publish our contributions to a cumulative developmental science, and also reduce the time we waste and the stress we endure while engaged in the reject/revise/accept manuscript-review process.

An important initial step toward publication is to select the appropriate journal where the manuscript should be submitted. This process should include not only exploring the criteria the journal lists for submissions but also scanning abstracts in the journal and reading some relevant articles to get a realistic perspective on the voices of our fellow authors and the ears of the audience we will be trying to speak to. Articles that have been published have met the requirements enacted by the community of reviewers. And, linking our manuscript to other articles in this journal increases our credibility and relevance. If linking our manuscript to these articles is not feasible, this journal is not the appropriate target. A metaphor that is pertinent here is to be aware of the destination of our travel before packing for the trip.

When I began submitting manuscripts for publication in the 1970s, a salient lesson for me was to shift my writing style to be more formal. The strategy that I used was to examine each change that was marked by a reviewer or a copy editor and to accrue a list of the words and phrases that this audience viewed as problematic. In subsequent submissions, I would scan the document for these words and phrases and alter them before submitting the manuscript. Over time, this process allowed me to become "bilingual" and write either formally or informally. Editorial guides and popular press books on writing style also helped me become articulate in this new language. In recent years, I have noticed that developmental science journals now publish articles that have a considerable amount of informal language and a large number of typographical errors. I am assuming that publishers are investing less money in copy editing, so shifting into formal language has become less important. However, I do believe that using informal language in published developmental science can be distracting and can undermine the credibility of articles, particularly for us older readers.

A much more important endeavor for increasing publication success is to become more aware of the review process by reviewing manuscripts. At the most fundamental level, this can be a collaborative context in which groups of graduate students agree to share their manuscripts and provide feedback to their peers. At a more sophisticated level, graduate students can ask their advisors to share manuscripts that the advisor is reviewing and allow the students to add their feedback to the review. This collaboration is a formally accepted policy for most journals. The next step is to contact the editors of relevant journals and volunteer to become a reviewer. As professional progress continues and a person's name has become associated with a particular topic, that person is increasingly likely to receive invitations to review all manuscripts on that topic.

The advantage of this evolution is that the manuscripts will be well reviewed and the reviewer will be aware of ongoing progress on his/her primary topic of interest.

We see another perspective on the review process when we receive reviews of our own manuscripts. It is tempting to feel inappropriately attacked when a reviewer gives us strong criticism of our procedures, analyses, or conclusions. However, our most efficient strategy is to view this as an example of a perspective that can be evoked by what we have written and then use this information efficiently to make appropriate adjustments. For some criticisms, the reviewer is correct and we need to consider changes. For other criticisms, the reviewer has not understood what we attempted to communicate, and we need to make changes in that communication so that the reviewer and other readers will not encounter this problem. Finally, some reviewers offer criticisms that are incorrect and in this situation, a cordial and collaborative communication with the editor can be helpful. I remember receiving a rejection of a manuscript in which I reported an important new tool, and the rejection I received was obviously based on the perspective of a colleague who had developed a tool that my tool could compete with and possibly replace. I shared this information with the editor, the manuscript was then reviewed by a different associate editor, received strong reviews, and was published.

Another aspect of efficient publication is to develop a publication plan in collaborative projects. For example, the plan should acknowledge the particular team member who should have first access to being the first author, and it should also explicitly acknowledge the other collaborators who will be included in the publication and who may face different professional obligations affecting publication timing (e.g., an upcoming review for tenure, postgraduate job hunting, etc.). To balance the needs of all team members, a broad timetable should be negotiated and signed with specific dates, stipulations of what must be completed by that date, and a plan for shifting responsibilities when deadlines are missed. If a team member fails to perform activities such as writing a component of the manuscript, performing statistical analyses, or reviewing the manuscript by an agreed upon date, stipulations can then alter aspects of authorship. And, if the manuscript is not submitted for publication within an agreed upon timetable, access to first authorship can be shifted to another member of the team. An obviously important perspective on publication planning is to discuss this topic with the research team and reach agreement before the collaborative research project begins.

Dissertations in some countries and in some domains of scholarship are expected to be created totally independently by the graduate student who seeks a Ph.D. Dissertations in the United States in developmental science are usually conducted in active laboratories and are linked to ongoing grants and projects. Thus, these projects are almost always based on collaboration among a graduate student, an advisor, and other personnel. This initial collaborative context leads to a dissertation that is proposed, conducted, analyzed, and defended under the primary control of a graduate student, but in the broader context of the collaborative laboratory. When the dissertation is completed, it can then be harvested in an array of publications with authorship that reflects the initial collaboration among the research team that spawned and supported the dissertation. This configuration seems obvious to me but it is salient because one of my first graduate students failed to recognize my collaboration as a basis for co-authorship. My subsequent policy on publication has been to clarify this with all of my graduate students. I also remember a moment in the planning of my own dissertation in which two advisors dictated a change in my research project that I did not agree with. My own policy on dissertation decisions is to clearly inform each of my students that their dissertation is their project. I will ask questions and offer advice about the dissertation, but the student who is conducting the dissertation has the final authority for all decisions in this project.

12.3 Acquiring and Maintaining Our Data Analytic Skills

Previous chapters have mentioned many contemporary tools for improved data analysis and noted the importance of being aware of these tools and knowing how to use them. All students who pursue graduate training in developmental science will encounter a curriculum that includes some training in statistics. However, that training will be much more sophisticated in Psychology Departments like the University of North Carolina at Chapel Hill that have a Quantitative Program with faculty who encompass a broad array of expertise on data analysis and are also scientists who are developing and implementing improved data analytic tools. Other Departments delegate data analysis teaching to faculty members who have some statistical skill and experience, or they delegate this training to faculty in statistically oriented departments. Access to strong training in data analysis during graduate school is an important attribute students should explore when choosing optimal graduate schools.

Some institutes and professional statisticians offer data analytic training in special sessions (often at a notable cost), and this is an opportunity that can be helpful for students and also for those of us who attended graduate school in previous decades or centuries. Textbooks are also published, and training is available online (e.g., see the impressive Institute for Digital Research and Education website offered by UCLA: www.ats.ucla.edu/stat/). Spending time and money on advanced data analytic skills can seem problematic, but most of us eventually realize that the savings we accrue by attaining better understanding of our tools almost always offsets the cost of that investment. The context here is statistical analysis, but the rule also applies more broadly to the use of computer programs such as Word or Excel, and the use of laboratory tools. And, to facilitate the ability to speak the language of modern statistics, learning the ancient Greek alphabet can make formulas and models much more readable. I remember an old joke about two photographers on a camping trip in Africa. They are relaxing and suddenly notice some approaching lions. One photographer runs away immediately while the other pauses to put on his shoes and socks. When he has enhanced his running tool, he quickly runs past his frantic, barefoot colleague.

Another strategy for improving data analysis is to establish a collaborative relationship with a statistical consultant. This can be a costly investment, but we can also find statisticians who volunteer their collaboration because they accrue benefits from co-authorship and engagement in research. I will also recommend being aware of a potentially problematic perspective: some statistical consultants may have a statistical bias that reflects their training and zone of expertise but is not necessarily or automatically the analytic approach that will best serve the harvesting of results in developmental science. As discussed in previous chapters, some statisticians will lean toward a formative approach rather than a reflective approach. Or, a statistician might apply Item Response Theory analysis to a set of data that are disjunctive rather than conjunctive. Some statisticians immediately engage in modeling and other sophisticated analyses without using Exploratory Data Analysis to get a view of what is happening before developing a sophisticated description. This reminds me of a series of meetings in which a statistical consultant helped my colleagues explore the efficacy of an intervention. I repeatedly requested a graph that would allow me to see the pattern of progression of each child in the treatment group and the control group and thus get a graphic perspective on the participants who were helped by the intervention in comparison to the participants who were not helped by the intervention. I also wondered about the rate of change in both groups and possible indicators of intervention efficacy such as gender, parental cooperation, demographics, etc. Instead of these graphs, our statistician continued to provide graphic representations of complex models, and many pages of Greek letters and numbers, and I never felt that I understood the actual outcomes in this study.

In our mentoring of students who are pursuing careers in developmental science, it is important for us to share our perspective on data analysis, and to also recognize our potential bias towards our own toolbox. There is some value in helping our students learn to use our data analytic strategies, but there is also value in encouraging our students to become proficient at newly emerging data analytic strategies. Dissertation defense meetings have become productive opportunities for me to learn about the implementation of new statistical techniques. It is important for all of us to avoid expressing potential resistance to data analytic techniques that are not what we would have used but that might be improvements.

12.4 Enjoying and Harvesting From Teaching

I have made extensive use of a metaphor in which I view a college professor teaching students in a classroom as a chef who is serving cooked food to individuals in a restaurant. One use of this metaphor is to view a professor who complains about how students are evaluating a class as comparable to a chef who is complaining because individuals do not like the chef's food. Another use of the metaphor is to view students who are not engaged in a course as comparable to individuals who order food and pay for it but do not eat it. Using this metaphor from a broader perspective, the academic world evolved during the 20th century and the chef was expected to also be a farmer (conducting research) by growing crops outside the restaurant and harvesting from them as part of the cooking process. Another shift was that restaurant staff (administrators) were hired to organize seating, prepare menus, handle reservations, process charges, clear tables and clean dishes, etc. In recent years, many universities have shifted back toward hiring chefs who cook using off-the-shelf raw material and do not do any farming (adjunct instructors). If this trend continues, research will be contracted to private industry that does not engage in teaching and to government institutions that are focused on research. If this evolution occurs, colleges and universities will return to their original zone of primarily teaching and training undergraduate students.

At present, most developmental scientists work in academic settings in which teaching is an important component in their job. Some developmental scientists are much more interested in research and find careers in which their research funding offsets their responsibility for teaching. Other developmental scientists focus on teaching and find careers in which their primary responsibility is to teach students about developmental science. Young professionals who prefer avoiding teaching may encounter a significant challenge as our educational system evolves to focus more on teaching as a primary goal and abolishes tenure because it can be seen as a self-serving anachronistic privilege that should be replaced with appropriate metrics of performance and relevance for a contemporary curriculum.

Whether or not developmental scientists enjoy teaching, teaching is an opportunity to learn more about something that developmental scientists are interested in or need to be more informed about. From my perspective, I have many examples of this benefit. In the semester before my daughter was born, I was able to teach a course on child care that facilitated my knowledge of a topic that would soon become prominent within my life. In the 1990s, the Psychology Department at Yale University did not have a Quantitative Program, so faculty were required to teach undergraduate and graduate courses on statistics. When I was asked to teach undergraduate statistics, this course was a very positive experience for me. Specifically, in previous years, I had learned how to calculate and interpret simple statistics, and I would have said that I understood them. However, when I faced the challenge of explaining these topics to my students, my level of understanding became much deeper. Finally, I taught an undergraduate course on research methods at Yale because this topic interested me, and when I began teaching at UNC-Chapel Hill, I shifted to teaching research methods at a graduate level. My multiple renditions of this course evolved into a series of presentations that are the core content of this book. Teaching a course on this topic not only led to my development of the chapters in this book but also led to my balance of reading traditional approaches and also reading modern approaches to stay informed on this topic. And, the comments and suggestions I have heard from and discussed with graduate students in this course have helped me consolidate and expand my set of classes/chapters on relevant topics.

Another course that I learned from was the First Year Seminar that I taught several times at UNC-Chapel Hill on "Human Infancy: The Emergence of Mind in the Human Infant." My goals in this course were to help students learn about the psychological development of human infants, evaluate the research procedures that inform this topic, and explore creative new procedures for assessing infant psychological development. I framed these general goals within the context of an overarching question: "When do human infants have minds and how do minds change during early development?" My preparation for class, engagement in dialogue with students, and reading their papers helped advance my own thinking on this topic. And, this opportunity to be engaged in a fascinating topic early in their college career led many students to their choice of major, some to their eventual completion of an honors thesis, and a few to graduate training in developmental science.

Almost all academic institutions attain anonymous feedback from students to evaluate the performance of the person who has taught a course. Receiving this formal feedback after your course has ended is helpful, but a more efficacious strategy is to attain some feedback shortly after the course has begun. My usual strategy was to insert a pause in class a few weeks into the semester and request that students write brief anonymous answers to a few questions that I posed regarding how they perceive the class, my performance, and zones of potential improvement. This form of feedback helped me make adjustments to improve my class and helped my students understand and appreciate my goal of offering an optimal educational experience for them. An additional strategy that emerged later was to set up a Qualtrics survey link that students could use to provide me with anonymous feedback in the format of an email at any point during the semester.

Finally, teaching can be viewed as an opportunity for better training of students and for broad communication about developmental science. When I teach "Introduction to Developmental Science," I see this as an opportunity to educate young adults who will eventually be parents and to recruit students who will eventually be developmental scientists. All topics in this course have some general relevance, and some seem particularly important to me or to my students. For example, when covering prenatal development, I am very explicit in noting how much development has occurred before many women notice that they are pregnant. When we then discuss various teratogens, I mention that some substances should be avoided when pregnancy is a possibility rather than an official occurrence. Another important example is my description of parent perception of infant intentionality and how some perspectives are incorrect and can lead to poor parenting. One additional recommendation for teaching any introductory course is to evaluate student performance based on their acquisition of relevant constructs, findings, etc. and their understanding of relevant theories and methodology. Despite the advice we receive from publishers of textbooks, these areas of expertise are more important than easily tested multiple-choice or true–false questions. It is also important to avoid blind acceptance of all facts in developmental science rather than including self-criticism on all topics in our evolving accrual of knowledge.

12.5 Attaining Efficacy, Efficiency, and Excellence

My unexpected "end game" with a diagnosis of amyotrophic lateral sclerosis has definitely undermined my credibility as a mentor for advice on how to manage one's life. However, I am confident that almost all of my friends and family agree that my disease is not a direct manifestation of a strategic error in my lifestyle that decimated my health. Here are my 10 top suggestions for attaining efficacy, efficiency, and excellence in life.

1. Meditation – Many of us became aware of various formats of meditation in the early 1970s. We were influenced by the Beatles and others, and found prominent experts such as Maharishi Mahesh Yoga and others. The basic idea is that various tools such as a mantra, yoga, or focused breathing can be used to attain a mental state that is an unusual mode of consciousness that can have many advantages. From a historical perspective, we can identify a wide range of cultures/religions that have incorporated various behavioral techniques for allowing us to spend some time in this state. For example, I remember watching my grandfather standing beside a radiator, wearing his yarmulke and tallis, and rocking back and forth as he prayed in alignment with memorized Hebrew text. Research and experience has shown that meditation is healthy and helpful in various ways. My original strategy was to meditate for 20 minutes each morning after waking up and before beginning my day and also for 20 minutes in the afternoon. Various complications steered me toward my current sustainable model, which I have been using for almost four decades: I meditate for 20 minutes every morning before leaving the bed. I am confident that spending this time in this state has nurtured my psychological health, my mental ability, and my creativity.

2. Maintaining a journal – In the spring of 1975, I read a book about intellectual development that suggested maintaining a daily journal primarily focused on activities and with some attention to emotional and psychological perspectives. I began writing daily entries in a composition book then, and I have continued my daily journaling since then. A convenient format emerged in which the length of the entries allowed me to complete one composition book each year. For easier indexing, I began adding pages at the end in which I listed major events that had occurred, every movie and concert that I had attended, every book that I had read, any travel, my participation in various exercises, etc. I realize that this will sound rather obsessive/compulsive, but obtaining and preserving this information has been very informative. When a question emerges about my past, my indexing makes it relatively easy to find the year and dates when something occurred, and I can then review the text to remember what happened and why. When I lost my ability to type using a keyboard in 2014, I began recording my daily journal electronically. The advantage of this new format is that it is easy to search for various words and I no longer have any page limits. The frightening disadvantage is that the electronic format I am currently using will eventually be replaced by

other formats, and old electronic documents could eventually become obsolete and inaccessible.

3. Sleeping well – It is very healthy to develop and maintain a daily routine that includes a specific time frame for deep sleep. When someone asks me "How did you sleep?" I tend to reply "I closed my eyes." A more accurate answer would also include the techniques that I use for maintaining my sleep. We are all aware of "counting sheep" as a strategy for shifting away from focal thought on an arousing topic, but we also have noticed that simple counting is not a very effective strategy. A better strategy is to learn a list and then use the recitation of that list to shift our focus. A list based on calculation (e.g., counting backwards) is too engaging. The best strategy is to learn a list that evokes an appropriate level of engagement. The list I use is American presidents. I initially learned the list of names in groups of five (when Ronald Reagan was president), and now when my sleep is distracted by an arousing topic, my mind works through the list. When I notice that my focus has shifted back to the arousing topic, I begin reciting the presidents again. If this does not work after multiple attempts, my next strategy is to open my eyes, look for a peripheral zone of light, and attempt to keep my eyes open and focused on what I can see. This becomes increasingly difficult at night, and when I notice that my eyes have closed, I attempt to reopen them.

4. Physical fitness – It is vitally important to include an appropriate amount of some form of aerobic exercise in our daily/weekly routine. My most effective strategies have been acquiring an elliptical machine in my home and using it for a timed routine at an appropriate level on a regular basis (usually while watching some form of video stream). I have also enjoyed jogging while thinking about an interesting topic (and often carrying a handheld recorder to begin saving my new speech, letter, song, or creative idea). Finally returning to the maintenance of social relationships, tennis provides a great opportunity for aerobic exercise in a social context.

There is one convenient form of exercise that I do not recommend: the plank. As a New Year's resolution in January 2013, I began doing a plank exercise each morning with the goal of improving my abdominal musculature. I began my routine with approximately a 10-second hold, fingers clasped, weight on my elbow and my toes. Day by day, I slowly increased my hold to approximately 5 minutes, and this included some time of solo support by my left elbow and some by my right. In March, I began experiencing back pain, stopped doing plank exercise, and the pain abated. In June, I began experiencing difficulty lifting my right ring finger, and this was my first symptom of ALS. I will always wonder if doing planks put extra pressure on my spine that affected the status of my motor neurons!

5. Developing an effective to do list – My to do list evolved for many years and eventually became my "Two Do List" because it is double-sided, with each side containing a two-dimensional set of rows and columns. The basic document evolved over the years, with a new version saved periodically. One side was labeled "Goals/Deliverables" and it contained information that was typed into the document and updated periodically. One column was labeled "Domain" and contained rows with labels like "research," "other work stuff," "Developmental Program," "domestic," etc. The three other columns were labeled "Must Do," "Should Do Eventually," and "Could Do Some Day." Items entered in these lists include possible research projects, books that could be written, administrative changes that could be instituted, places to visit, and other ideas, with the goal of having a virtually complete list of potential projects to scan when planning and prioritizing.

The other side of the document was labeled "Activities," and it contained boxes in which I would pencil in items, and erase and modify them constantly. One column was labeled "Action Now," the second column was labeled "Action Later," and the third column was labeled "Monitor." The two action columns were used to indicate the "now" agenda and "later" agenda for rows reflecting ongoing activities like a course being taught, a manuscript or grant being written, a research project being conducted, etc. Other rows were used for activities to do "on campus" and "off-campus." The final row had a list of people to contact via email or telephone. The "Monitor" column had rows for upcoming deadlines, items to schedule eventually, communication for which I was awaiting a reply, and items to include on the agendas of upcoming committee meetings.

This system is obviously very complicated, but I am sharing this format as an example of how to create a structured document in which potentially completed activities are arranged in a format in which they can be reviewed, prioritized, and monitored for completion. Having virtually all doable items listed in this way reduces the anxiety of feeling disorganized, and greatly increases the probability of completing activities that must be completed within an appropriate prioritization across items. The wise words I use here are: "If you bite off more than you can chew, you will remain hungry and food will become increasingly salient."

6. Office efficiency – I have collaborated with many colleagues whose office contains stacks of papers, bookshelves with a random array of books, and a desktop covered with inches of various items. I have never had a compulsively pristine office myself, but I have always invested some time in organizing my office to facilitate access to relevant material as needed. File drawers need labels, and sub-dividers within each drawer can help create a relevant arrangement. File dividers on the desktop allow a view of my "hot folders" and access to them as needed. Materials that can probably be discarded but could possibly be needed soon go into a pile that is periodically pruned by discarding some items at the bottom of the pile (i.e., the items that have been in the pile for the longest time). Replacing an ancient chalkboard with a large bulletin board creates a dynamic space in which relevant items can be pinned to the board. Finally, books do not need to be organized as a virtual library, but placing them in relevant labeled sections can be helpful.

7. Learning to use tools – One general strategy that applies across a wide range of tools is to spend time learning how to use them efficiently. Instruction manuals are often too detailed and esoteric to read, but investing some time in knowing more about our most prominent tools can yield extremely helpful information. Online guides, advisory websites, and helpful books are almost always worth the investment. Mentioning specific ideas here will probably be archaic. However, it is hard to avoid sharing strategies that work well for me and that I seldom see being used by colleagues. For example, I was one of the first members of my department to discover Dropbox as a tool to increase the chances that ongoing work on a document focuses on the most recent version of that document, and I shared this discovery with my colleagues. Working in Microsoft Word, I have a toolbar with icons I have selected because I use them frequently when adding or removing rows or columns in a spreadsheet; navigating to tracked changes and either accepting them or moving to the next change, etc. And, I save this toolbar information in a file that is present on each computer that I use. In Microsoft Outlook, I keep my inbox empty by distributing new emails into folders and subfolders, setting up rules that transfer incoming emails from specific senders or regarding specific topics directly into folders and subfolders that I review once a day, designating many email sources as junk, etc. Finally, icons for major programs are pinned to my toolbar. When I right click on most icons, I see a list of the

files I have opened most recently using that icon. And, I can pin particular files to always be accessible at the top of the file list.

8. Planning for good news or bad news – When you apply for something and go through the interview process, keep a to do list of things that you would do if you get the opportunity that you have applied for. Also, keep a list of things that you will do if you do not get the opportunity. The former list will help you be productive and creative, and accrue a useful harvest during the interview process. The latter list will help you cope with not getting the opportunity. It will not only prepare you for that possibility but also place you in a better position to behave rationally and thoughtfully despite the pain that comes with an unfulfilled expectation. This insight is emerging from my experience of being denied various administrative positions I had applied for. A related thought is an activity that always appeared on my opportunity to do list: I planned to contact the other candidates, meet with each of them, and attempt to discover any ideas/insights they had accrued through their preparation or interview.

9. Use administration as an opportunity to expand zones of life – One important aspect of administration is the opportunity to expand one's inventory of friends beyond one's department, area of expertise, and generation. My service on committees and in formal administrative positions allowed me to become familiar with peers in other departments on campus, and leaders in higher level administrative positions. It also provided a useful perspective for understanding the general goals and challenges in my educational institution. Was doing all of this administrative work a wise decision? Positives included: I enjoyed it, I accrued a wide array of new friends, and I was able to implement changes that I view as improvements. Negatives included: It reduced my contribution to developmental science and my opportunity for teaching. My recommendation is to consider the positives and the negatives when volunteering or being recruited for administrative activity, and to attempt to make an informed decision.

Another relevant level of administrative activity is service in professional organizations and as a reviewer for journals and funding agencies. It is easier to defend the time and energy that we devote to this level of administrative activity if we are aware of, and make use of, the important opportunities that allow us to advocate for positive changes in our profession. Service in our professional organizations also allows us to establish social contacts with a wide array of peers. When we become socially interconnected in our field, we have more opportunities to make changes and to learn about new topics of interest, tools, professional opportunities, etc. Organizing symposia at professional meetings helps us establish our connection with the topics we are most focused on and helps us establish cordial relationships with peers who are also engaged in these topics. Serving on grant review committees helps us maintain awareness of the current criteria for research funding and the progress that is being made by our colleagues on various important topics that are of interest to us.

Administrative roles in local institutions outside of our campus usually have very limited value from a professional perspective, but for those of us who enjoy administering and can do it well, these administrative roles allow us to improve the quality of life in our community and attain pleasure through many zones of interest. Family life at home needs appropriate focus and blocks of time, and this zone can be expanded to include neighbors and community events and other opportunities. More broadly, our engagement in politics can affect the quality of life in our community and in our various professional societies.

10. Maintain friendships – My episodic memory has always been relatively weak in comparison to my other types of memory, so I have always been aware of the need to archive information. One strategy that I began implementing many decades ago is to begin using an index card when I met a new colleague, student, or fellow committee member and update that person's index card with basic information such as where they are from, where they went to school, the names of members of their family, and other topics that emerged. Then, in preparation for an upcoming committee meeting, I would review my information about my colleagues and thus have that information in mind when we had time to talk. I would update my cards after the meeting.

Related, when I became aware of a person's date of birth, I would add that information to my yearly calendar. Then, on that person's birthday, I would contact them with sincere wishes for a happy birthday. I became engaged in this activity initially because I wanted to know someone born on every day of the year, but probability emerged quickly and I realized this was not very feasible. More important, I began to realize that my birthday monitoring was an effective and sincere strategy for maintaining friendships, and I still have contact with friends I have known for decades through my annual communication with them. I respect our newly emerging social media, but I never use Facebook for joining the list of people who are wishing someone I know happy birthday triggered by Facebook. My birthday communication is direct to the individual and a sincere effort to maintain our relationship.

My social engagements have created a remarkably large number of people who know me, respect my efficiency and diligence, and enjoy my unconstrained creativity. This leads me to the best wise saying I have invented and my bottom line (literally) for personal advice: "It ain't what you know and it ain't who you know: it's who knows you and what they think of you."

The end!

Bibliography

Achenbach, T. M., & Rescorla, L. A. (2000). *Manual for the ASEBA preschool forms and profiles*. Burlington, VT: University of Vermont Department of Psychiatry.

Achor, S. (2012). Positive intelligence. *Harvard Business Review*, January–February, 100–102.

Adolph, K. E., & Robinson, S. R. (2011). Sampling development. *Journal of Cognition and Development*, 12(4), 411–423.

Ainsworth, M. D., & Bell, S. M. (1970). Attachment, exploration, and separation: Illustrated by the behavior of one-year-olds in a strange situation. *Child Development*, 41, 49–67.

American Psychiatric Association. (2013). *Diagnostic and statistical manual of mental disorders* (5th ed.). Washington, DC: Author.

American Psychological Association, American Educational Research Association, & National Council on Measurements Used in Education. (1954). Technical recommendations for psychological tests and diagnostic techniques. *Psychological Bulletin*, 51(2, pt. 2), 1–38. doi: 10.1037/h0053479.

Anderson, C., Colombo, J., & Shaddy, D. (2006). Visual scanning and pupillary responses in young children with Autism Spectrum Disorder. *Journal of Clinical and Experimental Neuropsychology*, 28, 1238–1256.

Aslin, R. N. (2007). What's in a look? *Developmental Science*, 10, 48–53.

Babineau, B. A., Yang, M., & Crawley, J. N. (2012). Mainstreaming mice. *Neuropsychopharmacology*, 37(1), 300–301. doi:10.1038/npp.2011.168.

Barlow, D. H. (2010). Negative effects from psychological treatments: A perspective. *American Psychologist*, 65(1), 13–20.

Barrett, L. F. (2009). The future of psychology: Connecting mind to brain. *Perspectives on Psychological Science*, 4, 326–339.

Bauer, D. J. (2007). Observations on the use of growth mixture models in psychological research. *Multivariate Behavioral Research*, 42, 757–786.

Bauer, D. J. (2011). Evaluating individual differences in psychological processes. *Current Directions in Psychological Science*, 20(2), 115–118.

Bauer, D. J., Gottfredson, N. C., Dean, D., & Zucker, R. A. (2013). Analyzing repeated measures data on individuals nested within groups: Accounting for dynamic group effects. *Psychological Methods*, 18(1), 1–14.

Bauer, D. J., & Reyes, H. L. M. (2010). Modeling variability in individual development: Differences of degree or kind? *Child Development Perspectives*, 4, 114–122.

Bauer, D. J., Sterba, S. K., & Hallfors, D. D. (2008). Evaluating group-based interventions when control participants are ungrouped. *Multivariate Behavioral Research*, 43(2), 210–236. doi: 10.1080/00273170802034810.

Bauer, P. J., & Zelazo, P. D. (2014). The National Institutes of Health Toolbox for the Assessment of Neurological and Behavioral Function: A tool for developmental science. *Child Development Perspectives*, 8(3), 119–124.

Baumeister, R. F., Vohs, K. D., & Funder, D. C. (2007). Psychology as the science of self-reports and finger movements: Whatever happened to actual behavior? *Perspectives on Psychological Science*, 4, 396–403.

Baumrind, D. (1968). Authoritarian vs. authoritative parental control. *Adolescence*, 3(11), 255–272.

Bechtel, W. (1988). *Philosophy of science: An overview for cognitive science*. Hillsdale, NJ: Erlbaum.

Beck, D. M. (2010). The appeal of the brain in the popular press. *Perspectives on Psychological Science*, 5(6), 762–766.

Behrens, J. T. (1997). Principles and procedures of exploratory data analysis. *Psychological Methods*, 2, 131–160.

Berlin, L. J., Dodge, K. A., & Reznick, J. S. (2013). Examining pregnant women's hostile attributions about infants predict offspring maltreatment. *JAMA Pediatrics*, 167, 549–553.

Blair, C., Granger, D., Kivlighan, K., Mills-Koonce, R., Willoughby, M., Greenberg, M., et al. (2008). Maternal and child contributions to cortisol response to emotional arousal in young children from low-income, rural communities. *Developmental Psychology*, 44, 1095–1109.

Bollen, K. A., & Ting, K. (2000). A tetrad test for causal indicators. *Psychological Methods*, 5(1), 3–22. doi:10.1037/1082-989X.5.1.3.

Borsboom, D., Romeijn, J., & Wicherts, J. (2008). Measurement invariance versus selection invariance: Is fair selection possible? *Psychological Methods*, 13, 75–98.

Bradburn, N. M., Sudman, S., & Wansink, B. (2004). *Asking questions: The definitive guide to questionnaire design – for market research, political polls, and social and health questionnaires*. San Francisco: Jossey-Bass.

Buhrmester, M., Kwang, T., & Gosling, S. D. (2011). Amazon's Mechanical Turk: A new source of inexpensive, yet high-quality, data? *Perspectives on Psychological Science*, 6, 3–5. doi: 10.1177/1745691610393980.

Burchinal, M., Skinner, D., & Reznick, J. (2010). European American and African American mothers' beliefs about parenting and disciplining infants: A mixed-method analysis. *Parenting: Science And Practice*, 10(2), 79–96.

Cacioppo, J. T., Berntson, G. G., & Decety, J. (2012). A history of social neuroscience. In A. W. Kruglanski, W. Stroebe, A. W. Kruglanski, & W. Stroebe (Eds.), *Handbook of the history of social psychology* (pp. 123–136). New York, NY: Psychology Press.

Cacioppo, J. T., & Decety, J. (2009). What are the brain mechanisms on which psychological processes are based? *Perspectives on Psychological Science*, 4, 10–18.

Cacioppo, J. T., Semin, G. R., & Berntson, G. G. (2004). Realism, instrumentalism, and scientific symbiosis: Psychological theory as a search for truth and the discovery of solutions. *American Psychologist*, 59, 214–223.

Caelli, K., Ray, L., & Mill, J. (2003). "Clear as mud": Toward greater clarity in generic qualitative research. *International Journal of Qualitative Methods*, 2, 1–13.

Cairns, R. B., Elder, G. H., Jr., & Costello, E. J. (1996). *Developmental science*. Cambridge: Cambridge University Press.

Campbell, D. T. (Ed.). (1974). *Philosophy of Karl Popper* (Vol. 1). LaSalle: Open Court Publishing Co.

Campbell, D. T., & Fiske, D. W. (1959). Convergent and discriminate validation by the multitrait-multimethod matrix. *Psychological Bulletin*, 56, 81–105.

Cantlon, J. F., Brannon, E. M., Carter, E. J., & Pelphrey, K. A. (2006). Functional imaging of numerical processing in adults and 4-y-old children. *PLoS Biology*, 4, 0844–0854.

Carnegie, D. (1936). *How to win friends and influence people*. New York, NY: Simon & Schuster.

Carroll, J. B. (1993). *Human cognitive abilities: Survey of factor-analytic studies*. New York, NY: Cambridge University Press.

Chan, M. E., & Arvey, R. D. (2012). Meta-analysis and the development of knowledge. *Perspectives on Psychological Science*, 7, 79–92.

Chandra, A., Martino, S. C., Collins, R. L., Elliott, M. N., Berry, S. H., Kanouse, D. E., & Miu, A. (2008). Does watching sex on television predict teen pregnancy? Findings from a national longitudinal survey of youth. *Pediatrics*, 122, 1047–1054.

Churchland, P. M., & Churchland, P. S. (1998). *On the contrary: Critical essays 1987–1997*. Cambridge, MA: The MIT Press.

Cizek, G. J. (2012). Defining and distinguishing validity: Interpretations of score meaning and justifications of test use. *Psychological Methods*, 17, 31–43.

Cohen, A. B. (2010). Just how many different forms of culture are there? *American Psychologist*, 65(1), 59–61. doi:10.1037/a0017793.

Cohen, J. (1962). The statistical power of abnormal-social psychological research: A review. *Journal of Abnormal and Social Psychology*, 65, 145–153.

Cohen, J. (1977). *Statistical power analysis for the behavioral sciences*. New York, NY: Academic Press.

Cook, T. D. (1985). Postpositivist critical multiplism. In R. L. Shotland & M. M. Mark (Eds.), *Social science and social policy* (pp. 21–62). Beverly Hills, CA: Sage Publications.

Cooper, H., & Koenka, C. (2012). The overview of reviews: Unique challenges and opportunities when research syntheses are the principal elements of new integrative scholarship. *American Psychologist*, 67(6), 446–462.

Costa, P. T., Jr., & McCrae, R. R. (1992). *Revised NEO Personality Inventory (NEO-PI-R) and NEO Five-Factor Inventory (NEO-FFI) manual*. Odessa, FL: Psychological Assessment Resources.

Curran, P., Hussong, A., Cai, L., Huang, W., Chassin, L., Sher, K., et al. (2008). Pooling data from multiple longitudinal studies: The role of item response theory in integrative data analysis. *Developmental Psychology*, 44(2), 365–380.

Decety, J., & Cacioppo, J. (2010). Frontiers in human neuroscience: The golden triangle and beyond. *Perspectives on Psychological Science*, 5(6), 767–771.

DeFries, J. C., & Fulker, D. W. (1988). Multiple regression analysis of twin data: Etiology of deviant score versus individual differences. *Acta Geneticae Medicae et Gemeologiae*, 37, 205–216.

De Los Reyes, A., & Wang, M. (2012). Applying psychometric theory and research to developing a continuously distributed approach to making research funding decisions. *Review of General Psychology*, 16(3), 298–304. doi:10.1037/a0027250.

Diamond, A., Cruttenden, L., & Neiderman, D. (1994). AB with multiple wells: I. Why are multiple wells sometimes easier than two wells? II. Memory or memory + inhibition? *Developmental Psychology*, 30, 192–205.

Edwards, J. R. (2008). To prosper, organizational psychology should ... overcome methodological barriers to progress. *Journal of Organizational Behavior*, 29, 469–491.

Edwards, J. R., & Bagozzi, R. P. (2000). On the nature and direction of relationships between constructs and measures. *Psychological Methods*, 5, 155–174.

Elder, G. J., Shanahan, M. J., & Jennings, J. A. (2015). Human development in time and place. In M. H. Bornstein, T. Leventhal, R. M. Lerner, M. H. Bornstein, T. Leventhal, & R. M. Lerner (Eds.), *Handbook of child psychology and developmental science, Vol. 4: Ecological settings and processes* (7th ed.) (pp. 6–54). Hoboken, NJ: John Wiley & Sons Inc.

Enders, C. K. (2013). Dealing with missing data in developmental research. *Child Development Perpectives*, 7, 27–31. doi: 10.1111/cdep/12008.

Erceg-Hurn, D. M., & Mirosevich, V. M. (2008). Modern robust statistical methods. *American Psychologist*, 63, 591–601.

Erkut, S. (2010). Developing multiple language versions of instruments for intercultural research. *Child Development Perspectives*, 4(1), 19–24. doi:10.1111/j.1750-8606.2009.00111.x.

Fantz, R. L. (1958). Pattern vision in young infants. *Psychological Review*, 8, 43–47.

Feldman, R., & Reznick, J. S. (1996). Maternal perception of infant intentionality at 4 and 8 months. *Infant Behavior and Development*, 19, 483–496.

Fenson, L., Marchman, V. A., Thal, D., Dale, P., Reznick, J. S., & Bates, E. (2007). *The MacArthur-Bates Communicative Development Inventories: User's guide and technical manual*. Baltimore, MD: Paul H. Brookes Publishing Company.

Ferguson, C. F., & Brannick, M. T. (2012). Publication bias in psychological science: Prevalence, methods for identifying and controlling, and implications for the use of meta-analyses. *Psychological Methods*, 17(1), 120–128.

Fiedler, K., Kutzner, F., & Krueger, J. I. (2012). The long way from α-error control to validity proper: Problems with a short-sighted false-positive debate. *Perspectives on Psychological Science*, 7(6), 661–669. doi:10.1177/1745691612462587.

Firick, R. W. (1996). The appropriate use of null hypothesis testing. *Psychological Methods*, 1, 379–390.

Fisher, Sir Ronald A. (1935) Mathematics of a lady tasting tea. In J. R. Newman (1956, Ed.), *The world of mathematics* (Vol. 3, Part 8): *Statistics and the design of experiments* (pp. 1514–1521). New York, NY: Simon & Schuster.

Fiske, D. W., & Campbell, D. T. (1992). Citations do not solve problems. *Psychological Bulletin*, 112, 393–395.

Fox, E., Russo, R., Bowles, R., & Dutton, K. (2001). Do threatening stimuli draw or hold visual attention in subclinical anxiety? *Journal of Experimental Psychology: General*, 130, 681–700.

Gehlbach, H., & Brinkworth, M. E. (2011). Measure twice, cut down error: A process for enhancing the validity of survey scales. *Review of General Psychology*, 15(4), 380–387. doi:10.1037/a0025704.

Gilmore, J., Lin, W., Gerig, G., & Tamminga, C. (2006). Fetal and neonatal brain development. *American Journal of Psychiatry*, 163, 2046–2046.

Giner-Sorolla, R. (2012). Will we march to utopia, or be dragged there? Past failures and future hopes for publishing our science. *Psychological Inquiry*, 23(3), 263–266. doi:10.1080/1047840X.2012.706506.

Gopnik, A., & Wellman, H. M. (2012). Reconstructing constructivism: Causal models, Bayesian learning mechanisms, and the theory theory. *Psychological Bulletin*, 138(6), 1085–1108. doi:10.1037/a0028044.

Gottlieb, G. (2007). Probabilistic epigenesis. *Developmental Science*, 10, 1–11.

Gough, B., & Madill, A. (2012). Subjectivity in psychological science: From problem to prospect. *Psychological Methods*, 17(3), 374–384. doi:10.1037/a0029313.

Greenwald, A. G. (2012). There is nothing so theoretical as a good method. *Perspectives on Psychological Science*, 7(2), 99–108. doi:10.1177/1745691611434210 1.

Grothe, I., & Plöchl, M. (2008). Amplitude asymmetry: A direct link between ongoing oscillatory activity and event-related potentials? *The Journal of Neuroscience*, 28(49), 13025–13027. doi:10.1523/JNEUROSCI.4670-08.2008.

Gullo, M. J., & O'Gorman, J. G. (2012). DSM-5 Task Force proposes controversial diagnosis for dishonest scientists. *Perspectives on Psychological Science*, 7(6), 689. doi:10.1177/1745691612460689.

Gunnar, M., Sebanc, A., Tout, K., Donzella, B., & van Dulmen, M. (2003). Peer rejection, temperament, and cortisol activity in preschoolers. *Developmental Psychobiology*, 43, 346–358.

Haith, M. M. (1980). *Rules that babies look by: The organization of newborn visual activity.* Potomac, MD: Erlbaum.

Handy, T. C. (2004). *Event-related potentials: A methods handbook.* Cambridge, MA: The MIT Press (B&T).

Harmon, A. G., Hibel, L. C., Rumyantseva, O., & Granger, D. A. (2007). Measuring salivary cortisol in studies of child development: Watch out – what goes in may not come out of saliva collection devices. *Developmental Psychobiology*, 49(5), 495–500.

Hart, B., & Risley, T. R. (1995). *Meaningful differences in the everyday experience of young American children.* Baltimore, MD: Brooks.

Hartmann, W. E., Kim, E. S., Kim, J. H. J., Nguyen, T. U., Wendt, D. C., Nagata, D. K., & Gone, J. P. (2013). In search of cultural diversity, revisited: Recent publication trends in cross-cultural and ethnic minority psychology. *Review of General Psychology*, 17, 243–254.

Hedges, L. V. (2008). What are effect sizes and why do we need them? *Child Development Perspectives*, 2, 167–171.

Helms, J. E., Jernigan, M., & Mascher, J. (2005). The meaning of race in psychology and how to change it: A methodological perspective. *American Psychologist*, 60, 27–36.

Henrich, J., Heine, S. J., & Norenzayan, A. (2010). The weirdest people in the world? *Behavioural and Brain Sciences*, 33, 61–135.

Howell, R. D., Breivik, E., & Wilcox, J. B. (2007). Reconsidering formative measurement. *Psychological Methods*, 12, 205–218.

Hull, C. L. (1943). *Principles of behavior: An introduction to behavior theory.* Oxford, England: Appleton-Century.

Hume, D. (2003). *A treatise of human nature*. New York, NY: Dover.

Hyde, J. S. (2005). The gender similarities hypothesis. *American Psychologist*, 60(6), 581–592. doi:10.1037/0003-066X.60.6.581.

James, W. J. (1890/1981). *The principles of psychology* (Vol. 1). Cambridge, MA: Harvard University Press.

Jarde, A., Losilla, J., Vives, J., & Rodrigo, M. F. (2013). Q-Coh: A tool to screen the methodological quality of cohort studies in systematic reviews and meta-analysis. *International Journal of Clinical and Health Psychology*, 13(2), 138–146.

Johnson, V. E. (2013). Revised standards for statistical evidence. *Proceedings of the National Academy of Sciences*, 110, 19313–19317.

Jones, J. M. (2010). I am white and you're not: The value of unraveling ethnocentric science. *Perspectives on Psychological Science*, 5, 700–707.

Kagan, J. (2009a). Categories of novelty and states of uncertainty. *Review of General Psychology*, 13, 290–301.

Kagan, J. (2009b). Two is better than one. *Perspectives on Psychological Science*, 4, 22–23.

Kagan, J., Reznick, J. S., & Snidman, N. (1988). Biological bases of childhood shyness. *Science*, 240, 167–171.

Kagan, J. & Snidman, N. (2004). *The long shadow of temperament*. Cambridge, MA: Harvard University Press.

Klein, O., Doyen, S., Leys, C., de Saldanha da Gama, P. M., Miller, S., Questienne, L., & Cleeremans, A. (2012). Low hopes, high expectations: Expectancy effects and the replicability of behavioral experiments. *Perspectives on Psychological Science*, 7(6), 572–584. doi:10.1177/1745691612463704.

Kosslyn, S. M. (1999). If neuroimaging is the answer, what is the question? *Philosophical Transactions of the Royal Society of London, B*, 354, 1283–1294.

Kraemer, H. C., Yesavage, J. A., Taylor, J. L., & Kupfer, D. (2000). How can we learn about developmental processes from cross-sectional studies, or can we? *The American Journal of Psychiatry*, 157, 163–171. PMID: 10671382.

Krause, M. S. (2012). Measurement validity is fundamentally a matter of definition, not correlation. *Review of General Psychology*, 16, 391–400.

Krause, M. S. (2013). The data analytic implications of human psychology's dimensions being ordinally scaled. *Review of General Psychology*, 17(3), 318–325.

Kruschke, J. K. (2011). *Doing Bayesian data analysis*. Oxford, England: Elsevier.

Kuhn, T. (1962/1970). *The structure of scientific revolutions*. Chicago: University of Chicago Press.

Laborda, M. A., Miguez, G., Polack, C. W., & Miller, R. R. (2012). Animal models of psychopathology: Historical models and the Pavlovian contribution. *Terapia Psicológica*, 30, 45–59.

Lane, D., & Sándor, A. (2009). Designing better graphs by including distributional information and integrating words, numbers, and images. *Psychological Methods*, 14, 239–257.

LeBel, E. P., Borsboom, D., Giner-Sorolla, R., Hasselman, F., Peters, K. R., Ratliff, K. A., & Smith, C. T. (2013). PsychDisclosure.org: Grassroots support for reforming reporting standards in psychology. *Perspectives on Psychological Science*, 8(4), 424–432.

Leevers, H., & Harris, P. (2000). Counterfactual syllogostic reasoning in normal 4-year-olds, children with learning disabilities, and children with autism. *Journal of Experimental Child Psychology*, 76(1), 64–87.

Logothetis, N. K. (2007). The ins and outs of fMRI signals. *Nature Neuroscience*, 10(10), 1230–1232. doi:10.1038/nn1007-1230.

LoLordo, V. M. (1971). Facilitation of food-reinforced responding by a signal for response-independent food. *Journal of the Experimental Analysis of Behavior*, 15(1), 49–55.

Luck, S. J. (2005). *An introduction to the event-relates potential technique*. Cambridge, MA: The MIT Press.

Maccoby, E. E., & Martin, J. A. (1983). Socialization in the context of the family: Parent–child interaction. In P. Mussen (Ed.), *Handbook of child psychology* (Vol. 4). New York, NY: Wiley.

MacCorquodale, K., & Meehl, P. E. (1948). On a distinction between hypothetical constructs and intervening variables. *Psychology Review*, 55, 95–107.

MacKinnon, D. P. (2008). *Introduction to statistical mediation analysis*. Boca Raton, FL: CRC Press.

Madill, A., & Gough, B. (2008). Qualitative research and its place in psychological science. *Psychological Methods*, 13(3), 254–271. doi:10.1037/a0013220.

Magnusson, D. (1998). The logic and implications of a person-oriented approach. In R. B. Cairns, L. R. Bergman, & J. Kagan (Eds.), *Methods and models for studying the individual* (pp. 33–62). Beverly Hills, CA: Sage Publications.

Marcovitch, S., & Zelazo, P. (1999). The A-not-B error: Results from a logistic meta-analysis. *Child Development*, 70, 1297–1313.

Marshall, P. J. (2009). Relating psychology and neuroscience: Taking up the challenges. *Perspectives on Psychological Science*, 4, 113–125.

Maxwell, S. E. (2004). The persistence of underpowered studies in psychological research: Causes, consequences, and remedies. *Psychological Methods*, 9, 147–163.

McKnight, P. E., McKnight, K. M., Sidani, S., & Figueredo, A. J. (2007). Preventing missing data by design. In D. A. Kenny (Ed.), *Missing data: A gentle introduction* (pp. 65–87). New York, NY: Guilford Press.

Meade, A. W., & Craig, S. (2012). Identifying careless responses in survey data. *Psychological Methods*, 17(3), 437–455.

Medin, D., Bennis, W., & Chandler, M. (2010). Culture and the home-field disadvantage. *Perspectives on Psychological Science*, 5(6), 708–713. doi:10.1177/1745691610388772.

Meehl, P. E. (1978). Theoretical risk and tabular asterisks: Sir Karl, Sir Ronald, and the slow progress of soft psychology. *Journal of Consulting and Clinical Psychology*, 46, 806–834.

Mitchell, G. (2012). Revisiting truth or triviality: The external validity of research in the psychological laboratory. *Perspectives on Psychological Science*, 7(2), 109–117. doi:10.1177/1745691611432343.

Mook, D. G. (1983). In defense of external invalidity. *American Psychologist*, 38, 379–387.

Moore, D. S. (2015). *The developing genome: An introduction to behavioral epigenetics*. New York, NY: Oxford University Press.

Mussen, P. M. E. (1960). *Handbook of research methods in child development.* New York, NY: John Wiley and Sons.

Muthén, B. O. (2001). Second-generation structural equation modeling with a combination of categorical and continuous latent variables: New opportunities for latent class – latent growth modeling. In A. Sayer & L. Collins (Eds.), *New methods for the analysis of change* (pp. 289–322). Washington, DC: American Psychological Association.

Neuenschwander, E. (2013). Qualitas and quantitas: Two ways of thinking in science. *Quality & Quantity: International Journal Of Methodology*, 47(5), 2597–2615. doi:10.1007/s11135-012-9674-7.

Neuroskeptic (2012). The nine circles of scientific hell. *Perspectives on Psychological Science*, 7(6), 643–644.

Newton, P. E., & Shaw, S. D. (2013). Standards for talking and thinking about validity. *Psychological Methods*, 18, 301–319.

Nickerson, R. S. (2000). Null hypothesis significance testing: A review of an old and continuing controversy. *Psychological Methods*, 5, 241–301.

Palida, S. F., Butko, M. T., Ngo, J. T., Mackey, M. R., Gross, L. A., Ellisman, M. H., & Tsien, R. Y. (2015). PKMζ, but not PKCλ, is rapidly synthesized and degraded at the neuronal synapse. *The Journal of Neuroscience*, 35(20), 7736–7749. doi:10.1523/JNEUROSCI.0004-15.2015.

Pan, B., Rowe, M., Singer, J., & Snow, C. (2005). Maternal correlates of growth in toddler vocabulary production in low-income families. *Child Development*, 76, 763–782.

Pelphrey, K., & Morris, J. (2006). Brain mechanisms for interpreting the actions of others from biological-motion cues. *Current Directions in Psychological Science*, 15, 136–140.

Pelphrey, K. A., Reznick, J. S., Goldman, B. D., Sasson, N., Morrow, J., Donahoe, A., & Hodgson, K. (2004). Development of visuospatial short-term memory in the second half of the first year. *Developmental Psychology*, 40, 836–851.

Piaget, J. (1952/1936). *The origins of intelligence in children.* New York, NY: International University Press.

Piaget, J. (1954/1937). *The construction of reality in the child.* New York, NY: Basic Books.

Pinkham, A., Hopfinger, J., Pelphrey, K., Piven, J., & Penn, D. (2008). Neural bases for impaired social cognition in schizophrenia and autism spectrum disorders. *Schizophrenia Research*, 99, 164–175.

Popper, K. (1934/2002). *The logic of scientific discovery.* London: Routledge.

Popper, K. R. (1959). *The logic of scientific discovery.* New York, NY: Basic Books.

Porges, S., Doussard-Roosevelt, J., Portales, L., & Suess, P. (1994). Cardiac vagal tone: Stability and relation to difficultness in infants and 3-year-olds. *Developmental Psychobiology*, 27, 289–300.

Poulin, F., Dishion, T., & Burraston, B. (2001). 3-year iatrogenic effects associated with aggregating high-risk adolescents in cognitive-behavioral preventive interventions. *Applied Developmental Science*, 5(4), 214–224.

Pungello, E. P., Iruka, I. U., Dotterer, A. M., Mills-Koonce, R., & Reznick, J. S. (2009). The effects of income, race, sensitive parenting and harsh parenting on receptive and expressive language development in early childhood. *Developmental Psychology*, 45, 544–557.

Quine, W. V. O. (1951). Two dogmas of empiricism. *The Philosophical Review*, 60, 20–43.

Ratto, A. B. (2013). *The impact of cultural factors on the diagnostic process in autism: A comparison of Latina and European American mothers* (Doctoral dissertation). Retrieved from ProQuest *Dissertations Publishing database*. (Dissertation number: 3593268.)

Reichenbach, H. (1951). *The rise of scientific philosophy*. Berkeley and Los Angeles: University of California Press.

Reichenbach, H. (2006). *Experience and prediction: An analysis of the foundations and the structure of knowledge*. Notre Dame, IN: University of Notre Dame.

Reinhart, A. (2015). *Statistics done wrong: The woefully complete guide*. San Francisco: No Starch Press.

Rennie, D. L. (2012). Qualitative research as methodical hermeneutics. *Psychological Methods*, 17(3), 385–398. doi:10.1037/a0029250.

Reznick, J. S. (2007). Working memory in infants and toddlers. In L. M. Oakes & P. J. Bauer (Eds.), *Short- and long-term memory in infancy and early childhood: Taking the first steps toward remembering* (pp. 3–26). Oxford: Oxford University Press.

Reznick, J. S. (2008). *Inferring infant intentionality*. Berlin: VDM Dr. Müller.

Reznick, J. S., Baranek, G. T., Reavis, S., Watson, L. R., & Crais, E. R. (2007). A parent-report instrument for identifying one-year olds at risk for an eventual diagnosis of autism: The first year inventory. *Journal of Autism and Developmental Disorders*, 37, 1691–1710.

Reznick, J. S., Corley, R., & Robinson, J. (1997). A longitudinal twin study of intelligence in the second year. *Monographs of the Society for Research in Child Development*, 61(1, Serial No. 249).

Reznick, J. S., Morrow, J. D., Goldman, B. D., & Snyder, J. (2004). The onset of working memory in infants. *Infancy*, 6, 145–154.

Reznick, J. S., & Richman, C. L. (1976). Effects of class complexity, class frequency, and preexperimental bias on rule learning. *Journal of Experimental Psychology: Human Learning and Memory*, 2(6), 774–782. doi:10.1037/0278-7393.2.6.774.

Reznick, J. S., & Schwartz, B. B. (2001). When is an assessment an intervention? Parent perception of infant intentionality and language. *Journal of the American Academy of Child & Adolescent Psychiatry*, 40, 11–17.

Richards, J., & Gibson, T. (1997). Extended visual fixation in young infants: Look distributions, heart rate changes, and attention. *Child Development*, 68, 1041–1056.

Richman, C. L., Mitchell, D. B., & Reznick, J. S. (1979). Mental travel: Some reservations. *Journal of Experimental Psychology: Human Perception and Performance*, 5(1), 13–18. doi:10.1037/0096-1523.5.1.13.

Richters, J. E. (1997). The Hubble hypothesis and the developmentalist's dilemma. *Development and Psychopathology*, 9, 193–229.

Robinson, J. P., & Martin, S. (2008). What do happy people do? *Social Indicators Research*, 89, 565–571.

Rodgers, J. L. (2010). The epistemology of mathematical and statistical modeling: A quiet methodological revolution. *American Psychologist*, 65, 1–12.

Rosenberg, A. (2005). *Philosophy of science: A contemporary introduction* (2nd ed.). New York, NY: Routledge.

Rosenthal, R. (1979). "File drawer problem" and tolerance for null results. *Psychological Bulletin*, 86, 638–641.

Rosenthal, R., & Jacobson, L. (1968). *Pygmalion in the classroom*. New York, NY: Holt, Rinehart & Winston.

Salapatek, P., & Kessen, W. (1966). Visual scanning of triangles by the human newborn. *Journal of Experimental Child Psychology*, 3, 155–167.

Salmon, P. (2003). How do we recognize good research? *The Psychologist*, 16(1), 24–27.

Sanders, L. (2009). Trawling the brain. *Science News*, 176, 16–20.

Sanders, L. (2011). Residents of the brain: Scientists turn up startling diversity among nerve cells. *Science News*, July 30.

Schmidt, F. (2010). Detecting and correcting the lies that data tell. *Perspectives on Psychological Science*, 5(3), 233–242. doi:10.1177/1745691610369339.

Schmidt, F. L. (1996). Statistical significance testing and cumulative knowledge in psychology: Implications for training of researchers. *Psychological Methods*, 1, 115–129.

Schwartzer, J. J., Koenig, C. M., & Berman, R. F. (2013). Using mouse models of autism spectrum disorders to study the neurotoxicology of gene–environment interactions. *Neurotoxicology and Teratology*, 3617–3635. doi:10.1016/j.ntt.2012.08.007.

Scott-Phillips, T. C., Dickins, T. E., & West, S. A. (2011). Evolutionary theory and the ultimate-proximate distinction in the human behavioral sciences. *Perspectives on Psychological Science*, 6 (1), 38–47.

Shonkoff, J. P., & Bales, S. N. (2011). Science does not speak for itself: Translating child development research for the public and its policymakers. *Child Development*, 82(1), 17–32. doi:10.1111/j.1467-8624.2010.01538.x.

Simmering, V. R., Triesch, J., Deák, G. O., & Spencer, J. P. (2010). A dialogue on the role of computational modeling in developmental science. *Child Development Perspectives*, 4(2), 152–158. doi:10.1111/j.1750-8606.2010.00134.x.

Simpson, E. H. (1951). The interpretation of interaction in contingency tables. *Journal of the Royal Statistical Society, B*, 13, 238–241.

Skinner, B. F. (1972). *Beyond freedom and dignity*. New York, NY: Vintage Books.

Smedley, A., & Smedley, B. D. (2005). Race as biology is fiction, racism as a social problem is real: Anthropological and historical perspectives on the social construction of race. *American Psychologist*, 60, 16–26.

Staats, A. W. (1999). Unifying psychology requires new infrastructure, theory, method, and a research agenda. *Review of General Psychology*, 3, 3–13.

Steinberg, L., & Fletcher, A. C. (1998). Data analytic strategies in research on ethnic minority youth. In V. C. McLoyd & L. Steinberg (Eds.), *Studying minority adolescents: Conceptual, methodological, and theoretical issues* (pp. 279–294). Mahwah, NJ: Erlbaum Associates.

Sternberg, R. J., & Grigorenko, E. L. (2001). Unified psychology. *American Psychologist*, 56, 1069–1079.

Sulloway, F. J. (1997). *Born to rebel: Birth order, family dynamics, and creative lives*. New York, NY: Vintage Books.

Thompson, R. A. (2006). The development of the person: Social understanding, relationships, conscience, self. In N. Eisenberg (Ed.), *Handbook of child psychology* (6th ed., pp. 24–98). Hoboken, NJ: John Wiley & Sons.

Tudge, J., Putnam, S., & Valsiner, J. (1996). Culture and cognition in developmental perspective. In R. B. Cairns, G. H. Elder, Jr., & E. J. Costello (Eds.), *Developmental science* (pp. 190–222). Cambridge, England: Cambridge University Press.

Tukey, J. W. (1977). *Exploratory data analysis*. London: Pearson.

van der Worp, H. B., Howells, D. W., Sena, E. S., Porritt, M. J., Rewell, S., O'Collins, V., & Macleod, M. R. (2010). Can animal models of disease reliably inform human studies? *PLoS Medicine*, 7(3), 1–8.

Vaughn, B., Taraldson, B., Crichton, L., & Egeland, B. (1981). The assessment of infant temperament: A critique of the Carey Infant Temperament Questionnaire. *Infant Behavior and Development*, 4, 1–17.

Vul, E., Harris, C., Winkielman, P., & Pashler, H. (2009). Puzzlingly high correlations in fMRI studies of emotion, personality, and social cognition. *Perspectives on Psychological Science*, 4(3), 274–290. doi:10.1111/j.1745-6924.2009.01125.x.

Vul, E., & Pashler, H. (2012). Voodoo and circularity errors. *Neuroimage*, 62(2), 945–948. doi:10.1016/j.neuroimage.2012.01.027.

Wagenmakers, E., Wetzels, R., Borsboom, D., van der Maas, H. J., & Kievit, R. A. (2012). An agenda for purely confirmatory research. *Perspectives on Psychological Science*, 7(6), 632–638. doi:10.1177/1745691612463078.

Wainer, H. (2000). *Computerized adaptive testing: A primer*. Mahwah, NJ: Erlbaum Associates.

Weigold, A., Weigold, I. K., & Russell, E. J. (2013). Examination of the equivalence of self-report survey-based paper-and-pencil and internet data collection methods. *Psychological Methods*, 18(1), 53–70.

Wellman, H. M., Cross, D., & Bartsch, K. (1987). A meta-analysis of research on Stage 4 object permanence: The A-not-B error. *Monographs of the Society for Research in Child Development*, 51(3), 1–62.

Wellman, H., Cross, D., & Watson, J. (2001). Meta-analysis of theory-of-mind development: The truth about false belief. *Child Development*, 72(May), 655–684.

Wilkinson, L., & the Task Force on Statistical Inference. (1999). Statistical methods in psychology journals: Guidelines and explanations. *American Psychologist*, 54, 594–604.

Wilson, E. O. (1998). *Consilience: The unity of knowledge*. New York, NY: Vintage Books.

Wöhr, M., & Scattoni, M. L. (2013). Behavioural methods used in rodent models of autism spectrum disorders: Current standards and new developments. *Behavioural Brain Research*, 251, 5–17. doi:10.1016/j.bbr.2013.05.047.

Xiaolong, J., Shan, S., Cadwell, C. R., Berens, P., Sinz, F., Ecker, A. S., ... Tolias, A. S. (2015). Principles of connectivity among morphologically defined cell types in adult neocortex. *Science*, 350(6264), 1–10. doi:10.1126/science.aac9462.

Yarnold, P., & Soltysik, R. (2005). *Multiple sample analysis. Optimal data analysis: A guidebook with software for windows*. Washington, DC: American Psychological Association.

Yoshikawa, H., Weisner, T. S., Kalil, A., & Way, N. (2013). Mixing qualitative and quantitative research in developmental science: Uses and methodological choices. *Qualitative Psychology*, 1(S), 3–18.

Yuste, R. (2013). Electrical compartmentalization in dendritic spines. *Annual Review of Neuroscience*, 36, 429–444.

Zelazo, P. D., Carter, A., Reznick, J. S., & Frye, D. (1997). Early development of executive function: A problem-solving framework. *Review of General Psychology*, 1(2), 198–226. doi:10.1037/1089-2680.1.2.198.

Index